WOUNDED CHARITY

WOUNDED CHARITY

Lessons from the Wounded Warrior Project Crisis

10/12/2019

Carol —
Thank you for coming to the
Talkhouse tonight!

Doug White

Paragon House

First Edition 2019

Published in the United States by

Paragon House
www.ParagonHouse.com

Library of Congress Cataloging-in-Publication Data

Names: White, Douglas E., 1952- author.
Title: Wounded charity : lessons from the Wounded Warrior Project crisis / by Doug White.
Other titles: Lessons from the Wounded Warrior Project crisis
Description: First edition. | St. Paul, MN : Paragon House, 2019. | Summary: "Critically dissects allegations of Wounded Warrior Project mismanagement and the NGO's response. Provides a better understanding of how the nonprofit world operates, how it should work, and provides lessons for all charities and non-profits."--Provided by publisher.
Identifiers: LCCN 2019014687 | ISBN 9781557789402 (paperback)
Subjects: LCSH: Wounded Warrior Project--Evaluation. | Wounded Warrior Project--History. | Veterans--Services for--United States. | Disabled veterans--Rehabilitation--United States. | Nonprofit organizations--United States.
Classification: LCC UB357 .W524 2019 | DDC 362.1086/970973--dc23
LC record available at https://lccn.loc.gov/2019014687

10 9 8 7 6 5 4 3 2 1
Manufactured in the United States of America
The paper used in this publication meets the minimum requirements of American National Standard for Information Sciences—Permanence of Paper for Printed Library Materials, ANSIZ39.48-1984

This book is dedicated to all wounded warriors and their fallen comrades for safeguarding the rest of us and for preserving the noble ideals of our nation.

EPIGRAPH

"Americans of all ages, all conditions, and all dispositions constantly form associations. They have not only commercial and manufacturing companies, in which all take part, but associations of a thousand other kinds, religious, moral, serious, futile, general or restricted, enormous or diminutive. The Americans make associations to give entertainments, to found seminaries, to build inns, to construct churches, to diffuse books, to send missionaries to the antipodes; in this manner they found hospitals, prisons, and schools. If it is proposed to inculcate some truth or to foster some feeling by the encouragement of a great example, they form a society. Wherever at the head of some new undertaking you see the government in France, or a man of rank in England, in the United States you will be sure to find an association."

—Alexis de Tocqueville
Chapter V: Of The Use Which the Americans
Make of Public Associations in Civil Life
Democracy in America: Volume II

A BAD DEAL

"We may have disagreements on this, I don't know, you and I, but so far from my own research, I believe that Steve and Al at WWP were given a really, really, really bad deal."

—Ed Edmundson
Father and caretaker of a wounded warrior
November 17, 2016

AUTHOR'S NOTE

Veterans are America's treasure. Without their service, and that of their fallen comrades . . . who knows? The consequences to the nation would be unthinkable. This book is not a criticism of them.

Wounded Warrior Project is one of America's best charities. This book is not a criticism of its mission or good work.

Instead, this book is a criticism of the critics, as well as a brutal analysis of those appointed to oversee the charity's work—not the senior staff, but the board of directors.

IN APPRECIATION

Completing this book would not have been possible without the help and support of David Berg, Deanna Bosselman, John El-Maraghy, and Anthony Pulgram.

I send subtle but sincere thanks to all who spoke with me off the record. You know who you are.

I send a separate acknowledgment to Andrew Cardone for his gift of a Wounded Warrior Project medallion. It was with me for every word.

A special appreciation goes to my wife Susan. Thank you for your love and patience.

Contents

NOT EVERYTHING IS AS IT SEEMS

CONSIDER THE OPTICS AND RESULTS:

- The chief executive officer rappels down the wall of a luxury hotel.

- A former employee makes accusations of fraud, waste and abuse.

- An evaluator gives the organization a poor grade.

- A spokesperson stumbles through questions asked by a reporter.

- *CBS News* and the *New York Times* report this as a prime time, headline news story.

- The findings of an independent review refute the allegations in the news story.

- Nevertheless, the chief executive officer and the chief operating officer are fired.

- Support for the organization drops dramatically.

- This story is not about a government agency or a large corporation. It is about a charity: Wounded Warrior Project.

~

In *Democracy in America*, the French citizen Alexis de Tocqueville wrote of the *associations* he encountered during his listening tour of the United States in 1831. He discovered an early America whose citizens embraced a mindset rich with the welcoming possibilities of neighbor helping neighbor, a mindset that purposefully addressed community needs, such as the building of churches, hospitals, and schools, and the nourishing of the poor. He was surprised to see such outpourings of volunteer activity, mainly because in Europe governments, and not individuals, had for centuries provided the funding to address social problems. The nascent American government was far too poor for that.

The idea, however, of people gathering together in their communities to help one another because government wasn't able to do the job gave birth to almost all of the more than one million charities that now exist in the United States. Out of a national poverty has risen a robust aggregation of individual, non-governmental organizations that is today the envy of the world.

The nonprofit structure in the United States is large and complex enough that it has its own detailed taxonomy of causes, including education, the arts, the environment, animals, health, human services, international affairs, and religion. Within each of those broad groupings are several layers of subgroups. Deep inside one of the subgroups lies a category called "Military Veterans' Organizations." In there, if you look deeper still, you will find a charity named Wounded Warrior Project, based in Jacksonville, Florida.

～

For over 30 years I have studied how individual charities perform and, more broadly, what the nonprofit sector is doing. My recent pursuits—teaching, advising, and writing, with a long-standing and growing interest in ethical decision-making in the sector—have constituted a body of criticism of those who run charities, either as senior staff or board directors. This is not because I think the nonprofit world is essentially dishonest, but because I think it is essentially good. I so honor the role that charities play in society that I am offended, and think everyone else should be, too, when heads of charities play fast and loose with their mission or their money, the safekeeping of which is an important component of the public trust.

However we might normalize the shenanigans of those in government or the world of commerce, we can't become so inured to bad behavior at charities that we blithely, or cynically, accept it. Everyone has the right—obligation, even—to question how charities use their money. They occupy a unique and special place in society, and in our hearts. Nonprofit leaders therefore need to be more, not less, forthright, transparent, and diligent than business or government leaders. That is why I applaud public critical examination of charities. After all, individuals and news outlets—not regulators—perform the most effective oversight of charities. While state attorneys general and the Internal Revenue Service are statutorily assigned the roles of overseers, limited budgets, political considerations and the weight of bureaucracy work to inhibit their effectiveness. That is why the media must play an aggressive role to ensure that donors and other members of the public can be made as aware as possible of wrongdoing at charities.

Long ago, before I began trying to figure out the intricacies of the eleemosynary world, I spent time in journalism. I mention that here because the media play a central role in this story. The lifelong lessons of the news business are largely about separating fact from fiction, providing accurate and relevant context, and distinguishing credible sources from those not so credible—lessons that have served me surprisingly well in my work with charities and philanthropists.

Although it happens more frequently than in the past, it's not often that a charity, even a large one, captures the attention of a major network or lands a prominent placement in a national newspaper. When a charity is in the news it's usually bad news, and that's often because of how its news is related to a political issue. Think Red Cross, and criticism of its cleanup efforts after Hurricane Sandy in the northeast in 2012; Planned Parenthood, in light of the attention given over to abortion; and National Public Radio, whose chief fundraiser was caught making promises to a couple of people engaged in a conservative sting operation. Still, while these and other stories are well known, the number of them is relatively small.

While I support the investigation of charity activity, to be effective the criticism needs to be fair and accurate, and it must be relevant to the issues attracting the criticism; those doing the criticizing need to know what they're talking about. Otherwise, denunciations tend to be broad and cynical, and don't stand up to the weight of discussion and analysis.

∾

On an evening in late January 2016, I received a text message from a friend who asked if I had seen the *CBS Evening News* earlier that night. The lead story was about how badly Wounded Warrior Project (WWP) was being run. I hadn't seen the story so went online to watch it.

In the span of little more than a decade, Wounded Warrior Project grew to be the country's largest veterans' organization: it went from raising $10 million per year to almost $400 million per year. The growth was good for the organization in many ways, but the success it produced brought with it a vulnerability to criticism.

After watching the *CBS News* story, I emailed Dave Philipps, a reporter at the *New York Times* whom I knew to be working on a story about WWP. Some weeks earlier, he interviewed me at length about the organization's reputation, fundraising, and accomplishments. I spoke to what I knew: primarily publicly available information, as well as my thoughts based on the many years I had devoted to working in and studying the nonprofit world. The *Times* piece, as I understood our conversation, was to be a tough but fair investigation.

My concern on that late January evening, as I expressed it in my email to Philipps, was that *CBS News* was scooping the *Times*. Was he aware? Had he seen the report that night? Anyone who watched it would think that things must have been pretty bad at Wounded Warrior Project, so bad that donors could be excused for thinking they shouldn't send any more money. In fact, one significant donor would soon publicly denounce the organization.

My gut reaction to most news from the established outlets is that it is essentially accurate, and what they do get wrong I generally don't ascribe to intention. Yes, there is bias, but that's inherent in the recounting of any story. The question I ask myself is whether the reporter has made an honest effort to get the facts right, which is in part a function of the sources that are relied upon, the balance of the story, and the understandings I have developed over time, taking into account my own standards and skepticism, about the credibility of the news source. CBS, while far from perfect—and, really, what is?—has earned my respect over the years. In fact, I hold CBS in such high esteem that I serve as the chair of the Walter

Cronkite Committee at FoolProof, a charitable organization whose purpose is to promote critical thinking, particularly when it comes to making financial decisions. Cronkite's legend is among the best of anyone's in the history of journalism and *CBS News* is what it is today largely because of his high standards and reputation. It would take a lot to erode my trust in CBS.

I feel the same about the *New York Times.*

I could see that something at Wounded Warrior Project was lighting a fire—the CBS report was a major, three-part series—and so, fueled by many years of dissecting greed and hubris at charities, I was inclined to think the charity could very well have been guilty of what had been alleged: misusing funds, incorrectly portraying its results, and generally doing a poor job to help veterans, all the while falsely promoting itself as one of the best charities in America.

As far as my question of the moment for Dave Philipps, the answer came the next morning when the *Times* ran its own story under his byline. On the front page, above the fold, it was pretty much a duplicate of what *CBS News* reported.

My initial thinking was only to include the crisis among the many to which I had been devoting class time at Columbia University, where I was the director of the masters program in fundraising (now, nonprofit) management, as well as an instructor on board governance and ethical decision-making at charities. The twist in this story, for class discussion, would be an examination of the journalism itself, and the role news outlets play in shaping our ideas about charity and its purposes.

∼

On the Friday after the stories came out, I received a call from Peter Honerkamp, one of the founders of Wounded Warrior Project.

The prior day, as it turns out, an opinion piece I wrote, entitled "Charity Navigator Must Grow Up or Shut Down," was published in the *Chronicle of Philanthropy,* one of three major periodicals serving those who work in the nonprofit world. Charity Navigator, a nonprofit, advertises itself as a charity evaluator, and, in developing their allegations, the reporters at *CBS News* and the *New York Times* relied on Charity Navigator's assessment of WWP.

A friend of Honerkamp's read my commentary of Charity Navigator and Honerkamp called to ask if I would speak to Steve Nardizzi, the chief executive officer, and Al Giordano, the chief operating officer. Their take, he said, was that the news reports were flat-out wrong. This would be interesting, I thought, because I had the feeling the reports were flat-out right.

After talking with them, Nardizzi and Giordano asked me to conduct an independent review of Wounded Warrior Project. A financial audit was already in the works, but after that, they asked—say, in a month or so—if I would conduct a top-to-bottom review of policies, procedures, programs, morale, governance, and impact. At the time I was employed full-time and told them that I couldn't commit to such a large undertaking, but we agreed to revisit the issue later, after the financial audit was complete. I told them that, despite what they felt, I was inclined to believe that something pernicious was actually driving the stories, and that if I ended up conducting an investigation it would not necessarily spare criticism of them. In fact, I warned, given the news reports, I would be especially alert to uncover any wrongdoing on their part.

They said they would expect nothing less.

During the following weeks, *CBS News* and the *New York Times* reported more developments, including that one of WWP's major donors was jumping ship and calling for Nardizzi and Giordano to be fired. The narrative was consistent: How could a major charity, entrusted and funded to do so much good, so let down America's veterans?

As the sun was setting on March 10, 2016, a little more than a month after the media reports, I got a call from Timothy Sandoval, a reporter for the *Chronicle of Philanthropy* who had called for comment a month earlier when the reports first came out. "What do you think of the news?" he asked. "What news?" I asked back. "The leaders of Wounded Warrior Project were fired this afternoon."

The following morning, a shaken Peter Honerkamp called again, this time to ask, "What the hell happened?"

While Honerkamp was shaken because of the rupture in an organization he loved and helped start, I was surprised because at the same time the

WWP board announced the dismissals, it also announced the results of the financial audit. Basically, the announcement was this: the factual essence and the spirit of the media allegations were incorrect.

So why were board members firing their top guys?

INTRODUCTION

BIG QUESTIONS

IN 2013 DAN PALLOTTA, who calls himself a "philanthropy activist," opened his highly regarded, well-received and thought-provoking TED talk with this heresy: "The things we've been taught to think about giving, about charity and about the nonprofit sector are actually undermining the causes we love and our profound yearning to change the world." From there, he posited that, despite the conviction of many entrepreneurs, for-profit businesses can't do everything to save the world. Even though many think that businesses can lift up developing economies while charities will take care of the rest, he said, he pointed out that while the for-profit sector "will move the great mass of humanity forward, it always leaves behind that ten percent, or more, that is most disadvantaged, or unlucky." That's where philanthropy plays a role. "Philanthropy," he says, "is the market for love. It is the market for all those people for whom there is no other market coming."

After asking why some of our most prominent charities haven't solved or even adequately addressed some of society's larger social problems, such as breast cancer and homelessness, he answered by indicting a belief system in the United States that, he says, keeps charities tiny, too tiny to do the job expected of them, the result of an "apartheid that discriminates against the nonprofit sector." He then identified five areas—compensation, marketing, taking risks in pursuit of new ideas, time, and profit—where charities, relative to for-profit businesses, are forced into disadvantage, at least in terms of growth and getting the word out about their good works to attract money.

"You put those five things together—you can't use money to lure talent away from the for-profit sector; you can't advertise on anywhere near the scale the for-profit sector does for new customers; you can't take the kinds of risks in pursuit of those customers that the for-profit sector takes; you don't have the same amount of time to find them as the for-profit sector; and you don't have a stock market"—or, he might have added, any investors at all—"with which to fund any of this, even if you could do it in the first place—and you've just put the nonprofit sector at an extreme disadvantage to the for-profit sector, on every level."

Clearly, growth suppression in the charitable sector is a key concern for Pallotta. "If we have any doubts about the effects of this separate rulebook," he says, "this statistic is sobering: From 1970 to 2009, the number of nonprofits that really grew, that crossed the $50 million annual revenue barrier, is 144. In the same time, the number of for-profits that crossed it is 46,136. So we're dealing with social problems that are massive in scale, and our organizations can't generate any scale. All of the scale," he contends, "goes to Coca-Cola and Burger King."[1]

∽

While Pallotta has given all this a great deal of thought, some other people who also think a lot about the nonprofit world don't agree with him. Brian Mittendorf, a professor and the chair of the department of accounting and management information systems at Ohio State's Fisher College of Business, thinks the evidence doesn't support Pallotta's concerns, that nonprofit growth is *not* being deterred by negative perceptions of overhead and fundraising. "Among the ten largest for-profits," he wrote in an article for the *NonProfit Quarterly* in 2013, "only four view their advertising expenses as material enough to warrant separate disclosure. More importantly, among the remaining for-profit companies, advertising as a percentage of expenses is not noticeably different from that of their nonprofit counterparts."

Mittendorf admits that comparing the largest ten charities and the largest for-profit entities does not establish a statistically valid study, but he does say it's indicative. "Advertising among the nonprofits is not appreciably smaller than that of the for-profits," he says, and further notes of the two groups, "The (equal-weighted) average advertising percentage among the nonprofits is 1.2 percent, whereas it is 1.8 percent among the for-profits." Six-tenths of one percent, as Mittendorf says, "is hardly a note-worthy difference."[2] At the same time, it must be pointed out, it is also true that 1.8 percent compared to 1.2 percent is a difference, and an increase, of 50 percent, which some people might not characterize as hardly notewor-thy. Mittendorf's point, though, is that neither number is very large.

Pallotta also thinks that comparing percentages is problematic because the comparison ignores the scale to which the percentages apply. "In 2016," he says, "Susan Komen for the Cure spent a little under $2 million on advertising to bring in donations. L'Oreal, by comparison, spent just under $2 billion trying to get largely the same audience to part with their discre-tionary income to buy cosmetics and beauty products. Ironically, it is the constraints we place on nonprofits that prevent them from achieving the kind of scale L'Oreal achieves, which in turn prevent the percentage they spend on advertising from achieving the same decibel level that L'Oreal enjoys."

Moreover, he says, "Using percentage comparisons is like a David Copperfield illusion. That the percentage spends might be close hardly mitigates a massive inequity in public indoctrination. If Bill Gates and I each spend one percent of our income on housing, it hardly makes our housing comparable. And the small dollar amounts available to nonprofits mean that they are limited to cheap, annoying forms of advertising, like direct mail, while the giant consumer brands are able to wrap consumers in luxurious high definition television ads with giant production budgets and story-telling capability, on top of being able to deliver it at prime time to every American household."

It is also true that the marketing efforts at for-profits and nonprofits can often be fundamentally different. Direct spending on advertising at for-profits is often leveraged in a way that nonprofits cannot benefit from. Of Apple's 2017 operating budget of over $200 billion, a little less than $1 billion was devoted to advertising. But Apple isn't the only company adver-tising its iPhone. Retailers like AT&T, Verizon, T-Mobile and others also advertise the phone when they advertise their products. Automobile man-ufacturers gain similar leverage through advertising paid by car dealer-ships; even taking into account co-op buys, the effect of direct advertising is enhanced. No nonprofit ad campaign, no matter the size, benefits in the same way.

~

While Mittendorf wrote a factual rebuttal to Pallotta's thesis from an accounting perspective, others strongly disapprove of Pallotta's nonprofit ideology. One of them is Phil Buchanan, the president of the Center for Effective Philanthropy. In a 2013 blog posting, he began, "Dan Pallotta's TED Talk has received a lot of attention. Too bad, then, that it is built on so much ignorance about both the history and present-day realities of the nonprofit sector."

Buchanan refuted Pallotta's claims about the nonprofit world's lack of accomplishments. "It's absurd," he writes, "to cite the fact that social problems persist as evidence of the nonprofit sector's failings; indeed, it's fair to ask, *How much worse might they be without the work of nonprofits?*" To that, Pallotta responds, "I've never said that the persistence of these huge social problems is the fault of the nonprofit sector. I've said that if we truly unleashed the sector—gave it the same big-league freedoms we give to business—it has the potential to solve these problems. It has the potential to do transformative things."

Buchanan also took issue with Pallotta on the issue of inadequate salaries. "Pallotta, he says, "either ignores or is oblivious to the increasingly rich body of research that suggests that pay is in fact not a key driver of motivation and performance." In 2015 Buchanan earned in excess of $450,000 while operating a nonprofit whose revenues are forty times smaller than those of Wounded Warrior Project and whose CEO made about the same amount. Pallotta counters that Buchanan's argument is "absurd. People who command higher salaries are generally less fungible and less replaceable than those who do not. To say that you can find the same level of talent, at scale, for $100,000 and no incentives as you can for $400,000 plus bonuses and equity, flies in the face of the compensation rationale of the entire for-profit sector. You cannot simultaneously argue that for-profit corporations are greedy profit-feeders, and" at the same time "that they wantonly throw profits down the toilet by over-paying and over-incentivizing everyone.

At \$400,000 a year I can donate \$100,000 to charity and still be making \$300,000 more a year, so I satisfy my security concerns and my altruism simultaneously. The math is inescapable."

As for ineffective marketing, Buchanan echoed Mittendorf. "The notion that nonprofits haven't been effective marketers is simply false." To this Pallotta says, "Go ask 100 average people on the street how many have heard of Coca-Cola and compare that number to those who have heard of Charity Water—perhaps the best marketer the sector has—and see how that thesis holds up. You can have effective marketing skills, but if you don't have a penny to spend on it that's not going to mean very much."

On the topic of the public's current obsession with overhead costs at charities, Buchanan admitted that Pallotta has a point, but, he said, Pallotta "takes his argument to an extreme that ignores the fact that it isn't always irrelevant either. By lumping together fundraising costs that too often are, in fact, questionable, with investments in professional development or performance measurement, as Pallotta does, we do the cause of reducing the emphasis on overhead a disservice." Pallotta wonders who, exactly, has provided evidence that fundraising costs are "in fact, questionable."

Buchanan also took issue with Pallotta's use of the word "apartheid" in describing what Pallotta thinks is discrimination against nonprofits.[3]

This may sound like a dispute about how many angels can dance on a pin, a nerdy discussion that doesn't affect anyone outside of the nonprofit world, but in fact—because within it are profound questions that affect the public's willingness to support charitable causes and, indeed, zero in on why we have charities at all—the debate serves a profound purpose. Decisions made as a result of addressing such questions affect almost every human being in the United States.

～

Charity constitutes a distinct and important piece of society and its leaders have taken pains to emphasize their ethical place in the world. A common refrain is: *We do the good work that neither business will nor government can.* There's some meat to that sentiment, but at the same time, charities are, at least on a fundamental level, businesses. They have to balance their budgets and pay their people, they provide services, and they do it all to a significant degree by selling—getting people to give money for—a product. Even though it's an intangible product, it's also powerful: the opportunity, as Pallotta would say, to make the world a better place by investing, in the marketplace of love.

While Pallotta attracts criticism by challenging our way of thinking about the way charities should work, he has made us think about things we otherwise might not. And, to be fair, he gets more than a few things right. Perhaps most important, he identifies an essential conundrum in the nonprofit world: promoting an ethos in which people are led to believe that a charity's program services are somehow superior to the work of fundraising, the function that permits those services to be provided in the first place. Fundraising, according to Pallotta, is a process that "actively tries to engage more people in civil society and in important efforts to eliminate social problems—fundraising is an investment in strengthening civil society—in much the same way political contributions are used to get people out of their houses to vote. Fundraising," he says, "is the cost society pays for not giving spontaneously without being asked."[4]

If you take issue with the presumption that the image of fundraising is dirty, then why do you suppose that, currently, our system of evaluating charities is based in large part on the presumption that the less spent on fundraising, the better? Development professionals and other high-ranking employees, the people who raise the money for charities, know that the calling is noble, but somehow even they often get tongue-tied when asked to address the issue. *Yes, my role is crucial to the advancement of our mission, but, of course, we make sure the organization doesn't devote too much of the budget to that role.* This thinking, this fear of acknowledging a truth by submitting to the artificial measurements of what some say should guide charities, has led the public astray from constructive analyses of why they exist in the first place.

If Pallotta's thinking—and the extension of it—can be criticized, it might be in the following way. The sole purpose of charities is to improve society, while the sole purpose of businesses is to generate profits. That's a bit simplistic, actually, because the contours of decision-making in the for-profit world are more nuanced; as examples, Apple's watch can perform an electrocardiogram in 30 seconds and send it to your doctor, for free; Whole Foods promotes sustainable local farming; and Starbucks supports coffee farmers in developing nations. But it can also be persuasively argued that all the feel-good things that for-profit entities tell the public about their work are ultimately aimed at making money for management and shareholders. That's not true with charities, which is why they constitute a *separate* sector of our society.

Still, as is true at for-profit entities, charities need money to do their work. Instead of selling cars or smart phones or shoes, they sell dreams and hope and love.

That's what they sell at Wounded Warrior Project.

And they were criticized mightily for the amount they spent on raising money.

The role and scope of fundraising are only two uncomfortable themes charities need to confront. Others involve working in increasingly challenging environments, especially taking into account for-profit and government relationships, satisfying the expectations of today's philanthropists, deciding what transparency means in an increasingly sophisticated and critical world, managing a modern charity, and—the big issue—producing and demonstrating impact. Charities need to provide better evidence than they do now that the world is a better place because of their work.

These are the connecting threads in the confusing tapestry we call the nonprofit sector. The crisis at Wounded Warrior Project has given us a guide to confront important questions and to make sense of why that sector is so important to society.

CHAPTER 1

ALLEGATIONS

A Gloomy Day

The late winter afternoon was surreal. Although he had been told nothing yet, Steve Nardizzi knew the moment was at hand. He isn't the nervous type, but he still had trouble fending off angst as he tried getting his head around what he knew was happening. His career was darkening much like the sky was at that moment. In the cab from LaGuardia airport to midtown Manhattan, however, it wasn't so much his own future that occupied his thoughts but the future of the wounded veterans who returned from war after 9/11.

Nardizzi was the chief executive officer of Wounded Warrior Project. Also in the cab was Al Giordano, WWP's chief operating officer. Each had been a founder of the organization. Giordano wondered aloud, "What if we're being set up? What if we're being fired?"[5]

∽

As the sun began to set on that Thursday, March 10, 2016, the two men were told to wait outside the conference room of a high-end New York City-based business consulting firm, where their bosses—the organization's trustees—had already assembled. Although it was scheduled as a regular board meeting, this one would be different. Within three minutes after being invited in to join the group, after the board's chairman read aloud a short, prepared statement, Nardizzi no longer had a job and was brusquely escorted from the room. Immediately following, the same fate befell Giordano. In an instant they were gone; this, even though they were acknowledged as the architects of significant successes at the nation's fastest growing charity, and, by any measure, the largest and most effective of the over 8,000 independent 501(c)(3) organizations, that serve veterans.[6]

The board's news release that evening made no mention of what might have precipitated the decision to abruptly fire the two men, but it was clearly connected to reports, six weeks earlier on *CBS News* and in the *New York Times*, filled with disturbing claims: money was being spent frivolously on entertainment and travel, costs were too high, morale was bad, programs were failing, and charity watchdogs were giving the place warnings and bad grades. Charities occupy a special place in our lives, one that requires adherence to the terms of an unwritten but nevertheless demanding pact that calls for complex and unparalleled service to society, and, it appeared, Wounded Warrior Project reneged on the deal.

The CBS News and New York Times Reports

On Tuesday, January 26, 2016, six weeks before the fateful board meeting, Scott Pelley, the anchor of *CBS Evening News,* introduced the first of three damning reports aired that night and the following day. Also, in what would turn out not to be a coincidence, on that second day The *New York Times* published a strikingly similar story.

"What caught our attention," Pelley said on that first evening broadcast, "is how the Wounded Warrior Project spends donations as compared to other long-respected charities. For example, the Disabled American Veterans Charitable Service Trust spends 96 percent of its budgets on vets. Fisher House devotes 91 percent. But, according to public records reported by Charity Navigator, the Wounded Warrior Project spends just 60 percent on vets." Pelley briefly paused and then asked, "Where's the money is going?"

To partly answer that question, Chip Reid, the correspondent for the story, said *CBS News* had interviewed more than 40 former WWP employees. One of them, Reid's main on-camera resource, Army Staff Sergeant Erick Millette, was an Iraq War veteran who had suffered several injuries. "I was knocked unconscious six times," he said. "I suffer from traumatic brain injury. I have a spinal injury, as well as a left knee injury."[7] Millette also suffers from Post-Traumatic Stress Disorder. He was awarded a Bronze Star and a Purple Heart.

"Initially," Reid reported, Millette "admired the charity's work, and participated in its programs." Reid also mentioned a "shout-out" given Millette by President Obama, high praise that was, by all accounts, well deserved.

Millette, however, was not happy. "He took a job as a public speaker with Wounded Warrior Project in 2013," Reid said, "but he quit after witnessing what he calls lavish spending on parties for executives and staff." Their mission, Millette said, "is to honor and empower wounded warriors, but what the public doesn't see is how they spend their money." At charities, spending is closely scrutinized by the public because, unlike at for-profit organizations, people presume that every dollar not spent to further their mission is a dollar wasted. Reid reported that the former employees "described a charity where spending was out of control."

CBS News highlighted the spending at one conference in particular, the 2014 annual meeting held at the Broadmoor, a luxury resort hotel in Colorado Springs. The indicting comments were meant to be representative of problems at several conferences where, it was asserted, costs were unnecessarily extravagant.

Another person interviewed on camera, but whose identity was not revealed because, he said, of his fear of retaliation, said the Broadmoor event "was extremely extravagant—dinners and alcohol." The cost for the conference, which hosted 500 participants over a four-day period, was reported to be about $3 million. Millette said, "Donors don't want you to have a $2,500 bar tab. Donors don't want you to fly every staff member once a year to some five-star resort and whoop it up and call it 'team-building.'" This means, if the claims were true, that WWP was suffering from nothing less than wanton abligurition, a long cry from the image a charity that helps wounded veterans ought to be portraying. Reid wondered, "For a charitable organization that is serving veterans, all this expense on expensive resorts and alcohol, it seems—." Interrupting and completing the thought, the unidentified person said, "It's what the military calls fraud, waste and abuse."

Further, Millette said of his role as a spokesperson for Warriors Speak, one of several WWP programs designed to help veterans, "Wounded Warrior Project and those donor dollars trained me to speak and be a voice. And that's exactly what I'm doing. And I'm sorry, but I'll be damned if you're gonna take hard-working Americans' money and drink it and waste it." And this: "You're using our injuries, our darkest days, our hardships to make money. So you can have these big parties? Let's get a Mexican mariachi band in there. Let's get maracas made with the Wounded Warrior Project logo. Put 'em on every staff member's desk. Let's get it catered. Let's have a big old party. Staying at a lavish hotel at the beach here in Jacksonville on the ocean, and requiring staff that lives in the area to stay at the hotel?"

Reid pointed out that WWP's annual spending on conferences grew from "1.7 million dollars in 2010 to $26 million in 2014."

In an interview on National Public Radio, Dave Philipps, who researched and wrote the *Times* story, shared his own perspectives. "They would have it at far-flung places not close to their headquarters where the charity would fly in hundreds of employees to a five-star hotel," he said. "They would pay for drinks. They would pay for food. They would pay for outings. And the employees said there was not a whole lot of point to it and they sort of wondered what donors would think if they saw them all there."[8]

Charges also included that WWP's leaders spent $7.5 million for air travel. "Former workers recounted buying business-class seats," Reid reported, "and regularly jetting around the country for minor meetings, or staying in $500-per-night hotel rooms." He also pointed out, "About 40 percent of the organization's donations in 2014 were spent on its overhead, or about $124 million, according to the charity-rating group Charity Navigator."

~

Spending too little on programs that mattered and spending too much on activities that didn't weren't the only complaints. Millette claimed that Warriors Speak was nothing more than a fundraising machine. "They will tell you it's not" a fundraising vehicle, "but it is. I began to see how an organization that rakes in hundreds of millions of dollars a year is not helping my brothers and my sisters. Or at least not all of them." Reid reported that nearly all of the former employees were "concerned that the organization has become more focused on raising money than on serving wounded veterans." There was an unsubtle undertone that it was all being done on the backs of donors, many of whom were alone and elderly—easy targets and susceptible to appeals.

Too much money was spent to raise money. Fundraising costs doubled the year Steve Nardizzi took over in 2009 and he increased those costs "an average of 66 percent every year after, until 2015," the *Times* reported. "The Wounded Warrior Project spent more than $34 million on fund-raising in 2014, according to tax records."

The newspaper also took note of the hundreds of thousands of dollars spent on public relations and lobbying campaigns to deflect criticism of its spending and to fight legislative efforts to restrict how much nonprofits spend on overhead. WWP "hired the global public relations firm Edelman, which has represented Starbucks, Walmart, Shell and Philip Morris, to improve public perception of the charity and its overhead spending." WWP also donated $150,000 to the Charity Defense Council, a nonprofit started by Dan Pallotta that addresses what it considers misconceptions relating to charity spending on overhead and executive salaries. When Nardizzi joined its advisory board—as distinct from the governing board—some thought he was doing everything possible to justify his lavish spending.

WWP was also accused of *not* spending money. Wounded Warrior Project was sitting on a large surplus of cash that some said could be better used to provide services. Daniel Borochoff, the head of CharityWatch, another charity watchdog, said, "The group is sitting on a $248 million surplus, and not enough of it is being spent on veterans. It would be helpful if these hundreds of millions of dollars were being spent to help veterans in the shorter term in a year or two rather than being held for a longer term."

∽

Properly reporting its activities was also said to be a problem. Former employees said that WWP was inflating the amount it spent on programs by using illicit practices, such as counting some marketing materials as educational. "Wounded Warrior Project," *CBS News* reported, "says 80 per-cent of their money is spent on programs for veterans. That's because they include some promotional items, direct-response advertising, and ship-ping and postage costs. Take that out, and the figures look more like what charity watchdogs say—that only 54 to 60 percent of donations go to help wounded service members." This is a practice known as jointly allocating costs and WWP was being accused of fudging the numbers to make them look better than they were.

When Marcus Owens, who for ten years was employed as the director of the IRS's Exempt Organizations Division, was asked about his biggest concern, he said, "I couldn't tell the number of people that were assisted. I thought that was truly unusual." Owens was referring to the information reported in IRS Form 990, which all charities must file every year.

Morale was poor, too, according to the news reports. Several former employees claimed that they were fired unjustly.

One former employee, Dan Lessard, who ran a jobs-placement pro-gram, said, for example, that the number of placements the program was expected to make each year was too high, which reduced the amount of time specialists had to find good ones. He complained, "I would push back and they would get very frustrated and yell. By the time I left, we were just throwing guys in jobs to check off a box and hit the numbers."

Another, William Chick, a former supervisor who spent five years with Wounded Warrior Project, felt that that WWP's leadership fostered an environment of fear and mistrust. "It slowly had less focus on veter-ans and more on raising money and protecting the organization," he said. Chick, who was fired in 2012 after a dispute with his supervisor, said he saw Wounded Warrior Project help hundreds of veterans, but, like other former employees, said the group swiftly fired anyone whom leaders con-sidered a "bad cultural fit." The *Times* reported, "Eighteen former employ-ees—many of them wounded veterans themselves—said they had been fired for seemingly minor missteps or perceived insubordination. At least half a dozen former employees said they were let go after raising questions about ineffective programs or spending."

Other former employees said that Wounded Warrior Project lacked comprehensive programs for the treatment needed by wounded veterans. Erick Millette again: "I would raise issues. Why aren't we going to follow up? Why don't we have any case management?" When asked about outreach, he responded disparagingly, "We don't call warriors. Warriors call us. Again, as a disabled veteran, it just makes me sick. I think they want to show warriors a good time. I think they get these warriors to events. But where's the follow-up? A lot of the warriors I saw needed mental health treatment. They don't get that from Wounded Warrior Project." When asked what happens when employees suggest that there's a better way to serve veterans, Millette's answer was, "If you use your brain and come up with an idea, within a matter of time you're off the bus. They don't need you. It's their way or the highway."

In an effort to get WWP's perspective, after trying and failing to speak with Nardizzi, Chip Reid spoke with Captain Ryan Kules, the director of alumni at the time, who later became the director of combat stress recovery, and a recipient of the organization's services. As would be expected, Kules denied excessive spending on conferences. "It's the best use of donor dollars to be able to ensure that we're providing programs and services to our warriors and their families, and at the highest quality." Reid then asked, "Why go to a five-star resort in Colorado when you could just do it in Jacksonville and save a lot of money, and spend that money on wounded warriors?" "Like I've said," Kules responded, "the reason we're providing those All-Hands Conferences is to ensure that we're aligned and able to build as a team." Taking that as essentially a repeat of Kules's prior unsatisfactory answer, and after what seemed to be an edited-out back-and-forth that went nowhere, Reid said, "So you're going to just keep saying that, no matter what question I ask about the All-Hands Conferences?" An awkward silence followed as CBS caught a lingering and unfortunate shot on Kules's apparent inability to respond coherently, the implication being that the company line was shallow and indefensible.

At the end of that interview, Reid noted that although Kules disputed the $3 million bill for the Colorado conference, Kules did not attend and did not know what was actually spent.[9]

The message seemed to get through to people. One person said he once sat next to one of the leaders of Wounded Warrior Project on an airplane and, having been so taken with the group's mission he and his wife became devoted donors, but that, after hearing of the allegations in the news they discontinued their support. He said, "The group is obviously fraudulent."[10] Another person, asked when the topic of Wounded Warrior Project arose at her place of employment, responded by asking her own question, "Isn't that the fake charity everybody's been talking about?"[11]

$\backsim$

It's fair to say that any charity guilty of such claims ought to fire its staff leadership. The question might also be asked if the charity itself should continue to actually exist. After all, there should be consequences for donor dollars so misused and a public trust so violated.

How The Reporting Got It Wrong

As it turns out, however, the media got it wrong; in contrast to what was alleged, Wounded Warrior Project was actually pretty well run.

Although charities are required by law to freely make available to the public only the three most recent 990s, WWP makes all of them, back to its founding in 2005, available on its website. The same is true for its audited financial statements. Grant Thornton—the same accounting firm that has been used by the Department of Defense, the Department of Treasury, the Federal Reserve System, the United States House of Representatives, and many major corporations and other nonprofits in the United States—conducted the most recent audit prior to 2015. As with the 990s, all financial statements and annual reports from 2005 are available on the WWP website.

To ensure that things work well internally, WWP has an executive vice president who is responsible for financial operations, while the board of directors broadly oversees WWP's budget.

As for spending on conferences, WWP, as many charities do, hosted a small number of interoffice parties for the staff. As an example, for an event at the end of the fiscal year 2015, WWP brought in food from a local

Mexican restaurant and had a local mariachi band play for 30 minutes. No alcohol was served. It was a modest affair and not atypical.

Many charitable organizations spend money on off-site meetings to raise awareness of its mission, discuss strategic planning, and raise morale. Preparations for the large 2014 conference at the Broadmoor—the annual event was known as the All Hands Huddle—included deep vetting. The team of people charged with researching an appropriate site presented the senior staff with the top three selections, and, after much discussion, one that included cost, chose the Broadmoor. The Charity Defense Council pointed out, "Wounded Warrior Project sought bids from no fewer than fifteen hotels before deciding on the Broadmoor, which came in at the lowest price."[12] The cost, in fact, was not $3 million, but $970,000. Taking into account the type of event and the hundreds of people involved, it turns out that, at $150 per night per person, the place just wasn't all that expensive.

Although the reports made it seem that Nardizzi acted unilaterally on spending decisions, the board was aware of and approved the cost for the conference. In addition, through 2015 at least one board member had gone to every All Hands Huddle. Justin Constantine, a board member who went to the Broadmoor meeting, wrote on Facebook, "Have you ever attended a conference with 450 people super excited about their jobs who just want to keep doing great things for those they support? I just did . . . and am walking away very proud of the energy every employee puts into taking care of our wounded warriors and their families."[13] Although Erick Millette claimed he resigned from WWP because of the extravagance, and said that the Broadmoor conference was a catalyst for his concerns about spending, at the time he, too, wrote favorably of the event on his Facebook page. "That's how you start All Hands!" he wrote during the conference. "Love my teammates!!!"[14]

When asked about Nardizzi's ego-driven, extravagant conference entrances, Dave Philipps, the *New York Times* reporter, claimed that WWP employees characterized them as "absurd and a real waste of money."[15] Philipps did not attribute the sentiment to anyone. Nardizzi himself acknowledges that the CEO of any organization has an ego and that he is no exception. But, he says, "Look carefully at all of those dramatic entrances. I am in a wig and often in some of the most unflattering clothes imaginable, including lederhosen. No one, by the way, looks good in leder-hosen." So, why? And why the wig? "I came dressed as *FILIS*," a homonym for a woman's name but which also serves as an acronym for fun, integrity, loyalty, innovation, and service. "I was dressed in a way as to portray and remind everyone of our core values." Nardizzi wore the wig for his entrance every year. "If you were there," he says, "what you would have heard was resounding laughter—people making fun of me in a good way, but who also knew what it was all about and were responsive to it." The entrances, as it turns out, were neither a waste of money, as almost none was spent on the moment, nor absurd.

While it is true that WWP's spending on conferences and meetings for all programs had increased dramatically—in 2010 the amount was $1.7 million and by 2014 it was $26 million—the news stories were wildly mis-leading. Most of that money was actually spent on programs. In 2014, 94 percent of the $26 million conference budget went to program expenses.

Was a lot of alcohol consumed at these parties at WWP's expense? Was there, as Erick Millette claimed, a $2,500 bar tab? Hardly. WWP's alcohol policy prohibited alcohol at program events and required staff members not to drink at program events. The policy also prohibited the organization from paying for alcohol at All-Hands events. Of $251,000 of expenses relating to the All Hands meetings charged to WWP credit cards in 2014 and 2015, a total of two alcoholic beverages were purchased and charged to WWP by employees—about $20. "Overall," according to Al Giordano, "alcohol was paid for by WWP in extremely limited situa-tions, such as galas, fundraising events, and board meetings. Any improper purchases, such as the unauthorized purchase of alcohol, would be noted in an employee's review and, depending on the severity of the infraction, could lead to his or her termination. How could it be otherwise? Excessive alcohol consumption is directly linked to suicide efforts, one of the biggest problems veterans face. Not only is a claim that WWP condoned alcohol consumption one of financial excess, it irresponsibly attacks efforts to real-ize the mission."[16]

The *Times* reported, "Former workers recounted buying business-class seats and regularly jetting around the country for minor meetings." But that was not true. WWP's policy was and continues to be that, with some exceptions, no first class travel is authorized. Almost all of the paid air travel was in economy class. During the years prior to 2016, less than one percent was booked for employee travel in business or first class. Of approximately 25,000 flights over the prior several years, 232 were taken in either business-class or first-class seats—and over half of those were free upgrades.

The broader accusations on spending—that it "skyrocketed since Steven Nardizzi took over as CEO in 2009," that "Nardizzi doubled his spending on fundraising and increased it an average of 66 percent every year" when he was the CEO, and that WWP "spent more than $34 million on fundraising in 2014"—were isolated and inaccurate. Revenues increased by 66 percent annually, fundraising costs increased by 47 percent annually (not 66 percent), and programming expenses increased by 64 percent annually—but administrative costs, as a percentage of the budget, remained relatively flat.

According to Nardizzi and Giordano, neither ever received a complaint from an employee regarding how money was spent.

CBS News reported that nearly all of the former employees who were interviewed said they were concerned that WWP was more focused on raising money than on serving wounded veterans. Although Warriors Speak, the program where Erick Millette worked, initially included appeals for funds, after the first year WWP eliminated the fundraising aspect, and emphasizes this fact—that no fundraising is to take place—in its training. Millette, who incorrectly claimed the program was essentially a front for raising money, attended this training. One of the explicit requirements for those chosen to take part in Warriors Speak is that they must always be truthful.

As to his accusation that the program is "not helping my brothers and my sisters," metrics analyses showed that 90 percent of the alumni were satisfied with all of WWP's programs and services, including Warriors Speak. In another program, the National Campaign Team, a group of about three-dozen unpaid volunteer veterans and their family members told their stories, which, in fact, were used in fundraising and television advertising.

A vetting process for accuracy ensured that all participants in this group approved of the messaging. Millette was not part of this group.

As for Millette's comment—"We don't call warriors. Warriors call us."—verified records showed that WWP, in a program called Operation Outreach, regularly contacted veterans and their families. Both Nardizzi and Giordano, despite their executive status, participated in those calls. In 2015, staff members conducted almost 77,000 documented outbound wellness checks and outreach calls to veterans and their caregivers. From 2013 to 2015, WWP employees made more than 150,000 outreach calls and sent more than 114,000 outreach emails to wounded warriors. Furthermore, Millette was personally involved with the program. In fact, in what surely was a sign of his enthusiasm and support, he inquired about the Operation Outreach Coordinator position in December 2014. He ultimately didn't apply, however, because it was thought, he felt he was not qualified.

As mental and emotional health is critical to the overall well being of wounded warriors and their families, WWP offers additional support to ensure they are well adjusted in mind and spirit. Multiple WWP programs are specifically focused on mental health interventions and every employee is schooled with suicide-prevention training. WWP pays for mental health counselors. WWP spent over $1 million per month, for example, through the Independence Program to serve the most severely wounded and their family members in their homes.

When Marcus Owens, the former executive at the IRS, told CBS that his "biggest concern" after reviewing the organization's Form 990 filings was that he "couldn't tell the number of people that were assisted," he failed to mention that the form doesn't have a place to report the number of people assisted. Such information can be contained in a supplemental narrative, but it is not "highly unusual," even though Owens claimed it was, that it was absent in the 990. WWP provides detailed program participation numbers, from program metrics and alumni surveys, on its website.

Putting that aside, however, it's important to remember that Reid asked Owens about his "*biggest* concern." What was lost in what seemed to be feigned exasperation is that a formerly high-ranking IRS official could come up with nothing more important other than the absence of information relating to a question that is not asked on the 990. One could reasonably infer after giving the matter a little thought that nothing, apparently, in Owens's view, was wrong with the information provided in response to the questions that *are* asked on the 990.

Daniel Borochoff, the head of CharityWatch, criticized WWP for sitting on $248 million. It's easy to say a charity shouldn't be wasting money by sitting on it, but a fundamental reality in the nonprofit world is that reserves are important because they allow for long-range planning. Many large organizations have reserves and no one thinks the money is wasted.

The *Times* reported, "Eighteen former employees—many of them wounded veterans themselves—said they had been fired for seemingly minor missteps or perceived insubordination. At least half a dozen former employees said they were let go after raising questions about ineffective programs or spending." That's questionable. A forensic examination found that no employee had ever been fired for making a complaint about programs or spending. None of the former staff that spoke to the media sued WWP for wrongful termination, and there were no successful Equal Employment Opportunity Commission findings for them. Communications Executive Vice President Ayla Tezel said that some employees interviewed by the *Times* were fired for poor performance or ethical breaches.

Or worse. When WWP discovered that Neil Abramson, the director of major gifts, stole money, that Len Stachitas, the executive vice president of strategic giving, covered up the thefts, and that Theresa Nichols, the manager of major gifts, also mishandled money, Nardizzi and Giordano immediately fired them. All three were employed in positions that required sensitivity and integrity with money. Melissa Cain, a line staffer in the accounting department, received a public award (FILIS) for blowing the whistle on Abramson.

After Stachitas and Nichols were fired, they joined a Facebook page composed of dissatisfied ex-employees. One of the purposes of the group, according to Erick Millette, was to take down WWP.

The *Times* reported that by the time the board met to dismiss Nardizzi and Giordano, contributions were down. That is not true. In addition, contrary to what was strongly implied, Nardizzi and Giordano were not told that they were fired because of the findings in the internal investigation. When the *Times* reported that an independent review[17] "confirmed many of the findings by the *Times* and CBS," it was wrong.

As for the *CBS News* interview with Ryan Kules, it should be noted that Kules, as he was not a designated spokesperson for WWP, was not fully prepared to be interviewed. Still, tough interviews go with the territory at news outlets and Nardizzi regrets his decision to ask Kules to speak on behalf of the organization. "Ryan Kules is one of the brightest and most articulate young men I know," says Nardizzi. "I apologized to him and his wife. What the public saw –what *CBS News* chose to air—does not represent who Kules is. In fact, he is a great leader at WWP."[18]

WWP also taped the interview. At the end, after the CBS cameras had stopped rolling, Chip Reid said, "I'd much rather be doing a happy story about vets. But, I do love doing these stories when they're great. In fact, I have a whole file full of stories—Wounded Warrior Project stories that I have been pitching over time. And I haven't gotten . . . But anyway. Anyway, I gotta job and you gotta job."[19] His job, in other words, despite a preponderance of positive news, was to make WWP look bad.

WWP also recorded the words of several people interviewed by Dave Philipps. One of them was Jon Sullivan, the Vice President for Engagement. "They may first hear about us in their communities," he told Philipps, "but for a large part of the warriors that we serve, we're not necessarily going to meet them in the hospital. DOD [the Department of Defense] doesn't hand us a list and say, 'These are the warriors that were injured this month.' So we rely primarily on other warriors helping us get the word out to their fellow injured or wounded service members. We get a lot of people that reach out directly to our website. And I think the more awareness you have of the organization, the more visibility you have of the organization, the more traffic you generate, the more inbound traffic you generate for the people that you service . . . We're not just looking for anyone that can give us money. We're looking for people that can help us accomplish those three things: raise money, spread awareness, and then have a direct impact on warrior programs."[20]

Several other employees who spoke to Philipps discussed their roles with as much energy and enthusiasm, yet not one word of those interviews ended up in the published story. Al Giordano says, "The naysayers' thoughts appeared in print while those with a countervailing opinion ended up on the cutting room floor."[21]

Waiting and Disbelief

The first story aired on January 26, a Tuesday evening. Nardizzi watched it with a half dozen other senior staff in a conference room. "I was horrified," he says. "It was like a cartoon; it didn't seem like they were doing a report on Wounded Warrior Project. If not for the fact that our faces, and Millette's, and that our logo were all up there—if I had been listening to the report and not watching it and it didn't have our name, I would have said that's not our organization. It bore no resemblance to how we operated or to the great work we were doing or to the way we treated people."

Nevertheless, even though Nardizzi was shocked, he wasn't surprised. "Based on the tone of the emails we read in the run-up to all this," he says, "the opening salvo on CBS about where the money was going . . . I was sort of expecting that criticism. I fully expected it to be a hatchet job." But the rest, not so much. "It's when they started playing the video tapes out of context, and when you started hearing, particularly Erick Millette, with his—no other way to put it—his bald-faced lies—there was a mix in the room of both anger and shock."

The shock was about realizing that this wasn't just a criticism of how money was spent, but a portrayal of something much worse. "It's as if they were saying we were doing something illegal. They weren't just criticizing us. They were fabricating a story that made us look like we're some sort of fraudulent charity. "Yes," Nardizzi says defiantly, "there was anger—anger because we were watching people on the screen who were absolutely lying."

≈

A series of emails shows some concern at CBS—although not enough—about the stories. With an hour to broadcast—the first piece aired on Tuesday night, January 26—David Rhodes, the president of *CBS News*, was trying to ascertain what at least one influential advisor had called about. The advisor had received a heads up on the story. Rhodes missed the call, but knew the matter was urgent, even though the message provided no specifics. Shortly after the story aired the advisor wrote to Len Tepper, the chief of investigative projects at CBS, as well as to Leslie Moonves, the chairman and CEO of CBS Corporation, "Your piece was disgusting tonight. Do not air anything in the A.M. or tomorrow before we talk." That was to no avail, however, as CBS ran the second and third pieces the following morning and evening.

Two days later, Gayle King, the co-host of CBS This Morning received an email with this on the subject line: "Comments made by CBS reporter Chip Reid when he thought he was off camera at the conclusion of the hit piece CBS did on the venerable WWP." King, who was away and apparently had not seen the story, responded, "I will reach out to you when I get back. If you have spoken to Les, he will certainly sort it out. Very sorry to hear you are upset and want to hear what you have to say." By "Les," King meant Les Moonves. Clearly, although inner thoughts were not made public, there was at least some question within *CBS News* about a major story it had run.

A week later, King received another email. The sender said a charitable contribution to Wounded Warrior Project "would be a great way for CBS to make up for itself," as WWP's "finances, expenditures and organizational efficiencies were not at all accurately portrayed." The sender then wrote that Bill O'Reilly "is about to correct nationally after a full investigation he's doing. It confirms over 85% (not 60% reported by CBS) goes to veterans and life saving programs."[22]

⁓

Nardizzi heard a lot of expletives in the conference room the evening he and many staff watched the news. As this would be only the first of three *CBS News* reports over a two-day period, the staff could pretty much guess the tenor of the next two. "It wasn't as if we could assess the damage at that point," Nardizzi said. "We still had to sit through another day of this. We also had to wait for the *New York Times* story. The only thing we could hope for was that the *Times* piece would be more balanced. But it wasn't. It was also filled with lies and fabrication. But it was somehow less visceral in print and felt less sensational than the CBS reports. By then, too, because we had a night to think it through a little, we were getting numbed to the lies and the nonsense."

Nardizzi told his team that it was okay to be angry, but that they were not allowed to freeze up and do nothing. After the second day, when all three CBS stories had aired and the *Times* story had been published, Nardizzi responded. "We sent a demand to CBS for a retraction. We also prepared a statement for the staff to read. They knew the stories were all untrue, but they had friends and neighbors who would ask them what was going on. You have multiple audiences. What do we tell warriors who might have seen that? What about our donors? And the board?" The senior team had to craft messages to address everyone's concerns. They even called donors. In addition to the staff, Nardizzi was on calls every day. He also made two trips to Washington, DC for meetings with Congressional staff, including people in Senator Charles Grassley's office. "Our strategy was to try to get in front of the story, be an open book, provide all the information anyone wanted so that we could answer questions and document what was true and what was false."

The strategy of aggressive transparency, however, held only for a time. After they commissioned the financial review, board members told Nardizzi and Giordano that they were to make no public appearances and that they were not permitted to speak to the media. "I was allowed the corporate-donor calls, and the visits to Capitol Hill and Department of Defense staff, but that was all," Nardizzi says.

On February 1, 2016, the Monday after the stories were broadcast, *CBS News* reached out to Nardizzi. "We'd like to discuss more about Steven Nardizzi joining us live in New York City on *CBS This Morning* with Charlie Rose, Gayle King, and Norah O'Donnell. We want to give him an open platform to speak, completely unedited since it would be a live format, so that he can address any and all disagreements he has with the *CBS News* report. This is the best way for him to clear the air and to give his personal and professional perspective. We want to give him the opportunity to set the record straight, and to be able to fully defend the organization he has dedicated his time and effort to for so many years.

"We would dedicate a lot of airtime to the segment so that he can really speak in his own words in a smart and focused conversation. We normally spend around 3 minutes on air with a live guest, but we'd like to offer him double the amount of airtime so that his experience here is well worth it. We have other *CBS News* platforms we can offer as well if he is interested in expanding his audience even further, let me know and I can discuss these options with you. We would provide transportation costs—flight, hotel, and car service to and from the interview on our set."[23]

But no dice. The board was firm, even when the opportunity to explain things presented itself.

~

The muzzling was poor strategy, as it turns out, because in the void there was nothing to push back with against the growing negative public perception.

Nardizzi originally thought it was the result of bad advice from the media consultants the board had hired, but later came to think that board members, regardless of what would emerge in the report, might have already made up their minds to fire him.

The first inkling Nardizzi had on that point came when the board announced the financial review without his involvement. Nardizzi told Tony Odierno, the board chair, that sending an announcement without his discernible participation would send a negative message to donors and the public. "We should have put out a joint statement from both the board and me," said Nardizzi, "so that we could be unified in saying the media reports were wrong."

When he asked to change the statement, Nardizzi was told it was too late, that it was already on the wire for distribution to the media. This was the Monday following the news reports. "You do realize," he told Odierno, "that you will get calls, and not just media calls. Donors are going to call. Corporations are going to call. And we have no talking points for anyone." The board's response wasn't well considered, but that didn't seem to concern Odierno. He said that any calls could go to Abernathy MacGregor, the public relations firm, to which Nardizzi replied, "Well, that's fine for media calls, but what about donor calls? Are you going to have thousands of donor calls routed to the PR firm?"

The chaotic, unprepared approach led one corporate donor, Acosta, to withdraw a $6 million commitment because of the bungled follow-up. "The company and its shareholders might have weathered the storm," Nardizzi said, "had the message been: *Contrary to the media stories, WWP had things under control and there was no problem with the way the organization was being run.* But that wasn't the message. Instead, the message was: *Maybe there is a problem. We'll get back to you.*

Nardizzi told Odierno that if the board had already made up its mind regardless of what the financial report would conclude—which Nardizzi increasingly suspected—then an exit strategy needed to be prepared. "Don't wait," he said, "to create a secondary news cycle thirty days from now. If you've made up your mind, it's best to quickly rip the band aid off and avoid pain down the road." Odierno assured Nardizzi that wasn't the case. No one, he said, was talking about letting Nardizzi or Giordano go. It was a tepid and tellingly misleading comment, especially as it compares with the way at least one other major organization handled bad publicity aimed at its executive director.

In June 2016, the board of directors of the American Red Cross was confronted with blistering attacks on its executive director, Gail McGovern, charges that were made after ProPublica and National Public Radio conducted research involving the organization's 990s and program effectiveness, and after a withering report from the office of Senator Charles Grassley on the Red Cross's spending and openness. The Grassley report, born out of an 18-month inquiry about the Red Cross response to the 2010 Haiti earthquake, accused Ms. McGovern of gutting the charity's in-house ethics and investigation unit and trying to snuff out a Congressional review of the nonprofit's practices. Bonnie McElveen-Hunter, the Red Cross board chair, said in response to the criticism, "Gail McGovern is respected, admired, and really has 100 percent confidence of the board. Frankly, we think the nation should be casting laurels at her feet."[24]

Nardizzi and Giordano received no such support from their board.

Fired

At the meeting in New York, which had been scheduled to take place in Jacksonville, there would be no staff input on program, no updates on finances, and nothing on other matters that are components of a typical board meeting. "We want only you and Al to attend," Nardizzi was told, "as well as two other senior staff members." The board also told him to prepare a 30- 60- and 90-day operational plan for presentation at the meeting. Although this request had the markings of going forward without anyone being fired, Nardizzi, suspicious after the fiasco following the announcement of the financial review, thinks the directive was meant only to placate him.

Nardizzi and Giordano arrived at LaGuardia airport on March 10. The board meeting was held that afternoon in the midtown Manhattan office building where Abernathy MacGregor, WWP's public relations firm, was located. During a phone call on the taxi ride, Nardizzi learned that Dave Philipps contacted Abernathy McGregor to ask for a comment about the board's decision and the report. Nardizzi asked himself: *Why don't we know this? Why do the media know about the results of the report while none of us knows?* Actually, Nardizzi did know, if only in his heart at that point. "Once they moved the meeting, I knew."

As they were going up the elevator, Giordano asked Nardizzi when they would know. "We'll know when we walk in," Nardizzi answered. "The first sign will be if the attorneys are there, and if an attorney greets us as opposed to someone from the board. The second sign will be if they say they are going to bring us in separately. Then, the only remaining question will be whether they will fire just me or whether they will fire you as well." Nardizzi told Giordano that if he, Giordano, was not fired he should stay to ensure programmatic continuity and stability. Giordano responded, "I understand, but if they fire you I'm going to walk anyway."

After several minutes of waiting once they arrived, the conference room door opened and an attorney appeared. "Thanks for coming in gentlemen," he said. "Al, if you wouldn't mind, the board would like Steve to come in first."

The board members—Tony Odierno, Guy McMichael, Justin Constantine, Roger Campbell, Robert Nardelli and Richard Jones—and the attorneys were all seated on one side of the conference table. Nardizzi sat alone on the other side, at the end, directly across from Tony Odierno. Only one board member made eye contact with Nardizzi, who likened the moment to the way a defendant feels as the jury foreman is about to announce the verdict. "Tony picked up a piece of paper," he recalls, "and read a statement letting me know they decided to make a leadership change, that the change would be effective immediately, and that there would be no discussion about it." All the while, Nardizzi could see only the back side of the sheet of paper, as Odierno concealed his face while he read his statement. "He wasn't even able to look at me as he read it."

Giordano's experience was much the same. "I tried to look everybody in the eye. Nobody looked me in the eye. Didn't say a word." He looked around the room. "Literally," he recalls, "there were captains of industry, captains of Wall Street, and real captains—and the total lack of leadership was absolutely breathtaking. On the one hand they just got a report that said nothing was wrong, and on the other they said you're fired. At that moment, I realized that what we had done for wounded warriors was at its apex. *This day*, I thought, *March 10, 2016, is the high water mark for Wounded Warrior Project.*"

Furthermore, because of a conflict of interest, one of the trustees, Richard Jones, should not have been in the room.

∼

Immediately after, in a small room outside the conference room, the board's attorneys asked Nardizzi to sign a settlement agreement. Odierno had informed Nardizzi that he could characterize the change as a "resignation" rather than a "termination," but that he had only two hours to make that decision. "It would have provided me with $50,000," Nardizzi says. "There was a host of restraints, including a non-compete clause and a non-disparagement provision, which would have prevented me from telling the truth of what happened. I rejected the deal." Nardizzi also told the attorneys that although *they* might have only two hours, *he* was under no obligation to respond in such a short time, especially without counsel. The $50,000 offer soon rose to $200,000, but that too did not entice Nardizzi, the ability to tell his story and save his soul, as he put it, being higher priorities than being bought off. "I'm not going to get silenced," he said. "They smeared my reputation by allowing all these accusations to take place when they knew it was all false."

The attorneys in the impromptu post-firing gathering then asked for the company credit card and phone that Nardizzi had. After he surrendered those items and when the attorneys were leaving, he called out, "Wait. I still have the codes to all the bank accounts." Not only was a password needed to access the bank accounts, the codes were also crucial, as they were often changed for maximum security. Without the codes, accessing the accounts was impossible. Access to the codes meant access to hundreds of millions of Wounded Warrior Project dollars. Nardizzi had the keys to the kingdom in his pocket and the attorneys, who oversaw a carefully crafted, although rejected, letter of forced departure and who were entrusted with retrieving Nardizzi's company materials, almost walked away without realizing they hadn't remembered to retrieve the most important asset of all.

Incredibly, the same scene played out with Giordano. He had to ask them, after the attorneys asked for the keys and credit card, if they wanted anything else. "Do you have anything else," they asked. "Well, how would you like the codes to the bank account?" Giordano muses, "Theoretically, I could have transferred a hundred million dollars to the Bahamas."[25]

By the time Nardizzi and Giordano arrived back at their hotel, no more than 20 minutes after they left the building, CBS ran a teaser on a story that would run during its evening news about the two being fired. The short time given to Nardizzi, it turns out, was all about getting the agreement before the world would know. "The board tipped off CBS," Nardizzi said. "That was the only reason there was a two-hour window. The fact is, CBS knew I was going to be fired before I knew. And so did the *New York Times.*"[26]

CHAPTER 2

BEGINNINGS

"WE WERE ALWAYS A CLOSE FAMILY, a private family," Ed Edmundson said in 2016, but after his son Eric was severely injured in Iraq, the family was affected in many different ways. "We had to move. It affected us financially. It affected us spiritually. In every aspect of life it affected us. And it still does. It still has repercussions on us eleven years later."[27] Of course it would. Some wounds never heal. Such is the cost of battle.

On October 2, 2005, U.S. Army Sgt. Eric Edmundson, who was 26 at the time, and other members of his Stryker Brigade unit were hit near the Syrian border by an improvised explosive device. Badly injured and while waiting to be sent to a military hospital in Germany, Eric went into cardiac arrest. Oxygen stopped entering his brain. Without oxygen, a person can lose consciousness within 60 seconds. Damage to the brain can begin after about four minutes. Eric's brain didn't receive oxygen for 30 minutes. That deprivation induced a complex combination of traumatic brain syndrome and anoxic brain injury. It was so bad that when he returned home his doctors at the Veterans Administration hospital said that he would most likely remain in a vegetative state for the rest of his life.

Ed Edmundson thinks highly of Walter Reed Army Medical Center in Washington, DC, and has many good things to say about the treatment his son received there, but he thinks the post-discharge attention was badly flawed. [28] At once dissatisfied and hopeful, Edmundson looked elsewhere for help. On his own, he soon learned of the Rehabilitation Institute of Chicago, which is thought by medical experts to be the best of its kind in America.[29] There, after he waded through a massive amount of government red tape, and with the support of doctors and his family, his son's life active life slowly began again. He learned how to communicate again and he learned to move his arms and legs again; not in the way he was able to before he was injured, but enough to take charge of at least some parts of his life. Because his family members didn't accept the VA's ominous prognosis, and thanks to their determination, today, while his body is somatically challenged, Eric is vigorous and his life is full. In fact, he is both a husband and a father. He was a father of one child before his injuries and, because he and his wife found strength and not despair in their trials, he became the father of another after. He has a lot of life to live.

He will do that with the help of his family: his wife Stephanie, his sister Anna, as well as his parents, Beth and Ed. His daughter Gracie and his son Hunter are in their way more help than anyone else.

No small part of that new beginning—and its continuation—can be credited to the work and support of Wounded Warrior Project. "Wounded Warrior Project reached out to us as a family," says Eric's father. "They reached out to my son and they never forgot about us. They gave my son hope for the future."[30]

Coming Home From Vietnam

In the United States today there exists no more exalted citizen status than that of veteran.

And why not? What non-veteran can claim to have better served this country than those who have been willing to die for it? We owe something unique and special to the person who positions self and soul between our enemies and our way of life.

This is a strong and true debt that transcends political ideology. Many people, for example, might never have voted for John McCain, the former longtime Republican senator from Arizona, or for Bob Kerrey, the former Democratic senator and governor from Nebraska, for any public office because of his political philosophy, but they are likely to still fiercely regard the men—both of whom were severely injured in the Vietnam war—as symbols of our highest values. In surpassing politics, the concept of veteran reaches into our deepest understanding of what it means to be an American. Meredith Asbury, a student at the Columbia Middle School in

Missouri in 2013 when she won an essay contest, wrote that among the virtues of veterans is that they "watched out for one another on and off the battlefield," and that "they live by us and work by us, yet we don't even know who some of them are." Some, she noted, "are old and served in World War II while others are young and served in Iraq." Most poignantly, of what our country stands for, she wrote, "They were willing to lose their lives so that you and I can have these freedoms."[31]

Would that people always felt the same about the 42 million men and women who have served their country in the military since the American Revolution,[32] over half of whom—ponder this for a moment—are alive today.

But we haven't. For many people who came of age in the late 1960s and early 1970s, the image is searing: the returning solider from Vietnam derided, spat upon, disrespected for being a tool of those who conducted the war, the most unpopular in American history. Of the many protester chants, one of the more memorable was, "Hey, hey, L.B.J., how many babies did you kill today?"

"Implicit in the chant," according to Kyle Longley, a history professor at Arizona State University, "was the instrument of Lyndon B. Johnson's brutal, inhuman policy: the young men fighting in Vietnam. And it didn't take much for many Americans, especially war protesters, to decide that the soldiers were themselves brutal and inhuman—leading to an ugly backlash against returning servicemen. In one case," Kyle says, quoting from *The Killing Zone: My Life in the Vietnam War*, "a young man accosted a veteran missing an arm at a Colorado college in 1968. He asked, 'Get that in Vietnam?

"The veteran said 'yes.' 'Serves you right,' the man said."

Kyle writes, "Those returning received few parades or recognition, and often felt isolated from their countrymen. One remembered his sister asking, 'Who are you fighting for, the North Vietnamese or the other guys?' He lamented: 'I knew that nobody back here understood what was happening. Because if my own family didn't know, what hope did I have with somebody who didn't even know me?'"[33]

In 1968 *Time Magazine* described what veterans could expect when they got home. "This year, at least 900,000 more will muster out—all of them to face an adjustment problem unique among U.S. war vets. The men who fought in World Wars I and II and Korea found gratitude and the traditional heroes' welcome awaiting them at home: the Viet-vet returns with no fanfare to a nation whose response ranges from a non-committal 'Oh, you're back?' to—in some cases—downright hostility."[34] Another account explains, "In some instances, antiwar protesters reportedly spit on returning veterans and called them baby-killers. Although such incidents were rare, the stories were often repeated among U.S. soldiers in Vietnam and added to the soldiers' resentment of the antiwar movement."[35]

The *Oxford Companion to Military History* puts it this way. "At first, rather than giving returning veterans of the war welcoming parades, Americans seemed to shun, if not denigrate, the 2 million-plus Americans who went to Vietnam, the 1.6 million who served in combat, the 300,000 physically wounded, the many more who bore psychological scars, the 2,387 listed as 'missing in action,' and the more than 58,000 who died. Virtually nothing was done to aid veterans and their loved ones who needed assistance in adjusting." Television programs and films like "Born on the Fourth of July" and "Rambo," depicted Vietnam veterans as "drug-crazed psychotic killers, as vicious executioners in Vietnam and equally vicious menaces at home."[36] Combined, the news, the fiction, and the personal stories helped to create the image of a petulant and ungrateful nation during and immediately after the war.

But is the image real? In 1987 Bob Greene, a columnist for the *Chicago Tribune,* informed his readers that he had his doubts. "One of the most common things you hear about Vietnam veterans," he wrote, "is that when they returned from combat to the U.S., they were spat upon by anti-war protesters. Usually, the story is very specific. A soldier, fresh from Vietnam duty, wearing his uniform, gets off the plane at an American airport. He is walking through the airport, where he is spat upon by 'hippies.' For some reason, it is always an airport where this allegedly happened, and it is always hippies who reportedly did the spitting. I accepted these stories as an article of faith," he wrote. "After all, we knew that the veterans had not been welcomed home with parades and testimonial dinners. So it figured that maybe they had been spat upon."

Then Greene thought more about it and with more nuance. "Even during the most fervent days of anti-war protest, it was not the soldiers whom the protesters were maligning. It was the leaders of government, and the top generals. And even if you don't buy that, think realistically about the image of what was supposed to have happened. Hippies, no matter what else you may have felt about them, were not the most macho people in the world. Here's a burly member of the Green Berets, in full uniform, walking through an airport. Here's a hippie crossing his path. Do you think the hippie would have the nerve to spit on the soldier? And if the hippie did, do you think the soldier—fresh from facing enemy troops in the jungles of Vietnam—would just stand there and take it?"

So Greene, through his column, asked the approximately 2 million veterans who returned alive from Vietnam if the myth was real.[37]

There is no debate that Americans were divided over the war itself. In November 1969, 46,000 people—mostly students but many middle-aged men and women, as well as many priests wearing their clerical collars—from 44 states descended on Washington, DC to peacefully march single-file from Arlington National Cemetery across the Potomac River, around the Lincoln Memorial, to the White House and then to the Capitol. It was called the "March Against Death." Among the marchers were Dr. Benjamin Spock and William Sloane Coffin, Jr., both powerful anti-war voices of the time.

The first in line of the 46,000 was Judy Droz, a 23-year-old mother whose husband had been killed in Vietnam. She came, she said, "to express my feelings and those of my late husband that the United States should get out of Vietnam immediately. There is no light at the end of the tunnel, only the darkness that came over my husband." The day before, 186 people were arrested as they attempted to observe an "Ecumenical Mass for Peace" at the Pentagon.[38]

In his 1998 book, *The Spitting Image: Myth, Memory and the Legacy of Vietnam*, Jerry Lembcke, a Vietnam veteran and an associate professor at the College of the Holy Cross, makes a strong argument, backed by arduous research, that there was actually no evidence to show that Vietnam veterans were abused, that the stories add up to nothing more than an urban legend. But he does acknowledge the durability of the image. "Indeed, given the manipulation of information and images that began with the Nixon administration and continued at the hands of filmmakers and the news media during the 1970s and 1980s, it would be remarkable if a majority of Americans had not come to believe that Vietnam veterans were abused by the antiwar movement."[39]

By referencing the Nixon administration, Lembcke contends that the president tried to divide the public by creating an equivalency with the protests and a betrayal of the soldiers. In effect, he is saying, Nixon championed the myth to serve his political purposes. Political manipulation was nothing new at the time and it continues today, but how it applied during the Vietnam era stands out because Americans were divided about war in a way they never had been before.

Diane Mazur, a law professor the University of Florida, as well as a former Air Force officer and advisor to the National Institute of Military Justice, agrees with Lembcke. "The idea," she wrote in 2010, "that spitting on or mistreating Vietnam veterans was in any way typical or representative of anything in that era is completely false. It is by far the most powerful Vietnam War meme—a cultural unit of information passed from one person to another, like a biological gene—because it can be deployed instantly to silence difficult but necessary conversations about the military. For that reason alone the conventional wisdom is important, because it explains much about our civil-military dynamic today. It is also important, however, to understand why that accepted memory is untrue, and who benefits most from keeping it alive. The myth of the spat-upon Vietnam veteran is a difficult one to challenge."[40]

If the memory is a myth, if the mood was, in reality, not generally antagonistic, it was then at least indifferent and unwelcoming, and many of those who lived through the time, perhaps especially high school and college students for whom the unrest was an imprinting moment, acutely remember the era's unrest.

Bob Greene's experiment, however, showed him it was no myth. He received over 1,000 responses to his informal survey. He says he did his best to authenticate the authors and verified with the Veterans Administration that each sender had actually served in Vietnam. "There were simply too many letters, going into too fine a detail to deny the fact," he later wrote. "I think you will agree, after reading the letters, that even if several should prove to be not what they appear to be, that does not detract from the overall story that is being told."[41]

One of the people for whom the unwelcome feeling hit home is John Kerry, the former United States Senator, Secretary of State, and Democratic presidential nominee who served in in the Navy as a gunboat officer and who earned several military honors for his service in Vietnam. "There I was, a week out of the jungle, flying from San Francisco to New York. I fell asleep and woke up yelling, probably a nightmare. The other passengers moved away from me—a reaction I noticed more and more in the months ahead. The country didn't give a [care] about the guys coming back, or what they'd gone through. The feeling toward them was, *Stay away—don't contaminate us with whatever you've brought back from Vietnam.*"[42]

Another is Jan Scruggs, a Vietnam veteran and the founder of the Vietnam Veterans Memorial Fund, the charitable organization that built the Vietnam Veterans Memorial, the haunting polished black rock wall with the names of the more than 58,000 American service members who were either killed or went missing in Vietnam. The wall was officially dedicated on Veterans Day, November 13, 1982. "I'm aware of the people who say it never happened," he says, "but I have spoken to many people who say it happened *to them.* It happened enough times. It certainly didn't happen to 50 percent of all the veterans who came back but it happened enough that I'm convinced that it's not folklore. It did happen. I've had extended conversations with many people about it."

Scruggs returned from Vietnam in 1970, about a month before the shootings at Kent State University on May 4. More than two-dozen soldiers in the Ohio National Guard, called up by Governor Jim Rhodes, convened on the campus to stop a student protest against President Nixon's controversial decision, announced publicly five days earlier, to invade Cambodia. Four students were killed and nine others were wounded. One of the wounded suffered permanent paralysis. All were unarmed. While the Cambodian incursion had already become the subject of protest, the shootings at Kent State sent shock waves throughout the country.

"There was a mood among those in my age group," Scruggs recalls. "None of them were interested in fighting in the Vietnam War themselves, or even interested in hearing about what you had been through."

He remembers that he once met a woman for lunch just after he returned. "Someone who just got back from Vietnam had recently asked her out," Scruggs says. "This was just after all that stuff about Lieutenant Calley"—a reference to the My Lai massacre and William Calley, the Army officer who was convicted of murdering 22 unarmed South Vietnamese civilians in March 1968. Scruggs says the young woman didn't want to go out with the man who had asked her out. She told him, "I don't want to get involved with anyone like that because I might end up slaughtered."

The founding principle of Vietnam Veterans of America, a charity whose goal is to improve the public perception of Vietnam veterans, is "Never again will one generation of veterans abandon another." The mood was so bad, according to Reggie Cornelia, who returned from the war in 1967, "that some VFW posts around the country treated Vietnam vets very badly, in some cases refusing to admit them into membership. The sentiment was: *You assholes lost a war.* That was not an uncommon reaction, and the portrayal of Vietnam vets by the scurrilous cretins in the media and Hollywood served only to exacerbate these feelings."

The image of the drug-addled vet, while prevalent, was hardly accurate. As for the media treatment, Cornelia says, "Did these clowns ever think to compare the movies made about World War II vets with those made about Vietnam vets? It wasn't until Hamburger Hill that a semi-favorable portrayal was made, and that was made in 1987. And for them to not even mention books like *Stolen Valor: How the Vietnam Generation Was Robbed of Its Heroes and Its History* by B.G. Burkett, or the documentary 'The Long Way Home Project,' part of a project by the same name, is unfathomable."[43] "Hamburger Hill" portrays the American assault of a well-defended mountain near Laos in 1969. "The Long Way Home," which won the Golden Jury Selection Award at the Houston International Film Festival in 2002, provides what many feel accurately describes the war by those who served in Vietnam. But these were exceptions. Contrast that with the dozens of films about World War II, most made during or just after the fighting, all supportive of the war and it warriors.

Even though many protesters were going up against the government and the generals, and not the soldiers, it is also true that many other Americans did not distinguish between the war and those who fought it. Scruggs says, "Society was kind of fractured and people didn't separate the war from the warrior. People can debate the wisdom of our foreign policy decisions, but they can't really debate whether their neighbor's kid who volunteered for four years in the Marine Corps did the right thing for his country. *He did the right thing for his country.*" Those who came home from serving in the Vietnam War, he says, didn't think that soldiering was the kind of thing anyone would proudly list in a résumé, so he decided to do something to honor the people who served. "Which is what we did with the Vietnam Veterans Memorial," he says. "On one side of our thinking are the Vietnam War and the controversies, the debate over government policy. On the other are the people who served their country, who gave their lives, and I wanted to put their names up on a beautiful wall in Washington. So we were able to diffuse that sort of thing."[44]

Wounded Warrior Project, as well as the many other nonprofit organizations that serve veterans, are as strong as they are today because of the healing that began in 1982. Those who have come home since can, at least in part, thank Scruggs for his desire to distinguish the people masterminding the war from afar from those physically engaged in it with their boots on the ground. It is written in *The Oxford Companion to Military History,* "Not until after the 1982 dedication of the Vietnam Veterans Memorial in Washington, D.C., did American culture acknowledge their sacrifice and suffering, and concede that most had been good soldiers in a bad war."[45]

Chris Carney, one of the early volunteers for Wounded Warrior Project, says, "I have always believed that a great deal of the early success of WWP was due to the collective guilt the country shared over how the Vietnam era vets were treated when they returned home, and the willingness to correct that wrong."[46]

∼

Wounded Warrior Project should not need to exist. That men and women are sent to defend the United States and further its interests abroad may be a necessary evil, but the nation that sends them into harm's way ought to have the decency to properly care for those who return wounded. Although it may be difficult for Congress and the president to send our young into battle, it seems not so difficult to ignore many of their needs after they come home.

Perhaps the nation ought to also have a stronger spine going in. As Kevin Boylan, a military historian at the University of Wisconsin-Oshkosh and the author of "Losing Binh Dinh: The Failure of Pacification and Vietnamization, 1969-1971," has observed, the American commitment to engaging in Iraq and Afghanistan has not been all that different from our commitment to winning the Vietnam War. "The Communists didn't need American journalists and antiwar protesters to reveal that public enthusiasm for the war was fragile. [President] Johnson's refusal to raise taxes or call up the Reserves had made that obvious from the outset—just as our failure to impose new taxes or enact a military draft since 9/11 signals our enemies that America's will to fight is weak."

An examination of Boylan's indictment of our commitment in the 1960s and 1970s might be useful today. "Perhaps the key lesson of Vietnam," he wrote, "is that if the reasons for going to war are not compelling enough for our leaders to demand that all Americans make sacrifices in pursuit of victory, then perhaps we should not go to war at all. Sacrifice should not be demanded solely of those who risk life and limb for their country in combat theaters overseas."[47] If our resolve to properly engage in battle is underwhelming, how can we rally the resolve to salve the wounds the battle creates?

The mission of the Department of Veterans Affairs pays tribute to Abraham Lincoln's Second Inaugural Address, which he delivered as the Civil War was coming to a close: "To care for him who shall have borne the battle, and for his widow, and his orphan . . ." The VA's mission statement is completed with " . . . by serving and honoring the men and women who are America's Veterans." Those words are far more aspirational than real. If we're to be honest, we need to acknowledge that our country pays little more than lip service to its own ideal.

On the floor of the United States Senate, Bernie Sanders once expressed his frustration with the chasm between the aspirations and the realities at the Veterans Administration. "I believe from the bottom of my heart," he said, "that if we go to war, if we spend trillions of dollars on that war, that when our men and women come home from war—some wounded in body, some wounded in spirit—I don't want to hear people telling me it's too expensive to take care of those wounded veterans. I don't accept that. If you think it's too expensive to take care of veterans, don't send them to war."[48] But we do send them to war and we don't do enough for those who return.

While social needs unmet by the government are why charities exist in the first place, there is particular irony in the work of Wounded Warrior Project, as well as that of other organizations that serve veterans, because the government actually creates—not by omission, but by commission—the problem these charities address.

Backpacks

The idea was simple: distribute comfort backpacks to returning soldiers.

It was born in the heart and mind of John Melia, a Marine who, while serving in Somalia in March 1992, had been injured in a helicopter crash. It was a "fast-rope" training exercise, where, very much like sliding down a fire pole, Marines practiced a quick exit from a helicopter on ropes to a ship below. The helicopter malfunctioned and exploded. The crash killed four of Melia's friends and injured another 13. "My experience coming home as a wounded vet," he writes, "kind of showed me some of the gaps in service delivery to [wounded] military members." Melia describes how, after he got back to the ship where he would be treated for his burns, "They cut my clothes off, put me in a hospital gown—actually, put me in a pair of gym shorts—and that's all I had. I didn't have a toothbrush, playing cards. I didn't have any of my own stuff."

A decade later, long after he returned to civilian life, Melia saw on television a wounded Marine being loaded onto a helicopter. It just brought back a flood of memories for him and he thought, "I bet that guy's getting ready to go on the same type of journey that I did for a number of years, struggling to figure out what I was going to do after I was retired from the military." So in 2003, with $50, Melia began in his basement in Roanoke, Virginia. One day, he filled 50 backpacks in his basement with his wife and two daughters, and took them to Walter Reed. Two days later they asked for 50 more.

In March 2004 Melia told CNN, "While I got incredibly great care from the military, when I was hurt, I saw that there was significant gaps or lacks in service; things like family assistance, and just basic things like clothing for soldiers that are coming back. A lot of these guys are coming off the battlefield with just the uniform they have on. And the military really had nothing in place to clothe these guys. And nonprofits like myself got together and put together, you know, backpacks full of gear so that these wounded soldiers and sailors and airmen and Marines would have something when they came off the battlefield. A little bit of home, but also the things that they needed."

Asked if the government should do more for veterans, Melia did not find fault with the Veterans Administration. "We are not upset at the administration in any way at how they're handling the troops coming back. What we're trying to do is fill gaps that have been there for a long, long time. One of the problems is that we never seem, as a country, to learn from past experiences. These types of problems happened with veterans coming back from Vietnam and Korea, and even the first Persian Gulf War. And the mechanisms are not in place. This is not a VA issue. This is more of a military Department of Defense issue. There's kind of a hand-off between the military and the VA. It's kind of an invisible handoff." The idea was for WWP to "make that hand-off as smooth as possible."[49]

~

In addition to Melia, Steve Nardizzi and Al Giordano, each of whom also had extensive experience with veterans, were equally instrumental in founding Wounded Warrior Project.

Nardizzi's father and uncle served in World War II. Giordano also comes from a family with a tradition of military service. His father was a Marine officer and Al was born on Marine Corps Base Camp Lejeune in North Carolina. Both of his grandfathers served in WWI, his maternal grandfather as a medical officer with the American Expeditionary Forces in France. He had four uncles who all served: one in the pacific in WWII to include combat on Saipan and Iwo Jima, one served in Korea 1950-1951, and two others served in the Marine Corps. His brother was a West Point graduate and served in Germany during the 1980s. Giordano enlisted in the Marines, serving from 1981 through 1985, spending most of his time forward deployed in a Marine Amphibious Unit, and again from 1991 through 1993 in support of Operation Desert Shield/Storm.

Giordano and Nardizzi met when they were working, at the same time but at different organizations, to help veterans obtain benefits owed them by the Veterans Administration. When Giordano first walked into the Disabled American Veterans office in Manhattan in 1993 to file a disability claim—he had been injured in the line of duty—he asked the man behind the desk what he did. "He told me, 'I represent veterans before the VA.' At the time I was under the impression that, of course, the government takes care of its veterans. Boy, was I wrong." That, Giordano says, "was my defining moment."

For the next nine years Giordano worked at the DAV on behalf of veterans. "I really enjoyed the work and excelled at it. This was my calling in life." He worked thousands of disability cases. For some veterans he scoured records going back to 1946, the year after World War II ended, to identify veterans who were originally denied benefits, but he was able to prove the denials were in error, and so won these veterans years—some more than 50 years—of back pay. During this period he also attended and graduated from paralegal school, college and later on, Seton Hall School of Law. Overall, he estimates that he was responsible for approximately $70 million—perhaps more—getting into the hands of veterans who were owed money. The largest single amount he recovered was $409,000, for a Vietnam veteran.

"But Steve is an excellent technician," Giordano says. Also while at law school, and motivated by his father's military service, Nardizzi was doing similar work at United Spinal Association—it was Eastern Paralyzed Veterans Association at the time—and, Giordano remembers, "for many years Steve had the distinction of obtaining the largest award in VA history: $1.6 million. The VA had wrongly denied benefits to a World War II vet who had polio and Steve labored for several years on the case, eventually winning it at the Court level just prior to the veteran's passing."

In their work, the two men were witness to how the system works. "We talked with families, the children," says Giordano. "The father didn't get the right kind of treatment when he came back from combat and was under a lot of stress. Drinking problems, often. Couldn't keep his job. Maybe threw his hands at mom. Keep in mind that if it had a negative effect on your dad, it had a negative effect on you. If dad had kept his job or could get a better job, maybe the family would have had more vacations, or a vacation; maybe a better college, or a college, for the kids, maybe a happier childhood; maybe the family would have stayed together. The whole idea in coming home, or should be," he says, "is to reintegrate back into society. But wounds, both visible and invisible, are holding you back so you never fully integrate." Seeing directly the effects of that absence of help, Nardizzi and Giordano were deeply and personally affected. They asked, *What if?* "What if robust programs were available for vets in 1946, or 1953 or 1972? It could have changed the lives of so many returning vets, and had a cascading effect on their families too. Yes," Giordano acknowledges, "we could have an impact. We can get some money for veterans and their families"— as he and Nardizzi did for many years—"but you can't turn back the clock." So they instead thought about what could be done now.

∼

At 8:46, on the warm, clear and cloudless morning of September 11, 2001, a Boeing 767—American Airlines Flight 11, with 92 souls on board— crashed into the North Tower of the World Trade Center in New York City. At first, no one in the DAV office where Al Giordano worked knew what was going on. Some weren't even all that worried. At least one of the first reports said that a private plane had crashed into the tower. A colleague reminded Giordano that a B-25 bomber had crashed into the Empire State Building in 1945, and the building, while badly bruised, survived just fine. Still, Giordano and others left their offices several blocks to the north of the World Trade Center site to better see what was going on.

Seventeen minutes after the first crash, at 9:03, another Boeing 767—United Airlines Flight 175, with 65 souls on board—crashed into the South Tower. At that point Giordano evacuated his staff from the federal building and began walking downtown towards the buildings along with thousands of others that fateful day. While he was several blocks north of the towers, at 9:59, the South Tower collapsed. "The tower falls. *It falls!* It was like Dante's Inferno," Giordano remembers. "All of a sudden, there was a sound, a vibration like I'd never heard before. It was like I was sitting between two sets of railroad tracks and trains on each side came speeding through at the same time." For some moments, time stopped for Giordano. Then, the snow. Or what looked like snow. "The paper and ash falling through the air," he vividly remembers. "And the people falling, too." The North Tower fell a half-hour later, at 10:28 that morning.

By the time the South Tower was hit Giordano "knew it was war." As the next days wore on, amidst the chaos in New York and after the shock took its toll, he and Steve Nardizzi thought it through—in terms of a coming military engagement and its aftermath. "We knew we'd have wounded warriors coming back," Giordano says. "We knew how the system failed the previous generations. We knew we needed to change how we deal with veterans. We knew, after asking, that no other charities would change their approach. We knew we needed a new model of service."

Already enveloped in the deep and raw emotion bred from years of working on behalf of so many veterans who needed assistance and who received it only years or even decades later—or not at all—Nardizzi and Giordano would soon after, as circumstances and time permitted, use their energies to help start Wounded Warrior Project, an organization that would embody a new model of service for those returning from war in the wake of 9/11.

$\sim$

WWP began as a program called Vets First. Giordano and John Melia had the idea when Melia was working at Paralyzed Veterans of America. PVA didn't want the program, however, so Giordano asked Nardizzi, who was at United Spinal, if he would be interested. He was, and in November

2003 United Spinal's board voted to adopt the program. It was initially funded with $160,000, with Melia receiving $60,000 of that as his salary. Melia signed over the Vets First trademark to United Spinal. At that point, because Nardizzi was in charge of programs at United Spinal, Giordano and Melia reported to Nardizzi.

After the three men raised $5,000, mostly from friends and family members, Melia delivered wounded warrior backpacks to Walter Reed, as well as to Bethesda Naval Hospital in Maryland. They "were filled with things like underwear and socks and calling cards and a CD player, a T-shirt and a pair of shorts—the things that I wanted to have when I was evacuated," he says. "My family actually had to meet me at Dover, Delaware and bring me some of that stuff—my toothbrush and my razor and all of those kind of things—when I was flown back to the States. And I knew things in the military didn't change very quickly, and I knew that these guys would be going through the same type of stuff."

Melia wanted to honor wounded warriors. He distributed the backpacks, he said, "as just kind of a thank-you gift, and it just turned into so much more because every time we went there, warriors were inspired by stories that I told them about other wounded veterans, and I started seeing that families didn't have all the information that they needed to access their benefits."[50]

Matt Modine—who, among his many other acting credits, starred as Private Joker in the 1987 Vietnam War movie "Full Metal Jacket"—is a supporter of veterans and of Wounded Warrior Project. In 2014, he told an audience, "It was amazing to discover that somebody who had been wounded would wake up in a hospital and not have anything. They weren't provided for. They didn't even have the basics, like a toothbrush. The Wounded Warrior Project knew that and would give a backpack and put some toothpaste and a toothbrush, maybe a Walkman—shoes and socks sometimes—basic things that kids coming from the field wouldn't have when they woke up in the hospital."[51]

∽

After United Spinal took on Vets First, a lot of money came in for the cause, much of it coming from another activity that raised money when veterans got together to cycle across the country. The money was raised in the name of Vets First, but also by another as well: Wounded Warrior Project. Giordano and Nardizzi credit Melia for coming up with the name, which, along with its logo—at once haunting and hopeful—depicting a walking soldier carrying a wounded one, did well in direct mail fundraising appeals.

Within two years of adopting Vets First, also referred to by then as Wounded Warrior Project, as a program, United Spinal was experiencing severe financial problems, and Nardizzi left. As well, Nardizzi, Giordano, and Melia wanted to recover the trademark to Vets First.

As eleemosynary as the program was at United Spinal, it didn't yet constitute a freestanding charitable organization. Not knowing whether they could get back the rights to Vets First, the three men quietly set up a nonprofit in Virginia, which was named Wounded Warrior Project. Melia was the executive director, Giordano served on the board of WWP and was also its chief operating officer, and Nardizzi was the volunteer general counsel.

Two years later, in late 2005, United Spinal agreed to give the program Vets First, or Wounded Warrior Project, to the new nonprofit Wounded Warrior Project, and put up $2.7 million, approximately the amount it had raised in the name of the effort. By that time the purpose had broadened from delivering backpacks. WWP was "devoted to assisting the new generation of severely injured service men and women, as they transition into civilian life."[52]

∼

Even before Wounded Warrior Project became its own charity, when it was still a program of United Spinal, it scored a major legislative success. In large part that was due to Army Staff Sergeant (Ret.) Ryan Kelly, one of the returning soldiers from Iraq. He was in Iraq in April 2003, attached to the 3rd Armored Calvary Regiment when his team was tasked to help restore the local infrastructure. On his way to a conference about rebuilding the country's schools and hospitals, his convoy was ambushed with an improvised explosive device and he lost his right leg below the knee.[53]

Kelly worked with Steve Nardizzi and others to develop legislation that would "establish an insurance program that would financially assist soldiers as they recovered in stateside military hospitals from life-altering injuries." Nardizzi then drafted the bill. Known as the "Traumatic Injury Protection Amendment," or the "Wounded Warrior Law," the amendment was signed into law by President George W. Bush in May 2005. "With these major accomplishments and much more," United Spinal said, "the WWP had reached a stage of development whereby it could begin Phase II of its work—providing longer-term support for today's wounded veterans via compensation, education, health care, insurance, housing, employment, etc." United Spinal further said that the $2.7 million grant allowed Wounded Warrior Project to become a "stand-alone charity with its own identity and programs."[54]

On September 10, 2008, after Nardizzi wrote the application for accreditation, the Secretary of Veterans Affairs approved WWP as a Veterans Service Organization (VSO). This meant that WWP was now recognized as "a national organization for purposes of preparation, presentation, and prosecution of claims under laws administered by the Department of Veterans Affairs."[55] There are fewer than 40 official VSOs, chartered by Congress. For an organization to be listed, it must be a national nonprofit with a good reputation, in existence for a minimum of three years, and working on a wide range of veterans' issues.[56] Wounded Warrior Project was named a VSO as soon as the rules permitted.

∾

Soldier Ride

A little after John Melia began the backpack program in Virginia, something else was independently taking place that would expand WWP's ultimate purpose and, as well, generate a tangible narrative for the organization. In Amagansett, New York, a hamlet close to the eastern tip of Long Island, a few guys were sitting at a little saloon well after midnight. They'd had a few drinks.

The saloon is the Stephen Talkhouse, named after a Montaukett American Indian who in the mid-1800s made his living by regularly walking the 25 miles between Montauk and Bridgehampton, New York to collect and deliver mail at the train, which at that time reached only as far east as Bridgehampton.

"In the summer of 2003 there was a power outage in the northeast," recalls the bar's owner, Peter Honerkamp. "A lot of people thought it was a terrorist attack. It wasn't, but it blacked out a lot of the northeast," says Honerkamp. "I had a major act, Big Bad Voodoo Daddy, scheduled to play at my bar. We had no power, so it got canceled and was rescheduled for the fall." But because the Talkhouse doesn't usually offer concerts in the fall, Honerkamp thought he might do something extra. "I thought we could also raise some money for wounded soldiers. I wanted to do something, some gesture, for the soldiers who were starting to come back in. We'd already been at war in Afghanistan for nearly two years. We'd gone to war in Iraq in March 2003. The wounded were starting to come in."

Honerkamp called his congressman, Tim Bishop, to personally connect with local veterans. Bishop introduced him to John Fernandez, a West Point graduate who was captain of the varsity lacrosse team, even though—a tribute to his leadership skills—he wasn't a starter.

"He lost one leg and the other foot in a friendly-fire accident," says Honerkamp, referring to a bomb that was mistakenly dropped from a U.S. Air Force jet. "He went to sleep one night with his head stuck out of one end of the bunk. If he'd slept in the other direction, his head would have been blown off." "We call it fog and friction," Fernandez has said. "It's just like on the athletic field. There are so many variables. Who's to say I would not have been shot in the head the next day?"[57] Fernandez subsequently worked as a spokesman for Wounded Warrior Project for ten years.

The Big Bad Voodoo Daddy concert at the Talkhouse raised $4,000, but Honerkamp wasn't satisfied; it was a little light given his expectations and he was determined to do something more for returning soldiers. Hoping for better fundraising results, the following spring he rented the Patchogue Theatre, about an hour's drive west of Amagansett to put on a larger show with a number of bands.

While he was planning the performances, Honerkamp called members of the Fernandez family to ask if anyone other than the VA had ever helped their son at the hospital. They said yes. Honerkamp recalls, "There was this one guy, John Melia." At this point Melia was working at United Spinal with the backpack program. "I got hold of a guy there by the name of Al Giordano, who then set up a meeting with Steve Nardizzi, who at the time was an executive at United Spinal, and he told me about Melia's work, about this small operation that he had started in the basement of his family home in Virginia."[58] When he met with Nardizzi, Honerkamp told him about his plans for the Patchogue concert, as well as his hopes to put on additional, bigger shows. At that meeting, Nardizzi told Honerkamp about two other eastern Long Island veterans' families who could benefit from whatever could be raised at the Patchogue concert.

While that was happening, Chris Carney, a bartender and bouncer at the Talkhouse, who was aware of Honerkamp's desire to help returning soldiers, came up with the idea, late one night in his basement while talking with a friend, of bicycling across America to raise money. Carney didn't cycle much, but he had recently taken part in a short ride in Manhattan to benefit the National Multiple Sclerosis Society. "I was thinking, instead of having thousands of riders ride a short distance," he remembers, "why not have one rider ride a long distance?" Traveling mainly on back roads, that distance would be approximately 4,200 miles.

Honerkamp thought it could work. "I was in the gym with him and I leapt up from the floor and said, '*It's great! It'll get national attention. We're going to do it.*'" Shortly after, during a late-night conversation at the Talkhouse, a drink-laced back-and-forth essentially turned into an unlikely brainstorming session, when the ride across America was then developed and mapped out. "Chris is a very strong guy, so I knew he could pull it off," says Honerkamp. "We would use a bike ride as a mechanism to raise money and awareness for wounded soldiers. It was perfect—a civilian making this gesture to our military."

But, in the midst of their enthusiasm, Carney saw a problem: he would likely have to stay home. "We can only do the ride in the summer," he said, "but that's when all the people are in the Hamptons, and that's when I make all my money at the Talkhouse." Undeterred, Honerkamp then had this to say to his friend: "OK, think about this, but don't get mad at me. We're going to do it. And if you decide not to do it, are you okay if I find someone else?" That was merely faux bluster, of course, because, even if Carney wasn't yet hooked, Honerkamp hoped, and was pretty certain, that Carney eventually would be, no matter the season. "The cause was too important," says Steve Nardizzi. "I can't overstate how emotionally compelled and energized Peter and Chris were."

The excitement for the ride came at a good time. Even though it was bigger than Big Bad Voodoo Daddy's at the Talkhouse, the Patchogue concert, held on March 12, 2005, netted only $1,200 for each of the three families of wounded veterans. By Honerkamp's way of thinking, it was another disappointment.

Honerkamp went back to United Spinal, this time to talk with Nardizzi about the ride. "They had this brilliant idea baked up in a bar," Nardizzi says. Honerkamp explained how he was going to sponsor someone to cycle across the country and raise awareness for veterans' needs.

"Have you ever done that before?" Nardizzi asked.

Honerkamp said no.

"Have you ever planned a fundraiser like that?"

"No."

"But surely you have an avid cyclist, right? After all, this is going cross-country."

"No. Actually, it'll be a bartender who hasn't ever cycled seriously."

An attorney for United Spinal, present at the meeting, also had questions for Honerkamp.

"What if Carney gets hurt?"

"He'll heal and resume the ride when's he's able."

"What if he changes his mind?"

"He won't."

"America is only 3,000 miles from one end to the other across the country. So why 4,200 miles?"

"He's not a crow and he's not flying."[59]

Nardizzi thought Honerkamp was nuts, but somehow Honerkamp got past the interrogation.

John Melia, too, had his doubts. He thought Honerkamp and Carney were well meaning, but, he said, "Let's be clear, I wasn't ever under the delusion that any of these guys were MBAs and that they had a business plan."[60]

⁓

Honerkamp and Carney moved forward and, without any legitimate strategic planning, the separate ideas of providing backpacks and sponsoring a cross-country ride to raise the public's awareness to the needs of returning soldiers began to merge and solidify into a bigger idea that would lead to today's Wounded Warrior Project. Yes, there was very little planning," Nardizzi recalls, "but those two founded the heart and soul of a movement."[61]

In early May 2004, Honerkamp, Carney, Reggie Cornelia, Nick Kraus, and two others traveled to Washington, DC to meet Melia. Cornelia and Kraus were friends of Honerkamp's who would play a role in the development of Soldier Ride. They visited Walter Reed's amputee ward, off limits to almost everyone, where they met several soldiers who had lost their limbs. One of the patients was Ryan Kelly, who would later work on the traumatic injury protection amendment at United Spinal. Cornelia remembers his first impression of Melia, whom he met at Walter Reed. "A young man from California missing a leg whose girlfriend was back home and didn't have the money to travel to Washington. Right there, John Melia got on the phone. And boom, boom, boom, as Melia was standing at the bed and on the phone, the girlfriend was booked on a flight."[62]

The young men and women in that amputee ward, at once severely injured and full of promise, gave Honerkamp and Carney—although neither needed any—renewed impetus and purpose to their cause. "If we had any doubts before," Honerkamp says, "we knew then that we had to do the ride. The time with those vets at the hospital, more than anything else, hooked Chris."

The enormity of the project was running up against the adrenalin building inside Carney. He thought common sense and the light of day should have made him more skeptical. "We were just three guys from a bar and I was feeling like someone should put an end to this right now. I mean, someone was going to realize that we weren't qualified to do this." He thought others might ask, *Why are they even here?*[63] That thought process, combined with what he saw on the amputee ward, both humbled and inspired him.

Ride expenses would include shelter and food, and modest stipends for Carney and Tek Vakaloloma, the driver of the support vehicle. They calculated that they needed about $80,000. With anything less, they would abandon the ride and give whatever they had raised to Wounded Warrior Project. The fundraising was kept nonpolitical. "One of the first people who gave us something was the actor Alec Baldwin, who gave us $5,000," says Honerkamp. "That was from the left. And a lot of my conservative friends gave, too. They gave their time and money. Reggie Cornelia was one of them. We put a beer pitcher in front of the bar and set up a booth outside. Someone manned it every night and before every show I got up and explained why that booth was out there. And we raised the money to do it."

∼

On August 17, 2004, after dipping his back tire in the Atlantic Ocean on the eastern tip of Long Island, Chris Carney began his journey. Approximately 40 people, including Honerkamp, biked the first 20 miles with him. John Melia also took part in that first portion and rode a tandem bike with a blind soldier, Jeremy Feldbusch, on the back. A year and a half earlier, in early 2003, Feldbusch was hit with two rounds of enemy artillery that landed close by. The blast drove shrapnel deep into his face and head. He was blinded and suffered a traumatic brain injury. To save his life, he was sent to Brooke Army Medical Center in San Antonio, Texas, where doctors placed him in a medically induced coma that lasted for six weeks. For most of that time his survival was in doubt. He then spent nine months of intensive rehabilitation at home in Pennsylvania, where he underwent seven surgeries on his eyes and sinuses and one to remove additional shrapnel from his brain. Somehow, none of that mattered on this day as he rode down the road breathing in the ocean air close to the Atlantic coast.

The parade atmosphere at the beginning of the ride was soon subsumed by the intensity of the long, grinding haul across the country. Some days Carney would cycle 120 miles. On others the weather would prevent him from biking at all. Sometimes, a media opportunity meant he would bike only 30 miles, or less.

When Carney got to Colorado, two soldiers traveled from Walter Reed to join the ride. One was Ryan Kelly. The other was Heath Calhoun, who lost both of his legs when he was deployed as a squad leader for the 101st Airborne Division in Iraq in 2003, and a rocket-propelled grenade destroyed the Humvee he was riding in. Undeterred, Calhoun would later move to Aspen, Colorado to train for national and international alpine skiing competitions. He competed and earned honors in several events at the Para Alpine Skiing National and World Championships, including finishing second at the 2014 Winter Paralympic games in Sochi, Russia. He learned about adaptive skiing from a Wounded Warrior Project program for injured veterans.[64]

"Colorado is a tough place to bike," says Honerkamp. "You're climbing the Continental Divide. The first day was really tough on Heath. With a hand cycle you're really low to the ground. You're only using your arms. It's a lot harder to bike on a hand cycle. And you don't have the same circulation in your body when you don't have both legs because a double-leg amputee's body doesn't cool the same way a person's with both legs does. Heath puked his guts out on the first day after they'd gone only 10 miles. But he came back and did 30 the next day." After a couple of days, Kelly and Calhoun went back to Washington, and then returned to join Carney as the ride was about to end.

Another person who cycled the ride's last miles was Tony Snow. "By that time," says Honerkamp, "we were getting a lot of local and national publicity. Tony was a Fox radio guy who adopted us. He was later President George W. Bush's press secretary, but at this point he had his own radio show on Fox News. He called in to Chris fairly regularly: *Where are you now? How's it going? What do you need?* Chris would always tell Tony not what *he* needed, but what the *soldiers* needed. It was always about them. Snow followed Chris this way across the country, and he gave him an opportunity to say what he and the soldiers needed. The response was enormous. Every community came out *en masse* to support us."

On October 8, 2004, after 60 days and 4,200 hundred miles, Carney officially ended the ride in San Diego when he dipped his front tire in the Pacific Ocean.

Kelly and Calhoun told Carney that if he did it again, they'd do the whole country with him. "We thought they were crazy," says, Honerkamp, "but they were serious and made the commitment to do it." After Snow asked Carney to speak at a conference that turned into an event that produced both publicity and fundraising, he too made a commitment. "If you do it again," Snow said, "I'll follow you again."

Donations were growing. Snow urged his Fox News colleague Bill O'Reilly to talk about the ride on his show. When that happened, Soldier Ride, as it came to be officially called, raised over a million dollars in just one day, according to Honerkamp. "When the conservative O'Reilly was interviewing the liberal Alec Baldwin, they stopped screaming at each other for a few minutes during a commercial break and Baldwin told O'Reilly that there was one organization they could both agree on. And he told him it was Wounded Warrior Project."

With the publicity and support of Snow and O'Reilly, that first effort raised a total of approximately $2 million by the end.

∼

As this was happening, when United Spinal still had the Wounded Warrior Project program, Honerkamp drew up legal documents to ensure that the money they raised would be used solely for the wounded warrior program—for the men and women they saw in the hospital, and others in the same situation—and not for any other purpose at United Spinal. "It was a good thing that I had drawn up the legal papers," Honerkamp says. At the time, there were disputes between John Melia and United Spinal over how donations earmarked for WWP were to be spent. Melia wanted to be certain the money would be used to help wounded soldiers. At the time no one had any idea what might happen from a fundraising perspective.

Also, as his overriding goal remained to ensure that the money raised on soldier rides would benefit wounded veterans, in 2005, a few months before Wounded Warrior Project became an independent charity, Honerkamp founded a nonprofit and called it Soldier Ride. Honerkamp recruited Steve Nardizzi to serve as the new organization's first, and, as it turned out, only executive director. He took a 25 percent pay cut.

Soldier Ride's board consisted of Honerkamp, Chris Carney, and Nick Kraus's father. The charity was active for two years before its work was adopted in 2006 by the now officially IRS-designated charity Wounded Warrior Project. "We actually didn't want to start a nonprofit," says Honerkamp. "We didn't want to aggrandize ourselves with power or money. And we knew these guys—Steve, and we'd gotten to know Al, and John Melia—these were the guys who had the backgrounds to help veterans. John and Al were veterans themselves. They had connections and expertise. We always wanted them to run the organization."

In its first year, Soldier Ride granted money to Wounded Warrior Project to keep it from closing. Nardizzi cashed in his retirement account to keep both organizations afloat.

∼

The second cross-country ride, this time from the west coast to the east coast, took place one year after the first ride. On May 22, 2005, Ryan Kelly, with one leg, and Heath Calhoun, with no legs, set out to bike from Los Angeles to Montauk, New York, via, among other cities, Washington, DC. Tek Vakaloloma drove the support vehicle again, and, as there were three cyclists, as well as a videographer, Reggie Cornelia drove a back-up support vehicle. This time the group had more time to prepare and were better organized. The riders stopped at several major league baseball stadiums on the way, including those in Los Angeles, Denver, Kansas City, Philadelphia, and New York, to see the Mets, which substantially added to their growing positive publicity.

Harvey Naranjo, an occupational therapist at Walter Reed, was part of the effort. He had cycled in parts of both rides, and put up a notice at the medical center telling soldiers they could join the ride when it came through Washington. When President Bush went in about that time for his annual check-up, he saw the notice and invited the soldiers who signed up, a group of about 20, for a meeting at the White House. "Now, you have really major publicity," says Honerkamp.

In June 2005, while the second ride was taking place, Honerkamp arranged for two fundraising concerts. One was with Gary Sinise, the actor, at the Bowery Ballroom in Manhattan; the other was with Bon Jovi at the Talkhouse.

On July 18, Carney, Kelly, and Calhoun completed the second cross-country ride.

"I planned an outdoor concert to take place at the end of the ride," Honerkamp recalls, "in the hope of attracting a number of people and raising even more money. I booked Mary Wilson of the Supremes; a local act, Nancy Atlas; and a band called The Funk Brothers, who were getting a lot of publicity at the time, playing on more number-one albums than any other band in the world. They were the backup band for the Temptations, the Supremes, and lots of others. All those Motown groups had a session band, and this was the go-to for a lot of the big ones. The movie, 'Standing in the Shadows of Motown,' is about them."

All of this was going to be expensive and Honerkamp felt financial pressure. To raise money, he needed money, and, even though the two rides had attracted some attention, he wasn't hopeful. "My gut told me it wasn't going to work financially. I didn't put up any Wounded Warrior money, but I did get $10,000 from Martha Clara Vineyards, which hosted the concert. They knew they would sell a lot of wine. I also got $10,000 from WEHM, the local radio station." Honerkamp then put up $10,000 of his own money. "We were going to lose that $30,000 for sure," he recalls. "If our expenses went over that and our revenues were poor, the three of us—the vineyard, the radio station and I—were going to take the loss." He wasn't despondent, but he wasn't optimistic either.

As the concert date approached, Honerkamp had a long-shot idea. The morning before the event, he asked a friend who knew Jimmy Buffett for help. Honerkamp didn't know Buffett well then, but he played at the Talkhouse several times and over the years they developed a friendship. "My friend went to Jimmy at 3:00 o'clock that afternoon. Two hours later,

I got a call from Jimmy's manager, and he said Jimmy would come and play. We were able to get that out on the radio." Because of Buffett's participation, Honerkamp turned what he feared would be a $30,000 loss into a $40,000 net profit, which he shared with a local hospital. "Wounded Warrior Project got $20,000, and all the soldiers got to meet Jimmy Buffett and even get on the stage with him." A writer for the local paper cooed that she "enjoyed the sounds of Nancy Atlas, Mary Wilson and the Supremes, the Funk Brothers—the original Motown backup band, who played on more #1 albums than the Beatles, Rolling Stones, Elvis and the Beach Boys combined—and everyone's favorite margarita lover and East End resident, Jimmy Buffett." The writer noted that the concert marked "the end of the 4,200-mile cross-country journey of close to 100 disabled soldiers and local bicyclist Chris Carney that began in Los Angeles on May 22nd and was completed on July 18th at Montauk Point."[65]

∽

John Melia's backpack program and the two Soldier Rides combined to launch Wounded Warrior Project into a solid nonprofit, and paved the way for something unique and special. As for the rides, "It all came from that bar," says Honerkamp. "There were a lot of important players—John Melia, Al Giordano, Steve Nardizzi, and others—but without the Talkhouse and the Soldier Ride . . .who knows?

Donations resulting from that second Soldier Ride totaled well over $1 million. As successful as the fundraising effort was, however, Honerkamp came to understand that the rides were about more than money. They helped veterans come to terms with their injuries. "When soldiers joined us in Washington, I knew we had more than a fundraising tool. We had a rehabilitative tool. Instead of being relegated to hospital beds, where the wounded are talking only to their loved ones and their doctors, they could now feel like what they could be: vital young men and women again, empowering themselves, and each other. They were setting an example for the incoming wounded." As important, Honerkamp points out, "The wounded veterans were going out to the communities they sacrificed so much for. At least a few dozen soldiers have come to me and told me, *Soldier Ride saved my life.*"

Dealing with the complexity of the logistical challenges of the two cross-country rides, as well as the resulting exhaustion, led the group to think that, in the future, shorter, community rides were the way to go. The objectives at that point were to plan for enough time to train warriors on bikes and to ensure programmatic values—it wouldn't be just about riding but also about community. They ended up putting together a third cross-country ride, but that was mainly because of a prior commitment to U-Haul, a corporate sponsor.

~

The first community ride went from Miami to Key West, Florida in January 2006, between the second and third cross-country rides. Honerkamp says, "I literally banged on doors by myself at the Naval Air Station," as well as at a few other places. "It's the only time a human being has ever been on a military base, a jail, a church, a strip joint and a drag queen hangout in the course of an hour and a half for a legitimate reason. I should be in the Guinness book of records." Drag queens alone have raised over $150,000 on the Miami ride over the years. "It's one of the best rides," Honerkamp contends, "partly because it's flat there and so it's not as arduous as it is in other parts of the country, and partly because it's just a lot of fun. It's the one everyone wants to do." The flat rides were more accessible to veterans who were early on in their recovery as well as to those with more severe disabilities.

In 2008, just three year after his injury, Eric Edmundson and his father took part in a community Soldier Ride in Washington, DC. Ed and Eric's mother Beth described what turned into a bonding moment with the president, the DC police and other riders. Eric was using a side-by-side bicycle and, even though both sides use pedals, it was slow going. "They started out with the group," says Beth, "and we were wondering how they were going to keep up. But we had faith."

The ride started at the White House and would end up at the United States Capitol building, although the riders took an intentionally circuitous route to get there—to the Lincoln Memorial, across the Potomac River on Memorial Bridge to Arlington Cemetery, where they would turn around and then return across the Potomac on the 14th Street Bridge and ride on to the Capitol. "We were supposed to meet the other riders over at the Capitol," says Beth Edmundson. "President Bush blew the starting horn and off they went with the group. We promptly turned around to go meet them at the Capitol building." That meant she wasn't actually accompanying her husband and son; she was just going straight up Pennsylvania Avenue to the Capitol to meet the group. The ride, which was supposed to begin at 9:00 in the morning, was delayed until 3:00 in the afternoon. Traffic was congested. "We're on this bicycle during rush hour," says Ed Edmundson, "and Eric and I are backing traffic up. We were going slowly and it was horrific. Cars were going by and everybody's mad at us, blowing their horns and stuff."

They got only three blocks from the White House, when, Ed says, "two motorcycle policeman came up wondering why traffic was backed up. When we explained what we were doing, they said they would escort us. So they blazed a path and we followed them to the Lincoln Memorial and then to Arlington National Cemetery, across the river. As we were crossing Memorial Bridge into Virginia, we could see all the bikers crossing the other bridge—the 14th Street Bridge—on their way back to DC and the Capitol. That's how far ahead of us they were." When they rejoined the group, Ed and Eric got stuck on a hill and Steve Nardizzi, who was on the ride too, jumped out of the lead vehicle of the other group and helped by pushing them up a hill. "So then," Ed says, "the policemen started stopping all the traffic at all the intersections, and we ended up pulling up to the Capitol at the same time the group did." Meanwhile, Beth was waiting at the finish line with no idea of what was going on with her son and husband. "We were just in awe," she remembers. "We thought, wow they did it. They kept up with the group."[66]

~

The planning grew more sophisticated as the rides became more plentiful around the country. An outreach coordinator was in regular contact beforehand with the riders, who typically arrived on a Wednesday. By then a team of staffers has booked the hotels, arranged for the meals, and performed other logistical tasks. They would ride Thursday, Friday, and Saturday. In addition to the tangible tasks, Wounded Warrior Project personnel screened the soldiers. "We try to take soldiers who are in good shape, both physically and mentally," says Honerkamp. "We can't have someone on heavy medication and we want to check to be as sure as we can that someone's not going to have a meltdown." But the system isn't perfect. Once, one young man had seizures and wanted to go to a different hospital every night. But Honerkamp thinks he probably wasn't having seizures. "I'm pretty sure he wanted to go to a different place to get another load of opiates. So dealing with that kind of thing is a challenge."

There have been some trips outside of the United States as well: five rides in London and two in Israel, through 2016, although WWP stopped taking veterans to Israel because of the danger. "Plus," says Honerkamp, "you don't want to send people to the Middle East on their first trip outside of the country after they got back, where there are terrorist bombs going off." WWP also has hosted British and Israeli soldiers at rides held in eastern Long island.

Over the years, Soldier Ride became a symbol of Wounded Warrior Project's commitment to rehabilitating soldiers and promoting their camaraderie. Honerkamp says, "It's incredibly important. It's therapeutic. It gets the soldiers involved with other soldiers. I say to them, *you've* got to be the one to go out and get the soldier we missed. Chances are a lot of them need help that they are not getting. Find them, and get them to come on Soldier Ride. It's a tangible way for someone who's locked inside himself, with his own injuries—hidden or visible—and who can suddenly be around other people who have similar injuries, went through similar traumas, or who didn't but care about those who did. This is more than just getting a person on the phone telling you how to get a benefit, like at the VA. And it has the additional benefit of putting these soldiers out in the public eye. Americans didn't have a way to thank these soldiers before WWP—and one of the tangible ways is Soldier Ride, whether it was biking with them or lining the streets waving the flag, or being with them at the finish line to say thank you."

Honerkamp says soldiers have told him the ride provides context and purpose that so often offers an alternative to despair and depression. That's a large part of the soldiers' rehab, because they're otherwise alone with what happened to them. For this journey of their lives," Honerkamp says, "the Veterans Administration and the Department of Defense aren't there."

Meghan Wagner, WWP's Manager of Physical Health and Wellness as of 2016, told Dave Philipps, the *New York Times* reporter, that the rides have a huge impact. "Warriors are . . .we're changing lives. You see it over the course of four days. It doesn't happen instantly, but warriors are coming to us with interest in this program. They're coming for a variety of reasons, whether it's emotional, physical, mental. They seek out that camaraderie from other warriors, so having 50 warriors there, like-minded individuals for them to connect and realize, *I'm not alone. Someone else is going through the same thing I'm going through.* They build friendship and by the end, they're sharing contact information, creating Facebook pages, crying . . .. But they're also being shown a new activity in an adaptive way that maybe they never had before, so it's empowering in that physical health sense as well."[67]

Despite being told the raw thoughts of someone deeply immersed in the purpose and promise of Soldier Ride, Philipps, for whatever reason, chose not to see it that way. In a March 2016 NPR interview, he dismissively described Soldier Ride, along with other activities at Wounded Warrior Project. "A lot of what they do in terms of programs is kind of light," Philipps said after Nardizzi and Giordano were fired. "It's a lot of taking veterans out to baseball games, a lot of taking them on bike rides, and it's not a lot of getting them mental health. And what some of the staff said was that stuff was not as good for marketing. Having a big bike ride through a town is a really high-profile event that you can use to raise money, whereas helping someone with mental health is expensive and no one necessarily sees it."[68] Actually, WWP had canceled any fundraising or marketing events associated with Soldier Ride years before.

Honerkamp was not pleased. "I was shocked and disturbed by Philipps's ignorant assessment."[69]

Matt Modine thinks the same. After the soldiers' hospital stay, the most important part, he says, "is rehabilitating them to help them rotate back to the normal world." That's where Soldier Ride plays a big role. "I've done bicycle rides with WWP from Death Valley to Oceanside, California." Modine rode alongside "kids who have lost both of their legs and were using hand-cranked bicycles. The whole idea is to make them whole, to put them back together and to help them to come home. What's important for us to know is that when we see the physical pain that people have suffered, losing arms and legs, is a tremendous cost." The healing process, Modine points out, must all too often address the invisible wounds as well. "The people who I've met and who are most troubled don't have any bullet wounds, who don't have any burns, who haven't lost their arms or legs. The psychological damage of war is the same as it was with Private Joker. The real cost of war is what you have to spend the rest of your life with in your mind that you can't erase, and we have to do everything we can as citizens to help them. More than 20 veterans are killing themselves, taking their own lives every day. It's extraordinary and unprecedented in our country's history."[70]

Growing Pains

Wounded Warrior Project grew from a basement operation to one of the nation's most recognized and largest charities in the span of just over a decade. In 2006 the organization raised $10 million, much of that spawned by contributions related to Soldier Ride. In 2008, the year John Melia resigned from his position as executive director, the organization raised $21 million. In 2010, Steve Nardizzi's first full year as the chief executive officer, that number doubled to $40 million. The year following, WWP raised $70 million. The year following that, the number doubled again to $140 million. During that year, from 2011 to 2012, the number of employees increased from 248 to 340. In 2013, fundraising reached almost $225 million. By 2015 it reached $375 million.[71]

That kind of explosive growth is almost always a strong sign of good news, especially as much of it was the result of many small donations from people drawn to the mission. With more resources, more programs can be established and supported, and this is pretty much what was happening at Wounded Warrior Project. WWP does—or was doing, before the blowup—what government departments and other charities, including other veterans' service organizations, do not.

Surprisingly, among WWP's detractors—after Nardizzi and Giordano were fired—was John Melia, who said WWP grew too big, too fast. "I will tell you I never expected it to be as big as it is today," Melia told a television reporter in 2016. "I don't know if I wanted it to be as big as it is today. In fact, with what's going on today, I know beyond a shadow of a doubt it grew too fast, and it became exactly what we didn't want it to be become. We didn't want to be an old-guard veterans' service organization. We didn't want to have a massive fundraising plan, because frankly, you have to raise money to do what you need to do."

A good portion of Melia's criticism focused on salaries. In 2015 Nardizzi was paid $457,000 and Giordano made $385,000. WWP's budget that year was a little more than $350 million. Melia said that he recruited Nardizzi and Giordano and once considered them good friends. He hired them hoping they'd help grow his vision, but he said they "were steered by personal gain and lost their focus, rewriting the charity's history. I think they believed a theory that your salary should be tied directly to how much money you raise and the success of fundraising," Melia said. "I believe you need to have good people, and good people need to be compensated fairly, but there is a standard of reasonableness." Melia said that when he learned of the firings of Nardizzi and Giordano, he felt vindicated. "They did good work for a long time, but organizations need a conscience. I think in my tenure, while I was there, I was the conscience of the organization."[72]

Nardizzi refutes much of that narrative. "It's simply false. That is not my theory. Furthermore, he didn't recruit us; we helped him found the organization."[73]

Melia also expressed his satisfaction to *CBS News* when he said, "This is about restoring an organization that I love, that my family loves." He said he was "pushed out" after disagreeing with the way Nardizzi was running WWP; this, even though at the time Melia, not Nardizzi, was running the organization. Melia also said he wanted Tony Odierno, the board chair, to resign. "The same board that oversaw these problems, who approved the budget, is the same board trying to fix the problem. Tony is a good and honorable servant of our country, but Tony was frankly asleep at the wheel."[74]

Melia said after he left salaries grew year over year and so did the executive staff. "It's not rocket science to have 14 executive vice presidents—it isn't just wrong—it looks bad. All of those executive vice presidents made very good six-figure salaries, and the public is offended, and they should be." When he was at the organization, he said, he vowed to never make more than $199,000 a year in the job.[75] But square that with this: According to WWP's 990s, in 2009 Melia earned $200,588, and in 2010 he earned $230,000. He resigned in 2008, so in both of those years he was not even an employee.

In 2007, WWP was planning to open an office in Washington, DC. Even though Melia, as executive director, oversaw the staff, because this was a new venture the board wanted to be looped in to the hiring decisions at the new site. Melia and the board members orally agreed that he would inform them of important decisions relating to the new office, including the backgrounds of potential hires. Ron Drach, WWP's board president at the time, says, "It wasn't that the board would exert any real veto power, but that we wanted to know who was going to be hired and in what positions. We wanted to know that the best people were being considered. We also wanted a list of recruiting sources."

But the day after that agreement was reached, without consulting the board, Melia announced that he had hired all three of the people he wanted to staff the Washington office. "We got pretty indignant about it," Drach says, "because he went back on his word."[76] Another person close to the situation at the time said Melia wanted to fill one important position with a person "who wasn't up to the job and didn't know what he was doing." That person was a friend of Melia's—his former college roommate—who had no experience in the veteran space or, even, in the nonprofit world. The members of the board had questions about Melia's desire to hire the person and wanted to review the situation. "The board told Melia, *Don't hire anybody until we've had a chance to review this thing.* But he went right ahead and did it anyway."[77]

This insubordination took place when the board felt Melia didn't want much to do with the Department of Veterans Affairs, even though the board wanted to work closely with the organization. The desire for a strong relationship made a lot of sense because, even at its high point of $400 million and a few hundred employees, WWP's budget was a drop in the bucket compared to the VA's budget of approximately $180 billion and a few hundred thousand employees.[78] There is no way that WWP, or any other nonprofit, can possibly come close to providing all the services veterans need or in any way substitute for the VA. This is one of many examples where nonprofits supplement—although they do not replace—the work of government.

The board took no action against Melia but decided unanimously to allow him to resign. The board, with the support of Nardizzi, who was subsequently hired as the new executive director, and Al Giordano, the deputy executive director—in effect, the chief operating officer—decided to give Melia a golden parachute. "I think we gave him the equivalent of a year's salary and a pretty lucrative contract to do some consulting for the organization," says Drach.[79] For reasons no one seems to remember or wants to discuss, Melia's contract was not renewed after the first year.

When Melia describes himself as the conscience of the organization, even though he left at a difficult time for him, arguably no one can dispute him. What drove him in the first place to assemble backpacks? "His generosity," answers Eric Howard, who knew Melia from before he was in Somalia. "I served with John from United States Marine Corps Recruit Training and all the way up to his injury in the helicopter crash. On the day we graduated from infantry training," officially known as USMC School of Infantry, "we were both—and the only—members of our class offered to try out for Reconnaissance Battalion. We then ended up serving together in the Bravo Company, 1st Battalion, 1st Marines, which was the small-boat raid company of the 1st Battalion." Howard would normally have been on the helicopter but stayed on the carrier because that day he was assigned to ship's detail, temporary duty when Marines are assigned to assist the crew with various operational activities, such as mess detail, or work on the flight deck. "Would I have survived?" he wonders. "I don't know."

But Melia did, and his response to the accident: start a modest drive to help veterans that would grow into Wounded Warrior Project. "He has always been," Howard says, "a first-class person."[80]

～

Melia was out and Nardizzi was in. Did the environment within Wounded Warrior Project change after that? Yes. It had to. The charity was expanding. Its mission, while remaining true to its core, cried out for ongoing transformation. That's what many healthy service organizations do.

"It began as an organization where everyone felt as if he were flying by the seat of his pants," recalls one former employee. "It was a get-things-done attitude, and, boy did we get things done. We were building a plane in mid-air. People wanted to help, and we all knew we were becoming one of the largest veterans' organizations in the country, with a real mission and purpose. Morale was great. It was like magic in a bottle. It was the greatest job I ever had."

While that sentiment is shared by many, especially by those who were at Wounded Warrior Project from the beginning or near its beginnings, another sentiment began to emerge. "Later on, it was let's design the plane, get signatures, confirm the signatures, have conferences. It wasn't the same."[81] Another employees said he was "disheartened by how bureaucratic WWP had become,"[82] even though the same person acknowledged that large organizations need to be run differently from small ones.

The goal of honoring and empowering those who return wounded from battle demands a sweeping, growing vision. It began, importantly, with backpacks, but how the mandate should be fully realized into the future—with physical traumas and mental injuries that persist for life, and psychological problems undiscovered, undiagnosed and untreated until too much time has passed—is, frankly, anyone's guess, and achieving WWP's goals will require the best thinking by the best leadership. It does not take much to realize that the difficulty of the task would increase from offering tangible items at a few dollars a pop to addressing the intangible, often intractable, needs that would, prudently projected out over time, require some billions of dollars.

CHAPTER 3

PURPOSE

WHAT WE THINK WE KNOW about charities is based mostly on superficial and, often, misleading information. From the small talk at dinner tables and cocktail parties to discussions in the halls of Congress, many otherwise civically engaged people demonstrate their misunderstanding of charities by essentially reciting what they have been told is important. Almost all of the conversation is infected by advice that pushes the public to focus on how much a charity's top employees are paid, how much of a charity's budget is devoted to programs, and how little should be spent on fundraising. What more could anyone want to know?

Plenty. If society is going to stand a chance of being sustainably improved by our generosity—the central idea in the marriage of nonprofits and philanthropy—our expectations of charities must change. We all must ask not only how charities are run, but also why they deserve our beneficence.

Perceptions

- **Watchdogs and Overseers**

Over the years, the media and the public have became fixated on fundraising costs. This is the result of the "watchdogs" and what they have concluded about financial ratios. Charity Navigator says, "Those spending less than a third of their budget on program expenses are simply not living up to their missions."[83] The Better Business Bureau Wise Giving Alliance says a nonprofit should "spend no more than 35 percent of what it raises on fund raising."[84] CharityWatch says a charity is "highly efficient" when at least 75 percent goes to programs and when it costs 25 percent or less to raise money.[85]

Every one of these organizations has been drumming into the public consciousness that the meat of any charity analysis lies in the numbers reported to the IRS.

So it came as a surprise to many in the nonprofit world when, in the summer of 2013, the leaders of The BBB Wise Giving Alliance, Charity Navigator and GuideStar—the first two of which grade charities, while GuideStar provides only raw information and, for a fee, provides selected compilations of that information—affixed their signatures to a letter they called "The Overhead Myth." The three were writing, they said, "to correct a misconception about what matters when deciding which charity to support. The percent of charity expenses that go to administrative and fundraising costs—commonly referred to as 'overhead'—is a poor measure of a charity's performance. Focusing on overhead without considering other critical dimensions of a charity's financial and organizational performance does more damage than good. In fact," they claimed, "many charities should spend more on overhead."

They asked that donors "pay attention to other factors of nonprofit performance: transparency, governance, leadership, and results. When we focus solely or predominantly on overhead, we can create what the Stanford Social Innovation Review has called 'The Nonprofit Starvation Cycle.' We starve charities of the freedom they need to best serve the people and communities they are trying to serve." In fact, they said, overhead is good. "Overhead costs include important investments charities make to improve their work: investments in training, planning, evaluation, and internal systems—as well as their efforts to raise money so they can operate their programs. These expenses allow a charity to sustain itself (the way a family has to pay the electric bill) or to improve itself (the way a family might invest in college tuition)."[86]

While these observations might sound reasonable, the letter diverts attention from the culprits. In a beguiling *Who, me?* tactic, the watchdogs drew attention to a problem they essentially created—without taking responsibility for it—and implored that it be fixed. Even though they should take the lead in fixing it, they haven't.

∽

In the old days, before the late 1990s, people had to request financial information about charities by mail or in person from state officials or the charities themselves. Since then, GuideStar—founded in 1994, three years after the World Wide Web went live, with its extensive database of information on all nonprofits required to file a 990—has made the information easily and freely available. The watchdogs create their reports by focusing on a few select data points in the 990. The meat of the assessments, arrived at by simple division, takes on the visual shape of a pie chart with three pieces: overhead, fundraising, and program expenses. The grading system follows this rule: more spent on programs is good; more spent on fundraising and overhead is bad. In this misleading way, the public has been trained to equate value with less money spent on overhead.

Unconditional adherence to spending ratios is the enemy of a nonprofit. Charity Navigator and CharityWatch both use algorithms that are not relevant to realistically evaluating the work charities perform. Even though the public is best served by being made aware of a charity's impact, the current rating system is unable to measure impact. As they are currently constructed, charity watchdogs do more harm than good, and so critical comments about a charity's worthiness from the watchdogs have limited meaning. Even though Charity Navigator calls itself a "guide to intelligent giving," it is nothing of the sort, and actually dumbs down the conversation about the real impact charities have.

In 2005, the Stanford Social Innovation Review conducted a detailed study of the charity ratings agencies to determine how useful they are. "The results were sobering," the report concluded. "These sites individually and collectively fall well short of providing meaningful guidance for donors who want to support more efficient and effective nonprofits. The major weaknesses of the ratings agencies are threefold: They rely too heavily on simple analysis and ratios derived from poor-quality financial data; they overemphasize financial efficiency while ignoring the question of program effectiveness; and they generally do a poor job of conducting analysis in important qualitative areas such as management strength, governance quality, or organizational transparency."[87]

The headline of an article in the *Chronicle of Philanthropy* once asked, "Is Charity Navigator the 'National Enquirer' of Watchdog Groups?" Michael Soper, a nonprofit consultant, said, "In my view, Charity Navigator, its ratings, and its top ten lists are nothing more than great merchandising of a weak underlying product." Specifically, the methodology is flawed, according to Soper, because it examines only the financial health of a charity, not how effective it is at meeting its mission; it relies too heavily on the Internal Revenue Service's 990 informational tax return, which charities often interpret differently; and its ratings could be skewed depending on a charity's mission or the year Charity Navigator began examining a group. For example, Mr. Soper writes that if Charity Navigator were to begin looking at a nonprofit group at a time it is in a capital campaign, "Future ratings and rankings could show the nonprofit in decline as a result of the decreasing revenue."[88]

Al Giordano says that Charity Navigator "never seems to find the really bad small charities ripping off donors. In fact, "he says, "they oftentimes will rate those scams three out of four stars because all they are looking at are 990s. They manipulate the numbers on large, well-known charities for the sake of the attendant media coverage. Actually, when I say manipulate, that might not be a strong enough term. They often publish false financial data, as it is does not comport with GAAP accounting. Charity Navigator knows full well that even if a charity believed in the questionable accounting process at Charity Navigator, the charity *couldn't* use it to complete its financials as no CPA firm would sign off on them, which would defeat the requirement of an outside auditor. In WWP's case, Charity Navigator publically stated that our numbers—which were audited by several large public accounting firms over the years such as BDO [Binder Dijker Otteand] and Grant Thornton—were wrong and misleading. In the for-profit world, *Bloomberg, Forbes* and the *Wall Street Journal* wouldn't give them a second thought if a watchdog criticized the audited numbers of a publically traded company based on its own secret, non-GAAP voodoo math." In addition, Al Giordano says, "You can't trust their objectivity. If the umpire is calling balls and strikes and you can't trust them, then what? Charity Navigator is a parasite on the industry." [89]

The BBB Wise Giving Alliance (BBB's give.org) does more than examine information on a charity's Form 990. Through a detailed online questionnaire, it evaluates a charity's governance, effectiveness, reporting, finances, solicitation practices, and informational materials. Art Taylor, the president and chief executive officer of BBB's give.org and one of the signers of the overhead myth letter, believes in a more rigorous approach and, to a large degree, thinks his organization has one. "We are a standards-based evaluator," he says. "Much of the information is assessed in relation to a set of criteria developed with the assistance of a broad range of charity stakeholders. Our evaluations go beyond a few data points taken from financial reports and digs into core factors that determine whether a charity is trustworthy."

If the organization meets all 20 standards, it receives the designation of *accredited charity*. It is within this broader context of evaluation that BBB WGA is different from Charity Navigator and CharityWatch.

"We all want to help donors, but we have different approaches," Taylor says. "If a charity spends ten cents on every dollar on administration or overhead, you might feel really good about that organization. In fact you might feel better about that organization than one that spends 20 cents of every dollar on overhead. However, we know from our evaluations that if you relied only on that financial metric—or a group of them—you might miss other areas of significant deficiency. For instance," Taylor points out, "the charity's appeals may be misleading. Or board members may have material and unmanaged conflicts of interest. Or the charity might not be basing its reports on audited financial statements." Or other qualitative measurements that numbers don't capture. Taylor says, "There could be many operational weaknesses that would point to a lack of trustworthiness, even though it may have low overhead rates."

Taylor says it's easy to be critical, but he acknowledges that no charity is perfect. "None of us does everything in a way that the public would most appreciate. Even charity monitoring organizations have limitations. Some people claim that our evaluations can be too intensive." He says the criticism he hears most of Charity Navigator is that "its ratings are skewed toward financial performance and that those metrics don't go far enough in assessing a charity's trustworthiness."

For Taylor, trust is key. "All of our standards lead to understanding the charity's trustworthiness." But, he cautions, "That doesn't mean the charity is effective in achieving its mission." In fact, he says, "Demonstrating trustworthiness is more important than proving effectiveness. I expect some people might take issue with that, but the reason I feel so strongly is that it's challenging, and sometimes expensive, to measure effectiveness. It's difficult to even prove that a particular organization *caused* the change it is claiming." Further, he says, "If a charity doesn't achieve effectiveness, it may be through no fault of its own. It may be that it's working on a difficult societal problem. Another challenge with proving effectiveness is contextualizing the results achieved in relation to the resources employed."

As an example, he compares two charitable organizations that train people for better jobs. The goal for each is to place 100 people in one year. "The one organization has a budget of $20 million to do that, and succeeds by getting them all trained and placed. That charity can say they were highly effective because they met their placement goal. The other organization with the same goal places only 50 people in good jobs, but its budget was only $1 million. Taylor says, "Even though the second organization placed only half as many people, can we say it was less effective than the charity with a $20 million budget? If you looked only at the performance metrics you might say the first group is better than the second, but the second did its work with far less money. Placing too much pressure on charities to produce performance metrics can have a negative effect on the amount of risk they take. Given the challenging nature of the problems they take on, charities will employ speculative solutions, and many times the outcomes will be lessons learned.

"But," he says, "all charities can and should demonstrate trustworthiness. Ideally a charity will work to demonstrate both, but trustworthiness is *sine qua non*. Charities should always put forth their best efforts to achieve their objectives in an open, transparent and trustworthy manner. We should be rewarding them with donations for their trustworthiness, for ideas on how they propose to solve a problem, and for their commitment and drive to work in the manner in which they promised."[90]

In a 2018 survey, BBB's give.org reported that almost 75 percent of all donors replied that trust in a charitable organization is essential before supporting it. At the same time, however, less than 20 percent said they had complete trust in charities. On a list of perceived trust among 13 categories within the charitable sector, ranked at the top were, in this order: nonprofit hospitals, veterans' organizations, and social service charities. Educational organizations, environmental organizations, and civil rights and community action groups came in at the bottom of the ranking. Still, as a whole charities were found to be more trustworthy than organized religion (for purposes of the survey, give.org separated religious organizations from other charities) banks, business, the media, and government.[91]

GiveWell, another organization that produces evaluations, focuses its efforts on charities that work in global health and development, and offered top recommendations on nine charities in 2017. "In any given year, the number of extremely deep dives that we do," says Catherine Hollander, a research analyst focused on outreach at GiveWell, "is quite limited. Because our goal is to recommend top charities, and to provide comprehensive information about all our charities, we spend the most time on organizations that seem the most promising. Each charity is thoroughly vetted and we spend hundreds of hours reviewing each one to determine whether it meets our standards."

The driving forces that inform GiveWell's evaluations include examining evidence of program effectiveness and estimating cost effectiveness. GiveWell then develops narratives in addition to financial analyses, a process that goes further than any other evaluator to provide the public with relevant context. Hollander says, "Thoroughly understanding even one charity is a great deal of work."[92]

But it pays off. GiveWell is able to document donations where its research has played an important role. Even though it assesses so few charities, GiveWell is able to document that those it has recommended have cumulatively increased their donations by $117 million in 2017.[93]

GiveWell, however, is unique.

Jacob Harold, the president and chief executive officer of GuideStar, thinks the sector itself should share responsibility with the watchdogs for the perpetuation of the myths associated with the current ways we evaluate charities. "Donors have been lazy," he says. "A lot of journalists have been lazy, and I would also argue that nonprofits themselves should take on some of the burden for not explicitly and proactively offering alternatives." Referencing "The Overhead Myth" letter, which he signed, Harold says charities that do well in evaluations "essentially reinforce the myth when they cite a good rating in their materials."

Harold also thinks we should be asking different questions. "We're stuck in the wrong conversation about what it means to be a good nonprofit," he says. While the public is understandably keenly interested in how charities spend their money, he thinks there should be more to how we evaluate charities, and likens the growth of interest in the numbers on a charity's public information forms to what he calls the drunk-under-the-lamp-post problem: a drunk looks for his keys under the lamp post because that's where the light is; the key probably isn't there, but there sure is a lot of light, so that's where he looks. "The presence of financial data," Harold says, "has led people's attention to be focused on comparable financial metrics. While that is a very important component of nonprofit accountability, given the diversity of the sector, it tells only a tiny fraction of the story." [94]

～

Alone as an executive in the nonprofit world, Steve Nardizzi not only thought the watchdogs were up to no good, he treated them with contempt. "Most Americans ignore the ratings groups," he says, "and will give despite higher overhead and fundraising costs. WWP's statistics prove that." [95]

Nardizzi told an audience of fundraisers in 2015, "When a discussion takes place about costs, it's usually not with a positive tone; it's in the context of the conversation framed by the rating groups. In the benign sense, the message is: if only you could have been a more efficient charity; if only you could work a little harder to reduce your overhead costs, your administrative costs and your fundraising costs. In the unfavorable sense, the message is this: you are a horrible human being, and you should spend less on fundraising."

Nardizzi explained that his mission was the driving force for everything he did. "For those of you not familiar with us, our mission is to honor and empower wounded warriors. Our constituents are active duty service members and veterans—our Wounded Warriors—who are returning from the conflicts in Iraq and Afghanistan with severe, debilitating injuries. Over 50,000 with physical injuries including amputations, burns, and paralysis; hundreds of thousands more coping with the invisible wounds of war combat stress, post-traumatic stress disorder, and traumatic brain injury. In the short ten years from our founding we have grown from a small, grassroots organization to one of the largest nonprofit organizations in the sector."

Nardizzi said he had to flout the watchdogs. "We were only able to grow our programs, to further our mission, to achieve that impact, by ignoring conventional wisdom about how nonprofits should be run, by ignoring the pressure to not invest in our infrastructure and administrative operations, and by recognizing that without investing in fundraising you may have a lot of good intentions, but you're not going to help a lot of people."

Nardizzi said he was at times asked why Wounded Warrior Project got only a three star rating from one group or a C-plus rating from another group. His response: "We get that rating because we choose to. Let me say that again. I get a three-star rating on Charity Navigator; I get a C-plus rating by CharityWatch because *I choose to*. If I wanted to get a four-star rating, or an A rating, or a higher rating from any of these groups, I could. But the reality is when my team and I looked at their rating systems we realized that if we followed them we would make less of an impact—not more. So we chose to ignore them."[96]

When Nardizzi said "we," he meant it. The WWP board voted to ignore what Charity Navigator had to say about charities. It also voted to follow the guidelines set forth by the Better Business Bureau Wise Giving Alliance.

Art Taylor thinks WWP is an interesting case. "Under Steve Nardizzi," he says, "the organization took on some very novel approaches. He challenged the nonprofit status quo by basically saying, *If we're a $30 million organization right now, the only way we can become a $300 million organization is by investing more in fundraising and promotion.* And so they did that. For many years they were spending far more on fundraising than lots of other organizations that were similarly situated. Taylor acknowledges that the formula won't work with lots of organizations, but that it worked for WWP. "One of the reasons," he says, "was that the subject matter was helping veterans, a cause that provides a gravity that draws people in."[97]

~

Maybe the idea of evaluation needs to be better understood. The word *value*, inherent in the word *evaluation*, can most readily be understood as a monetary amount. The IRS defines fair market value this way: The price at which the property would change hands between a willing buyer and a willing seller, neither being under any compulsion to buy or to sell and both having reasonable knowledge of relevant facts.[98] But *value* has several other connotations and one of them—far more relevant to what a charity does for society—is *something of relative importance*; another, also close to how we think of a charity, is *a principle or quality intrinsically valuable or desirable*. In only its most unsophisticated reading can value, as it is used in connection with evaluation, be thought of as strictly monetary.

Jordan Ellenberg, a math professor at the University of Wisconsin-Madison, contends that it is dangerous to use numbers inattentively. "Working an integral . . . is something a computer can do quite effectively. Understanding whether the result makes sense—or deciding whether the method is the right one to use in the first place—requires a human guiding hand." In the mathematics classroom, this issue is paramount, yet it lends itself to a better comprehension of how well things work outside of the classroom. "The danger of overemphasizing algorithms and precise computations is that algorithms and precise computations are easy to assess. If we settle on a vision of mathematics that consists of 'getting the answer right' and not more, and test for that, we run the risk of creating students who test very well but know no mathematics at all."[99]

One might wonder how many charities perform well on the watchdog exam but poorly at addressing their mission, or the opposite.

Jacob Harold put it this way. "None of us as American taxpayers would use our 1040 to tell our story as human beings, so how is it that the nonprofit sector has come to rely on the 990 as the means to communicate what nonprofit organizations are all about?"[100]

- **Bad Charity**

Identifying charity leaders who have misbehaved over the years is a far easier task than it should be. Starting with William Aramony and ending not so long ago—perhaps this morning—we have had to acknowledge a sad truth regarding the sector whose sole role is to facilitate good in society.

Although, as head of the United Way of America—now United Way Worldwide—from 1970 to 1992, Aramony increased the organization's annual revenues four-fold, from $787 million to over $3 billion, he was forced out when, as a *New York Times* obituary told the story, "an internal investigation and news reports disclosed his expense-account living and luxury travel, including trans-Atlantic flights on the Concorde. Federal investigators began examining accusations that for years Aramony had also spent lavishly on a young Florida woman with whom he had begun an affair in 1986, shortly after her high school graduation. In 1994, Aramony and two associates were indicted on 71 counts of fraud, conspiracy, tax evasion and money laundering, accused of stealing $1 million from a United Way corporate spinoff. Some $80,000 was said to have been given to his lover, Lori Villasor, and more for vacation trips with her to London, New York, Egypt and Las Vegas, and for champagne, flowers and even a fax machine for him to send love notes."[101]

That's pretty bad—so far the gold standard for nonprofit perfidy—and no one else at a charity has since gotten into quite the same amount of trouble, although, it seems, not for a lack of trying. Even though one might think that the crimes Aramony was convicted of and jailed for—crimes for which the United Way had to endure years of humiliation, and that might be seen as the birth of today's levels of skepticism aimed at charities—would be a cautionary tale, it seems only to have emboldened others.

∽

The public was shocked, for example, to learn in January 2015 that FEGS—Federation Employment & Guidance Service, one of New York City's most prestigious health and human services organizations—was about to close its doors after hiding a $20 million revenue shortfall. Its operating budget was $230 million. Part of the shock was the realization that the problems were long in the making and its leaders were hiding the problem. It was revealed that FEGS engaged in risky behavior and was drowning in debt, all the while looking for, and getting, money to continue financing its operations, even as those operations were failing.[102] The accounting was a mess and no one outside the organization seemed to notice. At the end, Gail Magaliff, who as chief executive presided over the demise of FEGS, argued that she was owed a hefty amount of what was left—$1.2 million in deferred compensation; this while some workers were looking for new jobs and hundreds more had not received their severance pay.[103]

A few years before, there was the case of Susan G. Komen for the Cure. It found itself in hot water in 2012 when its CEO, Nancy Brinker, announced $684,000 in cuts to Planned Parenthood's breast cancer screening and education program. Komen was accused of "yielding to long-standing pressure from anti-abortion groups." Komen denied this. "The main factor in the decision," a Komen spokesperson said, "was a new rule adopted by Komen that prohibits grants to organizations being investigated by local, state or federal authorities. Planned Parenthood was therefore disqualified from financing because of an inquiry being conducted by Representative Cliff Stearns, Republican of Florida, who is looking at how Planned Parenthood spends and reports its money." Cecile Richards, the head of Planned Parenthood at the time, claimed, "the change in financing criteria was written specifically to address the political pressure that they've been under."[104] Komen's spurious, specious logic was practically an invitation for a political hack with an ax to grind to provide cover for the organization as it impaired a critical operation at Planned Parenthood.

The decision was reversed but, according to a Harris poll at the time, did little to stave off sharp opposition. Robert Fronk, Executive Vice President and Corporate Reputation Practice Head at Harris Interactive, said, "Since it was first surveyed in EquiTrend, Susan G. Komen for the Cure has in many ways represented the 'gold standard' among non-profits measured in our study, consistently reporting high scores for quality, the willingness to recommend and, most importantly, trust. Now, Komen finds itself near the bottom of the pack on all of these items."[105]

Unsurprisingly, fundraising at Komen dropped dramatically. In 2011 the group, including all its chapters nationwide, raised $350 million, which made it the 41st largest charity in the United States in terms of fundraising. By 2015, Komen raised just under $200 million, a drop of more than 40 percent, which took the charity to a ranking of 127th of all charities. The year after the news broke, the decline was around $70 million, but if only the central organization is considered, the percentage drop is even more dramatic—from $160 million in 2011 to just over $77 million in 2014, according to its IRS filings. That's a decline of more than half.

The problem wasn't just the bad press. The losses were also linked to changes in fundraising strategy and expenses. Komen raised $101 million the following year,[106] but over the next few years shut chapters in six states. "National Komen officials say that the closing was related primarily to the expiration of lease agreements and reduction of staff to no full-time employees," the *NonProfit Times* reported, "but what they do not mention is that the measure is among a number of closings in the midst of a continuing revenue drop that began when the organization dropped its grants to Planned Parenthood for breast cancer screenings in 2012 and then tried unsuccessfully to spin communications about the internal decision-making process for that cut."[107]

FEGS or Komen is each an entirely different kind of organization from Wounded Warrior Project, although it's also true that both are far different from each other. We might better wonder, in the search for context at WWP, if any scandals have erupted at organizations that serve veterans.

∼

Enter Help Hospitalized Veterans, a California charity whose purpose is "to support the healing and enrich the lives of veterans and military personnel. Healing arts and crafts," the group says, "provide a therapeutic experience for all veterans including those who are hospitalized, in shelters, in convalescent homes and those undergoing therapy for a wide range of physical and mental challenges."[108] A CNN investigation, however, found that things weren't as they seemed. "Most of the donations sent to veterans' hospitals around the country," CNN reported, "amounted to so-called 'craft kits' for recovering soldiers to use while hospitalized. The kits included instructions for making paper airplanes." This amounted to the organization providing needless trinkets, all the while raising money by saying it was doing something big and important for veterans.

The worst of it came in 2012 when the California Attorney General's office fined the charity $2.5 million. As part of the deal the majority of its executives, including its executive director Michael Lynch, resigned. Most of the donations, it turned out, funded what the state called "excessive compensation" for its executives. Attorney General Kamala Harris said they had "improperly diverted" donated funds to themselves as well as purchased country club memberships, and in one case a suburban Washington condominium for the use of its officers. "I am pleased that this settlement forces these officials to resign, in addition to paying restitution," Harris said.

This case was a long time coming. "Help Hospitalized Veterans has been the subject of state and federal inquiries for several years," CNN reported. "In 2008, a House Oversight Subcommittee hearing led by Rep. Henry Waxman, D-California, spent a day seeking testimony from the charity's founder Roger Chapin, as well as other Help Hospitalized Veterans executives." Waxman told CNN in 2012 that executives of the charity "ought to be put in jail."

Only $500,000 of the fine was paid by the charity; the rest was paid from the estate of the founder's wife. Lynch was gone, after 35 years, but collects a pension of $160,000 per year.[109]

Help Hospitalized Veterans did not close, although it changed its name and is now known as Help Heal Veterans. It still favors healing through arts and crafts, but it suffered financial consequences. In 2011 the group raised $30 million. By 2014 fundraising dropped to $20 million.

In response to the scandal, the Veterans Administration banned Help Hospitalized Veterans from having anything to do with its veterans' hospitals or patients, something the charity never bothered to mention on its website.

But the story doesn't end there.

∼

Before the name change, the organization's board hired someone to succeed Michael Lynch as the executive director. The decision was a disaster and in 2014 CNN, again, was on it. Anderson Cooper opened the story by asking Drew Griffin, who had reported on Help Hospitalized Veterans the first time, with this, "Tonight the focus is on a discredited charity, one that is amazingly still doing business, if you can call it that. And not only that, it's who we've learned is now running this outfit. It is truly mind bending. And it comes on a day when VA officials took the heat, a whole lot of it, for yet another scandal involving veterans. The hospital mess."

"Help Hospitalized Veterans," Griffin reported, "is one of the most troubling charities we've ever reported on. Its mission is to take in donations and then help hospitalized veterans by sending them arts and crafts kits, models, to occupy the time of vets who are hospitalized. The charity has been raking in donations for more than 40 years. And in 2011 and 2012, the last two years the charity filed tax returns, it collected $64 million. Those same filings showed its officers were paid hundreds of thousands of dollars in salaries, donated money, paid for $80,000 in golf club memberships, and directors and their spouses were approved to travel first class for any function related to the charity. All money supposedly donated to help hospitalized veterans."

The reason CNN was on the story to begin with was a report by the Office of Inspector General about the deaths of veterans awaiting care at the Veterans Administration hospital in Phoenix, Arizona. In an initial report the OIG went out of its way to say there was no proof that anyone died waiting for care, but in a later report acknowledged the team actually didn't examine all of the deaths of veterans who died waiting for care, and didn't look at the records of thousands of veterans—approximately 5,600— who were waiting for care. "The bottom line from this hearing," said Drew Griffin, the CNN reporter, "is the Phoenix VA . . . appears to be still somewhat of a mess. No one really has been fired in all of this. And despite the fact that there are 9,300 VA hospitals under investigation across the country, and the FBI brought into investigate possible criminal violations, no one has ever been charged with a crime."

As bad as that is and as relevant as it is to veterans, how does the story connect to what was then Help Hospitalized Veterans? After summarizing the organization's malfeasance reported on a few years earlier, Griffin said, "But in a surreal twist, the charity survived. How? By hiring this woman to run its operation. And this is where poor management of the VA, the actual Department of Veterans Affairs, and the very bad veterans' charities intersect."

"This woman" was Diane Hartmann, who had been an administrator with the Veterans Administration for 20 years. She was available for the top job at Help Hospitalized Veterans because she had been forced to leave her government position. In 2010 the Office of Inspector General issued a report entitled "Abuse of Authority, Misuse of Position and Resources, Acceptance of Gratuities, & Interference with an OIG Investigation National Programs & Special Events." And, yes, it was all about her. The summary said:

> We substantiated that Ms. Diane Hartmann, Director of National Programs & Special Events (NPSE), Office of Public and Intergovernmental Affairs (OPIA), misused official time and travel; failed to properly record compensatory time for her subordinates; and improperly used hundreds of hours of unauthorized compensatory leave herself.

> We also substantiated that Ms. Hartmann interfered with an Office of Inspector General (OIG) investigation when she destroyed evidence, allowed a subordinate to destroy evidence, made a false theft report, and allowed a subordinate to file an erroneous theft report. Further, we found that after OIG officially notified Ms. Hartmann of the investigation, she attempted to have a subordinate destroy emails, asked a second to withhold material information, and tried to coerce a third by threatening exposure of a personal indiscretion from many years earlier.

> We further substantiated that Ms. Hartmann accepted, and allowed a subordinate to accept, gratuities valued in excess of $20 from a prohibited source, and that she circumvented acquisition

requirements by repetitively splitting a recurring contract for photography services.

In addition, we substantiated that [REDACTED] misused his official time and travel, interfered with an OIG investigation, made false statements to us while under oath, and misused his VA computer systems for improper activities; that [REDACTED] interfered with an OIG investigation and intentionally made false statements to us while under oath; and that destroyed evidence.

We also substantiated that Mr. Daniel C. Devine, Special Assistant to the Acting Under Secretary for Health, formerly the Acting Assistant Secretary for Congressional and Legislative Affairs, interfered with an OIG investigation when he improperly informed Ms. Hartmann that she was under investigation and when he intentionally made false statements to us while under oath.

The 44-page report concluded with 20 recommendations, the first of which was "appropriate administrative action against Ms. Hartmann for abuse of authority, misuse of her position, misuse of her and her subordinates' official time, and misuse of Government resources for private gain."[110] She wasn't fired, however; she retired a year later. As CNN reported, "This disgraced charity was looking for a new CEO, and a disgraced former VA administrator apparently was the perfect fit."

At the time, the organization's "Leadership" page pointed out, without mentioning why she left, that Hartmann brought a "wealth of experience" from all her time at the VA.

Drew Griffin reported that he was unable to get Hartmann to speak with him.

"You know, what makes me so outraged about this," said Anderson Cooper, "I mean, these people are so sleazy, they're taking people's money. And if they were a real charity, if they were a legitimate charity, they would at the very least give you an appointment. They would be completely transparent. They should be completely willing to say, *Oh, here is how we deliver, you know, kits to veterans in hospitals even though we've been banned by the veterans' hospitals we supposedly deliver these kits to. Here is how we do it."*

This exchange between Cooper and Griffin ended the report:

Cooper: These guys are, to quote Mike Wallace from "60 Minutes," they're running away like cockroaches, like scuttling from the cameras.

Griffin: That's exactly right. And the problem is, their target audience, the people who are sending in money are mostly—I hate to say it, Anderson. They're not watching our show. They're elderly people, they're people who are soft sells through the mail, and they don't get the information that we're delivering right now to all of our viewers that if you get something from Help Hospitalized Veterans in the mail, you should be very suspicious when they're asking you for money. We can't tell that story enough.

Cooper: And obviously, I mean, the name is so manipulative. Of course you get something if it's Help Hospitalized Veterans, you want to do whatever you can. Obviously the state of California here agrees with this. The veteran's administration agrees. Yet they continue to exist taking donations. Is there nothing that can be done to shut them down?

Griffin: You know, like I said, this is what can be done. People need to stop giving to this group. It's unfortunate. But the laws are extremely weak, and there is no push to make them any stronger. We did receive a statement from this charity's new chairman of the board, basically saying that they did know, by the way, about that most recent letter that bans them from the VA and that the charity was trying to reinstate itself, get access to the hospitals hoping for a more favorable outcome, and that the new chairman also blamed employees that are no longer there. They are trying—they say they are fully focused on rebuilding the trust that was shaken. But they're not going to say that on camera or answer questions.

Cooper: You know, how about—yes. How about one of these sleazy people actually come on camera and do an interview with you, with

me, with us both, together, I mean, rather than just give out statements, which are—you know, oh, yes, we're aware that the VA has
banned us. Well, yes, I would hope you—you know, they are, I'm
sure they're aware of that. That's nothing new. Anyway, it's just out-
rageous. [111]

Shortly after the CNN report aired, Diane Hartmann left the employ of
Help Hospitalized Veterans. Help Heal Veterans, as it is now known, is still
doing little to help, or heal, veterans.[112]

～

Then there was John Thomas Burch and the so-called charity he ran,
National Vietnam Veterans Foundation. That organization, which raised
almost $30 million from 2011 to 2014, helped him buy a Rolls Royce, even
though only two percent of what was raised went to actually helping veterans. Of the $8.6 million raised in 2014, $7.7 million was paid to professional telemarketers. Burch received a relatively modest $65,000 from
the charity, but—and this is weird—he was at the same time a full time
employee—and a lawyer, at that—of the Department of Veterans Affairs,
earning $125,000. "Yes, you heard right," said Drew Griffin of CCN when
he reported the story. "The man who runs one of the worst charities *for* veterans works at the agency dedicated *to* veterans."[113] Soon after the report,
Burch was fired.

But Burch's troubles continued. It turns out that he embezzled about
$150,000 of donations to spend on women he was involved with by claim-
ing reimbursements for visits to clubs, meals and hotel stays that were not
related to National Vietnam Veterans Foundation. After pleading guilty to
wire fraud in late 2017, he was sentenced to five months in prison.[114]

～

Would that Help Hospitalized Veterans and National Vietnam Veterans
Foundation were the only bad apples. But there are more in the veterans'
space, and more yet when all charities are considered. In the summer of

2013, Kris Hundley, from the *Tampa Bay Times,* and Kendall Taggart, from the Center for Investigative Reporting, teamed up to research charities that didn't do so well with the numbers. The criteria for the report, "America's Worst Charities," were simple: Which charities used outside solicitors and, among them, which ones received the least from the solicitors' fundraising efforts? Examining fundraising costs is just one component of an evaluation, and is often misleading; relying on it alone would reinforce the overhead myth. Still, the numbers were so egregious they led to further investigation and an understanding that the charities were, actually, poorly fulfilling their mission.

That methodology has been the basis for a long-running annual report from the Charities Bureau, which is part of the New York State Attorney General's Office. That report, "Pennies for Charity," lists fundraising campaigns conducted by professional fundraisers registered to solicit charitable contributions in New York. "Many donors," the Charities Bureau reported in 2016, "are not aware how large a share of their donations can go to professional fundraisers handling charities' solicitations." Outside solicitors retained about 33 percent that year, or $403 million of the funds they raised, while charities retained $822 million. Also, 13 percent of the time, or in 131 campaigns, expenses exceeded revenue for a total loss of over $9 million.[115]

∽

"America's Worst Charities," was an extensive compilation. The reporters combed through state and federal records to identify nearly 6,000 charities that paid for-profit companies to raise their donations. Then, based on the money they diverted to boiler room operators and other solicitors over a decade, they looked for the worst charities. "These nonprofits adopt popular causes or mimic well-known charity names that fool donors," the reporters wrote. "Then they rake in cash, year after year. The nation's 50 worst charities have paid their solicitors nearly $1 billion over the past 10 years that could have gone to charitable works. Until today, no one had tallied the cost of this parasitic segment of the nonprofit industry or traced the long history of its worst offenders."

Among the findings:

- The 50 worst charities in America devote less than 4 percent of donations raised to direct cash aid. Some charities give even less. Over a decade, one diabetes charity raised nearly $14 million and gave about $10,000 to patients. Six spent nothing at all on direct cash aid.

- Even as they plead for financial support, operators at many of the 50 worst charities have lied to donors about where their money goes, taken multiple salaries, secretly paid themselves consulting fees or arranged fundraising contracts with friends. One cancer charity paid a company owned by the president's son nearly $18 million over eight years to solicit funds. A medical charity paid its biggest research grant to its president's own for-profit company.

- Some nonprofits are little more than fronts for fundraising companies, which bankroll their startup costs, lock them into exclusive contracts at exorbitant rates and even drive the charities into debt. Florida-based Project Cure has raised more than $65 million since 1998, but every year has wound up owing its fundraiser more than what was raised. According to its latest financial filing, the nonprofit is $3 million in debt.

- To disguise the meager amount of money that reaches those in need, charities use accounting tricks and inflate the value of donated dollar-store cast-offs—snack cakes and air fresheners—that they give to dying cancer patients and homeless veterans.

"Over the past six months," the report recounted, "the *Times* and *CIR* called or mailed certified letters to the leaders of Kids Wish Network and the 49 other charities that have paid the most to solicitors. Nearly half declined to answer questions about their programs or would speak only through an attorney. Approached in person, one charity manager threatened to call the police; another refused to open the door. A third charity's president took off in his truck at the sight of a reporter with a camera."

The 50 worst charities were clustered into just a few causes: kids, cancer and other health issues, firefighters and police, and, yes, veterans. This isn't surprising, as donors often think with their heart—and who can resist the plight of the vulnerable in these groups?

The worst charity of all was Kids Wish Network; its hired guns kept $116 million—98 percent—of the $138 million it raised.[116] Another on the list was the aforementioned National Cancer Coalition, which AMC, the entertainment company, removed from its website "savewalterwhite. com"—Walter White, the lead character in Breaking Bad, suffered from cancer—when the report was published.[117] Apparently, the charity didn't learn much between 2013, when it was publicly shamed, and 2018, when California, by bringing charges for egregiously bad behavior, essentially put the charity out of its misery.

Despite the way *CBS News* lauded other veterans' organizations to provide contrast with Wounded Warrior Project, most charities that serve veterans don't do a very good job. In 2003, the Supreme Court took up the case of *Madigan v. Telemarketing Associates*, which was about high fund-raising costs. Vietnow, a small veterans' charity in Illinois, hired a tele-marketing firm that retained 85 percent of what it raised. While the court ruled, unanimously, that a charity can spend as much as it wants raising money—which means that Lisa Madigan, Illinois's attorney general, lost the argument—the case did little to assuage those who think that overhead at veterans' charities is too high and their impact too low. In fact, looking at only the numbers, as a group, veterans' charities perform dismally. As an aside, Vietnow, even though its fundraising approach was legally exon-erated, seems not to have learned much; over a decade after the Supreme Court decision, according to its 990 filing in 2016, Vietnow's fundraising costs and overhead accounted for 97 percent of its budget, leaving only three percent for programs—and no one knows how much of that goes to actually help veterans. Truly, the veterans, as well as the larger public, would be better served if Vietnow and others like it—and there are many that do not provide much in the way of services—stopped the charade and went out of business.

- **Relatively Speaking**

CBS News compared Wounded Warrior Project with two other

charities: The Disabled American Veterans Charitable Service Trust and Fisher House Foundation, both of which, as does WWP, serve the veteran community. Scott Pelley, the anchor for the broadcast, said, "The Disabled American Veterans Charitable Service Trust spends 96 percent of its budgets on vets. Fisher House devotes 91 percent." *CBS News* said it obtained this information from Charity Navigator.

The DAV Charitable Service Trust is interesting because it reported out only $77,909 for fundraising-related expenses, while obtaining, as it did in 2014, almost $5.6 million in philanthropic support, which translates to a fundraising expense of an unrealistic 99 percent efficiency rate. In addition, the charity reports zero expenses for salaries—this for an organization whose budget was $6.7 million.[118] Its website explains nothing about those curious numbers, but it does inform the public that Bridgette Schaffer, in her role as the administrator of trust and foundation administration, oversees the day-to-day operations of three charities.

In neither of the other two, the DAV National Service Foundation and the Disabled Veterans Life Memorial Foundation, are any salaries noted. The 990 for the Disabled Veterans Life Memorial Foundation does show, however, that its CEO, Fredric Fenstermacher, earned $434,866 while overseeing an organization that raised $12,424 and had expenses in excess of revenues by more than $9.6 million. Discerning how Ms. Schaffer is paid at the DAV Charitable Service Trust or how the three charities are actually intertwined is confusing, but it is fair to conclude that simple comparisons of what might seem like relevant data often tell the public very little.

Actually, it's like comparing apples and oranges. On his website at CharityWatch, Daniel Borochoff, explains,

> A charity's reported program percentage can sometimes vary greatly from the portion of donor funds that actually end up being used directly for charitable services, and that is very much the case with Disabled American Veterans Charitable Service Trust (the Trust). *CBS News* referenced that the Trust "spends 96 percent of its budget on vets" when it was comparing some veterans charity program ratios as part of its coverage in early 2016 concerning

accusations that the popular Wounded Warrior Project (WWP) was wasting donations on lavish spending. The Trust did in fact spend 96% of its budget on grants to veterans organizations, according to its 2014 IRS Form 990 filing, but comparing the Trust's program spending to that of WWP (which was 54 percent in fiscal 2014, based on CharityWatch's calculations)[119] was rather unfair given that WWP operates its own veterans service programs and the Trust does not. When a charity does not conduct its own programs but instead makes grants for other organizations to conduct programs, a high program percentage should be expected.[120]

But there's a further issue at play here, and it exposes the misleading simplicity of CBS's report. The Disabled American Veterans Charitable Service Trust is an affiliate trust of Disabled American Veterans, and its numbers are far worse than WWP's—and with fewer programs. Al Giordano sees it this way: "They rate WWP, a $400 million charity, against the Disabled American Veterans Charitable Service Trust, a $6 million operation with *zero staff*? No wonder their program ratio is 96 percent. A fair comparison would have been trust to trust, such as to the WWP Long-Term Support Trust, or WWP to the DAV, but that wouldn't fit their false narrative."

As for Fisher House, the other charity *CBS News* mentioned favorably, it too reports an unrealistically positive fundraising efficiency—98 percent—and, although *CBS news* quoted criticisms of Steve Nardizzi's salary of $496,415 in 2015, running an organization with $248 million in expenses, the report did not note the $494,202 salary that year of David Coker, the top executive at Fisher House Foundation, an organization with $50 million in expenses.

As with the DAV Charitable Service Trust there's more here than meets the undisciplined eye. Fisher House only builds houses. It then gives them to the government to operate. There are no ongoing expenses. "They also compared WWP to Fisher House," says Giordano. "Fisher House is doing good work, but in this instance the charity raises money for building centers, which they engage outside contractors to build, and, once completed, turn them over to the government to be run at taxpayer expense. No future costs means very low staff for their few other programs, such as airline miles, which is, again, not a fair comparison."

Giordano says, "CBS used these examples in its shoddy journalism to create a false picture to conclude that the DAV Charitable Service Trust spends 96 percent on programs, while WWP spent only 56 percent or 72 percent or 81 percent, depending on what you look at. Most folks don't know the distinction between the national level DAV and the trust so they think WWP is doing something wrong if DAV can be 96% and WWP can't come close to that."[121]

~

In his CBS story, Chip Reid said, unapprovingly, "According to the charity's tax forms, spending on conferences and meetings went from $1.7 million in 2010, to $26 million in 2014. That's about the same amount the group spends on combat stress recovery—its top program."

Actually, according to WWP's information returns, there appears a clear and easily seen number—one that CBS chose not to show—right next to the one showing $26 million spent on meetings. That number is $24,392,338, and it represents the portion representing the programming costs incurred during the meetings. (That number comes from the 2014 990; the graph below includes information from the 2015 990.) That means 94 percent was spent on programming activities that took place at the meetings that year. In fact, pursuing WWP's mission through programs was the primary purpose of the meetings. The numbers also show that, over the years, the portion devoted to programs, relative to the total cost of conferences, has increased over the years.

WWP's 990s show the increase of the cost of conferences from fiscal years 2009 to 2015.

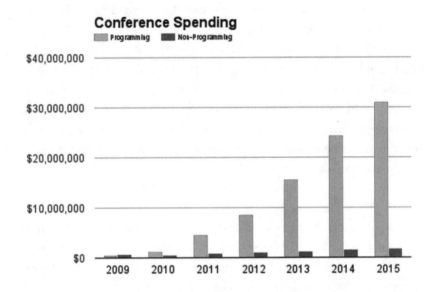

The percentage of programming activity at conferences between 2009 and 2015 rose from 38 percent, in 2009 when the total conference budget was $1.1 million percent to 94 percent, when the conference budget was $32 million. Between 2008 and 2015, the growth in all program activity was well over 200 percent. Part of the problem is that, because of the way the Form 990 is designed, it could, deceptively, look like $26 million was spent on nothing more than fun and games.

Part of the dispute about efficiency at WWP boils down to an accusation—not stated overtly, but implied nonetheless—that WWP's 990s are inaccurately compiled. If we go down that road we have to understand a few things that bedevil almost all charities with multifaceted finances: subjectivity in allocating expenses. Many people think that anything related to accounting is part of an exact science, but that is not the case; there is much gray area to traverse when completing financial documents. That's why we need professionals in accounting firms who not only can competently use a calculator, but who blend a sense of balance and fairness with their experience and understanding of the complexities in the nonprofit world.

One complexity is something called "joint cost allocation," which was a significant element in the allegations against WWP. Most of the guidance on this topic comes from the IRS or Generally Accepted Accounting Principles (GAAP). While the actual allocation process can be complex, the concept is fairly simple: Apply expenses to the correct categories of activity. The process needs to be accurate, but it falls well within the bright lines of the rules.

Suppose a charity's CEO spends 50 percent of her time administering the charity and ensuring legal compliance, as well as conducting other administrative duties, and the other 50 percent of her time raising funds. We would expect to see the CEO's salary allocated 50 percent to administration and 50 percent to fundraising.

Charity Navigator ignored the joint cost allocation rules in its analyses of WWP. When asked why, the former CEO of Charity Navigator, Ken Berger, justified this erroneous reporting on the grounds that the public doesn't understand the rule. At least one accounting firm, Carr, Riggs & Ingram, has called Charity Navigator's formula "mad science." The firm says, "It's smart to keep an eye on fundraising costs, but nonprofit organization executives shouldn't spend too much time worrying about the algorithms watchdog groups use to rate charities."[122] Over the years, many accountants who specialize in nonprofits have acknowledged that Charity Navigator causes confusion because it employs unacknowledged accounting procedures.

Steve Nardizzi didn't care. He simply didn't care what the ratings agencies thought of Wounded Warrior Project, and he certainly was not cowed by criticism of failure on their terms. For him, it wasn't about anything that could be found on a form sent to the IRS.

～

This is not to say that how much of a donated dollar goes to programs and not to overhead is unimportant. How public dollars are spent should always be of interest to the public and should be of ongoing and acute concern to those responsible for good management.

But Brian Mittendorf, a professor and the chair of the Accounting and MIS department at Ohio State University's Fisher College of Business, says that charities actually don't know for sure. "It's not so straightforward," he says, especially for charities, such as the Red Cross, that provide help after natural disasters. "It's difficult to say, *Of this, this is the precise amount going directly to those in need*." He thinks an honest answer is to provide a range and stick to it. Furthermore, acquiescing can create problems. "If donors come and say we want 90 cents on the dollar to go towards the cause," he says, "the simplest way for a charity to accomplish that is to take the dollar that was given to them and grant it to some other charity and let some other charity deal with the administrative costs. And we see that often," he says. "Some of the highest rated organizations are ones that just pass the money on to someone else. And that's not exactly what the donor wants."

Then there is the argument that overhead, instead of being a drag on the charity or a representation of unearned benefits to administrators, actually serves the charity's programs.

Congress has created a unique and protected place in society for 501(c)(3) organizations. Because they pay no taxes on their net income or investment gains, and because donors are permitted to deduct their charitable gifts to those organizations, all charities should be diligent about how money is used. For the average person, the quest for finding or evaluating the good charity requires balancing the good the charity does for society with how efficiently it spends its money, all the while taking into account the realities of the increasing costs of just about everything.

It is far wiser for charity executives and boards to manage the mission, and not the ratings. Impact is the most important measurement of any charitable endeavor. "In the end," says Brian Mittendorf, "we ultimately want organizations that don't just say I gave it to the cause, but operate, do the actual hands-on work." That's where he sees charities, including the Red Cross, facing unfair criticism. "They are doing the hands-on work and so we would expect them to have more administrative costs when they do that. They need offices in multiple locations. They need to train staff." He says that so much attention to overhead may actually push an organization "to be so lean that it isn't able to accomplish anything." Mittendorf says a complex organization's value to society cannot be measured solely by its administrative overhead. [123]

Actually, this is true at all charities.

Making A Difference

It's an adage in the sales world: facts tell and stories sell. While that may be true, the veracity of any one message depends on which facts and which stories are being pushed. Here are a few facts, written in a 2011 *Huffington Post* article, that are pertinent to Wounded Warrior Project:

- Twenty-five percent of veterans experience combat-related problems such as post-traumatic stress disorder, traumatic brain injury, depression or anxiety disorders.

- More veterans are committing suicide than are dying in combat overseas—1,000 former soldiers receiving care from the Department of Veterans Affairs attempt suicide every month.

- About 50,000 veterans are experiencing chronic homelessness.

- The unemployment rate for 18 to 24-year-old veterans is 21 percent, much higher than the 16.6 percent rate for non-veterans of the same age.

The article acknowledged, "To fill in the gap, veterans' charities are a crucial resource—providing financial assistance and job training, funding medical research and rehabilitative services, and helping veterans obtain government benefits. Every year, Americans give millions of dollars to such groups, expecting that the money will assist those who've served their country."[124]

Even though Wounded Warrior Project was racking up mediocre results from the watchdogs, Steve Nardizzi and Al Giordano were creating and growing programs that racked up significant impact to help the people who counted on the organization for help. They had impressive facts and persuasive stories.

The allegations brought against Wounded Warrior Project are a canary in the coalmine for the nonprofit community. Charities often come under heavy fire regarding the way their finances are managed, and for good reason. Transparency is an essential component in establishing and maintaining trust.

As nonprofits put a focus on being outcome-driven institutions, our methods of holding them accountable must be equally outcome driven. There are organizations that do have lower fundraising or administration costs, but there are few organizations that can match the difference WWP makes in their communities and the lives they change with their programming; this is the quintessential item to keep in mind. There is, and must be, a focus on prioritizing the allocation of funds to services; but there must be an equally equitable means of balancing that with the capacity to enact such services. Using irresponsible reporting methods and un-vetted sources to make wild accusations of charities will only damage the relationship nonprofits have with the public and diminish the capacity the nonprofit sector has to create meaningful, lasting impact in the lives of those who deserve it most.

∾

Dan Corry, the chief executive of New Philanthropy Capital, a charity think tank based in London, has written this about impact. "Achieving good is about outcomes—the changes or benefits that result from what a charity or project provides. It means really making a difference. It's not just about the number of signatures on a petition or lives touched or mentoring sessions delivered, but the effect a service has on people's lives. And these effects have to be additional to what might have happened otherwise.

"This is surely what drives us as a sector. And if we don't try to get a handle on it we cannot know if we are really making a difference or work out how to improve what we do—instead relying on anecdote and stories, and potentially misallocating precious resources."[125] While the so-called charity watchdogs give lip service to the importance of impact, none of their algorithms is built to take it into account. And, despite the growing conversation, very few charities have done much to measure the impact they have on their communities.

Interviews with employees at the time of the WWP scandal, as well as those who left the organization prior to the scandal, made it clear that WWP took steps to not only create impact, but also to measure it. Here are two representative examples of what grant makers who knew, and funded,

WWP's programs said: "WWP is doing more for veterans than any other organization in America, short of the VA"; and, "There's a lot of good intentions out there but not a lot of execution. WWP has great programmatic execution."[126]

- **Programs and Impact**

While Soldier Ride was the most prominent program at Wounded Warrior Project, it wasn't the only one of significant value to veterans. By the beginning of 2018, almost 100,000 wounded veterans had registered with the charity. They were looking for help to transition to civilian life and to being well-adjusted citizens, both physically and mentally. Almost 15,000 family members, many of whom were the primary caregivers to the wounded, had registered as well.

WWP's motto is *The Greatest Casualty is Being Forgotten.* Its mission is to honor and empower wounded warriors; its vision is to foster the most successful, well-adjusted generation of wounded service members in our nation's history; its purpose is to raise awareness and enlist the public's aid for the needs of injured service members, and to help injured service members aid and assist one another, to provide unique, direct programs and services to meet the needs of injured service members.

Consider the Combat Stress Recovery Program. It tackles the mental health and cognitive needs of veterans by addressing key issues linked to combat stress, including post-traumatic stress disorder (PTSD), Traumatic Brain Injury (TBI), the stigma attached to mental health, access to care, and interpersonal relationship challenges. WWP says it "challenges warriors to think about goal-setting and understanding their 'new normal.'"

Or consider the Independence Program, designed for the most severely wounded warriors who rely on their families and other caregivers. This idea gave birth to what became known as the Long-Term Support Trust, which WWP established to provide the economic means to assist with the long-term care the catastrophically wounded would need. While all of the approximately 20 programs serve veterans, it was the commitment to long-term care, which could be 50 years or more, depending on the life expectancies of those wounded in battle, that best illustrated WWP's sober and prudent commitment to the future. The WWP leadership calculated the dollar terms of such a commitment to conservatively be approximately $1 to $2 billion.

The effort to help wounded veterans become independent makes clear why the Edmundson family experience was so important. After helping the Edmundsons find the Rehabilitation Institute of Chicago, WWP stayed with Eric and the family. "The Wounded Warrior Project has been involved in Eric's life in many aspects of it since he got injured," Ed Edmundson says. "That's why we are such strong advocates of WWP. They stuck with him. They helped him. They have been there for him. He's able to have gone where he has gone, and done what he has done, and things like that because he has had the WWP support behind him. They gave my son hope for the future."[127] "Actually," Steve Nardizzi says, "Eric was the inspiration for the Independence Program, which helped him achieve his goal of becoming a professional hunter."[128]

That's impact.

Unfortunately, this Long-Term Trust's growth came to a halt after Nardizzi and Giordano were fired.

∾

In 2016, Wounded Warrior Project operated 15 substantive programs. Following are a few descriptions and what WWP said then about their impact.

- **The Independence Program** helps "warriors live life to the fullest, and on their own terms." Also, until the organization cut its programs, granted funds to the WWP Long-Term Support Trust, which WWP established to provide the economic means to assist with long term care in the event of the warrior's separation from his or her current caregiver, by reason of the caregiver's death, disability, or other reasons.

- Impact: The Independence Program served 493 alumni, and 347 caregivers. Seventy-seven point three (77.3) percent of respondents reported their quality of life has improved since entering the independence program. By the end of fiscal year 2015, there were 164 alumni enrolled in the Long-Term Support Trust.

- **The Combat Stress Recovery Program** addresses the mental health and cognitive needs of returning service members and those who have already made the transition back to civilian life.

- Impact: WWP distributed $21,400,000 in grants to the academic medical centers during the year ending on September 30, 2015. There were 2,668 participants in project odyssey, and 2,879 served through CSRP continued-care during fiscal year 2015. Ninety percent of Project Odyssey participants reported they learned useful or very useful PTSD coping skills. Eighty-nine percent of continued care participants have sought or are receiving mental health support 90 days after program participation.

- **Soldier Ride®** is the unique cycling opportunity for wounded services members to use cycling and the bonds of service to overcome physical, mental or emotional wounds.

- Impact: The soldier ride program served 1,845 participants in fiscal year 2015. Ninety-five percent of participants said soldier ride made them feel more confident that they can meet their physical fitness goals. Total soldier ride expenses were $19,467,915 for the year.

- **The Warriors to Work® Program** is one of the cornerstones of WWP's efforts to achieve its strategic goal of economically empowering wounded warriors.

- Impact: In fiscal year 2015, 8,698 warriors and family members participated in the Warriors to Work® program, with 2,555 participants placed in part-time or full-time employment, and an economic impact of $87.7 million from employment compensation. Total Warriors to Work expenses were $10,637,714, including grants of $635,000, for the year.

Although there are measures of activity alongside descriptions of impact, WWP was attuned to the need to report relevant evidence of its worth to its clients, its donors, and the general public.

In addition to being comprehensive, the descriptions and measurements shown here are a model of transparency. That Wounded Warrior

Project put such effort into not only its programs and their growth, but into measuring their results, would be accomplishment enough, but the underlying energy and philosophy emanating from senior leadership that drove it all also must be taken into account. WWP isn't just another charity. It's not just another veterans' service organization either. In growing as it did and in tackling issues the way it did, it was an innovator in defining the way a nonprofit can make a big difference in a world where the Veterans Administration, the government agency statutorily assigned to help, cannot meet all the legitimate needs of veterans.

∼

Innovation at charities, regardless of type or size, is crucial. The authors of a 2017 article in The Stanford Social Innovation Review define innovation "as a break from practice, large or small, that leads to significant positive social impact." A survey of the leaders of 145 organizations said, "Innovation is more than just a catchall slogan—it's an urgent imperative to which 80 percent of them aspire." Regardless of type or size, the authors identified six elements for building innovation capacity:

- Catalytic leadership that empowers staff to solve problems that matter

- A curious culture, where staff look beyond their day-to-day obligations, question assumptions, and constructively challenge each other's thinking as well as the status quo

- Diverse teams with different backgrounds, experiences, attitudes, and capabilities—the feedstock for growing an organization's capacity to generate breakthrough ideas

- Porous boundaries that let information and insights flow into the organization from outside voices (including beneficiaries) and across the organization itself

- Idea pathways that provide structure and processes for identifying, testing, and transforming promising concepts into needle-moving solutions

- The ready resources—funding, time, training, and tools—vital to supporting innovation work

"The problem is," they wrote, "just 40 percent of these would-be innovators say their organizations are set up to do so. This gap worries us, because most respondents say that if they don't come up with fresh solutions to the social sector's myriad challenges—such as improving the academic performance of at-risk middle schoolers, increasing African farmers' crop yields, or dramatically reducing the number of diarrhea-related deaths of young children worldwide—they won't achieve the large-scale impact they seek.[129]

They didn't mention helping veterans, but they might as well have, for it is as urgent and as in need of innovation as any other cause. With that in mind, program growth and impact evaluation at WWP were not only in good shape, they were necessary ingredients to successfully addressing the mission.

There can be no doubt that, while some might point to flaws or only-yet-to-be-realized dreams, Wounded Warrior Project could not be accused of a lack of effort, success, or transparency connected to its work to create an impact on its community. Far too many evaluators and critics do not have the authority to complain or criticize without first understanding the complexities of running a modern charity or, at WWP, the programs that help tens of thousands of wounded veterans, their families, and their caregivers.

- **Myths, Misconceptions, and Mistakes**

Shortly after *CBS News* and the *New York Times* ran their stories, Jacob Harold, of GuideStar, in addressing the issue of the public focusing on the wrong numbers, wrote on the organization's website, "Much of the critique of WWP has, tragically, been focused on overhead ratios. We at GuideStar have said it before and we will say it again: impact is what matters. It is a myth that overhead ratios tell you anything about the quality of a nonprofit's work. Organizations have to invest in themselves and their fundraising to achieve that impact." Then he went linguistic. "Language matters here," he wrote. "Even the venerable *Washington Post* used the misleading phrasing that a certain percentage of *Wounded Warrior Project's money goes toward its mission*. For every nonprofit," as Harold sees it, "100% of the money should go toward the mission. That does not mean that 100% goes to program expenses—every organization must also invest in administrative and fundraising costs. When responsibly used, administrative and fundraising costs are absolutely central to an organization's work to achieve its mission."

He also took note of how the inherent difficulties related to dramatic growth. "Wounded Warrior Project grew very, very quickly—from $41 million in 2010 to $342 million in 2014. Fast growth is difficult to manage. Just ask any successful technology start-up in Silicon Valley. Different-sized organizations need different systems, decision-making structures, governance processes, and different cultures. It takes work (even staff retreats) to manage that kind of growth. In general, growth is good: more resources for an organization to advance its mission."

Although the issue of executive salaries was a minor part of the overall criticism WWP received, it did come up. Dave Philipps wrote in his *New York Times* report that Nardizzi and Giordano "together earned nearly $1 million per year."[130] The topic comes up a lot when the media examine a charity's activities and expenses. According to Harold, "Good people can disagree about the right level to pay nonprofit executives. The bar should be high for justifying nonprofit compensation. But let us remember that senior executives at a for-profit company with $342 million in revenue would most likely be paid far more than those at WWP (according to one analysis, three times as much). Do we want less capable executives running nonprofit organizations? Don't our veterans deserve to have experienced professionals running veteran-serving nonprofits? Nonprofit compensation requires attention and accountability. Nonprofit leaders have difficult jobs. Let's hold them accountable, yes. But let's also treat them like professionals."

Harold also addressed transparency, the road to understanding whether or not a charity makes an impact. "In the end, nonprofits exist to achieve results for the people, communities, and ecosystems they serve. Sharing that data is a prerequisite for having meaningful conversations about nonprofit performance." WWP, he noted, provides much information for its GuideStar profile. That's in addition to what is reported on WWP's website. "We need this kind of transparency," Harold wrote, "if we are to shift to the conversation that matters, a conversation about results. The work of social change is hard. Some people do it well. Some do it poorly. A few scoundrels darken the work for all of us."[131]

If only we all could add nuance to our understanding of the charitable world, so that we could better figure out for ourselves the difference between the operations of a small charity and a large charity, as well as the difference between a charity that honestly works in the public interest and one led by scoundrels.

- **The Modern Charity**

A modern charity is run like a business while pursuing its charitable purposes. Neither is secondary to the other. Its leaders are concerned not only with efficiency, but also with impact and effectiveness. They pay their employees a decent wage. They have an infrastructure that supports their mission. They have a long-term outlook. They measure not only activities but also outcomes. They perform tactical functions while every day remembering the vision set forth by their predecessors. Board members purposefully align their fiduciary duties, their need to plan strategically, and their generative vision and oversight.

They ask how the world would be different if the charity were no longer in existence. They then answer the question by honestly addressing difficult truths. They balance the tangible needs of running an organization with the far less tangible aspects of pursuing a dream.

Roger Woodworth is a founder, former president, and former chief executive officer of Veterans One-Stop Center of Western New York, a 501(c)(3) that helps veterans return to civilian life by empowering them to achieve housing stability, economic success, and emotional health and well being. Veterans One-stop was a recipient of Wounded Warrior Project grants.

Woodworth has worked not only in the veterans' community, serving on several local, regional, and national committees, including as a member on the Veterans Administration's Federal Advisory Committee on Homeless Veterans, but also in mental health advocacy, homelessness, and behavioral health care. In addition, he has experience in the for-profit world, where he has had leadership roles overseeing management, financial performance measurement, internal valuation, cost accounting, and for-profit board participation. He has had substantial experience in both the for-profit and nonprofit sectors. He knows something about the full costs needed to run a large nonprofit.

"For years," Woodworth says, "the public thought of a charity as the enterprise and the people who work there as charitable, meaning that the people would work for below-market wages and where it was all about doing good. Employees would gather donations and then redistribute them directly to the market. Also, success was measured in activity. That's the traditional thinking."

A modern charity is run more like a business, which, he says, "is part of the "professionalization of philanthropy." These days, "People think of their donations more as philanthropic investments, whereas before the thinking was mainly about how little you could spend on infrastructure and how much could go towards programming." While there has been a change, however, it has been slight; plenty of people are still stuck on overhead. But Woodworth thinks such simplistic thinking is not a sustainable model. "You starve yourself of the very things you need in order to generate impact." And to do this right, he says, "charities need sophisticated measuring tools, much like what is found at large corporations."

Woodworth says charities have to look at the issue by asking what they want to accomplish in the long term. "What's good in the short-term is not always good for the long term," he says, and compares how we look at the desire to drive a stock price up with accomplishing a goal of social change. "To make that change, it takes sustained improvement over time, it takes consultants, it takes accountants, and it takes training and retention of staff. And it takes a sophisticated model to show what you will be accomplishing, the value you're adding beyond what you're bringing in."

Furthermore, he says, "It takes money that isn't always forward-facing or programmatic. Capacity—people, systems, strategy, expertise—is expensive and not always directly programmatic, yet it is required to maximize impact and sustainability in the long term. You've got to fully fund and develop your capacity in order to deliver impact and value in the short term, but more importantly to sustain its delivery over the long term." To have an impact and to be sustainable, he says, requires "an organizational and administrative structure that plans, manages, measures, seeks opportunities and mitigates risk over both the short and long term, as well as executes." Woodworth likens it to what's needed to fly a commercial airplane. "The ticket price doesn't represent just the direct cost to fuel the plane and pay the pilots and staff. There is a component of cost to maintenance, training, marketing, safety, and several other things. Why would we expect the nonprofit world to be different?"

Wounded Warrior Project has all of this, he says. "For the programs at WWP, not only were there measurements of volume, numbers attending, and so forth, but there were numbers showing longitudinal improvement in self-reported metrics. WWP then took it one step further to show economic impact—people who were employed and education benefits."

A modern charity is a business, but with a twist. It's a business of social impact.

Woodworth acknowledges that the modern charity feels uncomfortable to the uninitiated. "If you look at somebody like my grandmother who will write a check for $20—or $200, or whatever—to charity, in her mind that money is being taken by somebody who is donating his or her time to give to somebody else to do good. It gets scary when that donation goes into a pile of other money that is set aside in a trust, used to pay an accountant or to build a website, or pays for an All-Hands meeting to generate team building."

Woodworth connects what happened at WWP with its growth into a modern charity. "A nation's enemies multiply according to its successes," he says, employing a military analogy. "I think that, as we look at groups like WWP and other successful charities, other places feel a little bit threatened. Instead of counting only the number of visits or the number of people served, which are, in the end, only activities, we're starting to ask if we're moving the dial and if we're generating impact. And that gets scary. It's scary to the uninitiated and it's scary to those charities that aren't at that level."[132]

∿

Many people close to WWP couldn't put their finger on why, but they knew that what they saw and read in January 2016 was not the organization they knew. Many of the people were unwilling to speak about this on the record, however, because they were concerned about how a public condemnation of the board's response to the stories would look.

Somehow, everyone knew that the board should have done something more.

Charlie Battaglia, a former WWP board member, is gently critical of the board's response. "The organization had 25 staff in 2006, and it grew fast," he remembers. "It grew fast and did well, and so it attracted the ire of outsiders." About the disparaging allegations, he wrote, "The reports were alarming, and while in the end many of the allegations were proven to be untrue, the concern they sparked left many donors confused and unsure about whether to continue their support. That is incredibly frightening, because the people that will be hurt the most are the ones most in need of our support." He also heard the same comments that others heard. The "constant refrain of wounded veterans was: *WWP saved my marriage*, *WWP saved my job*, or most pointedly, *WWP saved my life*." This "convinced me of how incredibly important the life-changing programs run by the organization and the money that funded them were."[133]

This is not unimportant. It is not mere posturing or public relations. The central idea, put forth by almost everyone—other than the 40 or so anonymous disgruntled former employees, except for Erick Millette, who complained publicly—is that Wounded Warrior Project is a good and important charitable organization. Battaglia also wonders if those close to but critical of WWP fully understood the whole picture. "Did the whistle blowers have any access to all the financials? Were they just extrapolating things without realizing costs were not what they thought?"[134]

Despite allegations that WWP did not receive criticisms well, Nardizzi and Giordano welcomed whistle-blower comments. As with any allegation, however, what a whistle-blower says must be vetted; that is, just because a person holds himself or herself out to be a truth-teller, the accuracy of the claim must be shown. Almost no one interviewed for this book saw any truth, when it came to putting his or her comments into context, in what the media or Erick Millette said. As Charlie Battaglia wrote, "There is the adage that one's perception is one's reality. There is also Daniel Patrick Moynihan's observation that everyone is entitled to his own opinions, but not his own facts. WWP may recover its funding support over time, but it will be the wounded veterans it is serving with excellent programs who will suffer in the interim."[135]

Voices

No organization, whether it's a nonprofit or a for-profit, grows without incurring pain. Wounded Warrior Project inflicted some pain on itself, but its growth during its first decade was nothing short of spectacular. That growth fueled much criticism, some of which came from jealousy, some from a perceived unseemliness on the part of a charity, and some from a limiting territoriality felt by other nonprofits and the military. One criticism aired in the media reports of late January 2016 centered on morale, on whether people who worked and volunteered for Wounded Warrior Project enjoyed their days.

The question of morale raised by those who were fired by the organization, however, must be juxtaposed against the high morale reported in independent and anonymous surveys. In 2013 the *NonProfit Times* reported, based on the answers to questions in a comprehensive survey, that WWP was the best nonprofit in the United States to work for.[136]

～

Who has Wounded Warrior Project helped? That's one of the more important questions anyone can ask of a charity. As a respite and a salve amid the swirl of accusations and calculations, it is helpful to focus elsewhere for a moment, to relax angst just a bit, and take in thoughts representing WWP employees, caretakers, veterans, and others.

• **Trevor Dombeck**

Trevor Dombeck worked as a member of the major gifts team at the New York City office of WWP while he was a graduate student earning his masters in nonprofit management at Columbia University. Even as a fund-raiser Dombeck was trained in all aspects of WWP's activities, including suicide prevention.

That fact alone made him suspicious of what Erick Millette was claiming in January 2016. When asked about the organization's culture, Dombeck acknowledged he was not at the Broadmoor for the 2014 All-Hands meeting, but said that kind of meeting "is a good way to get people from 25 offices together. Most of the time people at these events put in some pretty serious work time during the day. Company policy was that drinking alcohol was prohibited in the presence of warriors," he says, "and the occasional team happy-hours were always paid for with employees' personal finances."

He participated once in Soldier Ride on Long Island and remembers, "Morale was awesome." He didn't know Steve Nardizzi well, but says, "he regularly took two hours of his day during orientation for new employees." As for Al Giordano, "I enjoyed my interactions with him. There was no one he wouldn't help." An assistant who had been there for ten years, "and not shy with her opinions," Dombeck remembered, told him that there was "nothing negative" at WWP. "A big takeaway for me," he said, "is that, although not all are from post-9/11 military engagements, half to two-thirds of the employees at WWP are veterans."

One of Dombeck's courses at Columbia was in nonprofit financial management, and he was taking that class when the allegations about WWP broke in the news. His financial management teacher, Terry Cook, he remembers, "saw right through them. We were learning all about the 990 and "he knew the numbers that were being reported on CBS were wrong. And he knew, and taught us, that there is so much more than what's on the 990 in evaluating a charity." Dombeck also said, "CBS reached out to several employees who left who said good things about WWP. Why none of that was used in the media stories, I don't know." Someone in the New York office recognized the silhouetted person in the CBS story and said he was fired for cause. And, yes, Dombeck says staff did make calls to warriors. "Birthdays and holidays are particularly important. We care. Everybody called, even the top staff. Doing that gives you energy."[137]

- **Scott Alpaugh**

"This country," Scott Alpaugh says, "is the greatest country in the world. I see it in a completely different light since my time at West Point and my deployment overseas. I'm incredibly patriotic and I take a lot of pride saying that. I would have happily given my life for our country."

Even so, Alpaugh, who served in the Army during the war in Iraq, had some barriers to overcome after he was medically discharged. He was working in the private sector, at Consolidated Edison, the principal energy company serving New York City, and had just finished having ACL (anterior cruciate ligament) replacement surgery on his knees at a Veterans Administration hospital, the result of a wartime injury, which was why he was discharged from the military. "Shortly after," he says, "I received a $40,000 bill. Now, who goes to the VA to pay for surgery?" It's a good question because no veteran is charged anything at a VA hospital when the reason for the care is service-related. One would think it would have been easy to sort out, but the red tape was overwhelming. "Not only are "the hospitals scary and dark—not places you would want to visit—the VA is a thick briar patch. You'd have to be the luckiest person in the world to find your way through." He says he didn't know where to go. "There's nobody to guide you through the VA, and I had to try to piece together things by myself. This," he points out, "after I fought for my country." He doesn't fault the everyday workers at the hospitals, but does think the VA has a leadership problem.

After a frustrating several months, Alpaugh, who later worked in the finance industry, reconnected with John Fernandez, a West Point friend and fellow lacrosse player—and, incidentally, the veteran whom Peter Honerkamp had found a few years earlier when he was looking for veterans from Long Island. Fernandez lost both legs early on in the Iraq war. "But," Alpaugh says, "he was able to re-engage in society."

Fernandez introduced Alpaugh to Al Giordano. "Al has a legal background. He was senior. I didn't know much more than that, but I did know that Johnny vouched for him." Giordano personally steered Alpaugh through the VA's thick briar patch. He had Alpaugh sign a power of attorney and got him invoiced into the system. Then, "as if by magic, the claim was taken care of in a fairly quick manner. "Al didn't know me," Alpaugh says, "not really, but he connected me and stewarded me. I was fighting for years to go an inch, and he got me a mile in a week and a half."

Giordano advised Alpaugh on some other problems, too. "Whatever—PTSD, reintegration problems or fighting for more disabilities for my knees so this wouldn't happen again. I can't tell you the number of times I went to the VA to say, *Listen, I'm never going to run again in my life. This is a serious disability.* The doctors would say it's just pain, or something else. I told them that I'd had four knee surgeries and that they needed to acknowledge that. It was horrible."

He was getting back on his feet, the beginning of a long-lasting relationship with both Giordano and Wounded Warrior Project. "I introduced friends to WWP," says Alpaugh, "and I gave a few speeches. Told my story."

During that time, Alpaugh was going through a divorce. "Al—a senior person!—called me weekly to see how I was doing. *What do you need? What can we do?* he would ask. I said, *nothing.* They had done so much already."

At one point, however, Alpaugh needed vocational rehabilitation, but the VA wouldn't give him disability. "The VA said I was only ten-percent disabled and so I wasn't eligible. But they were lying. In fact, as I found out from WWP, ten-percent disability was okay for rehab." Once he was able to cut through that set of red tape, again with help from WWP, the VA also retroactively paid costs for business school. He says, "The thing I remember so well is that Wounded Warrior Project convinced me not to walk away from schooling; it was tough for me." A counselor, one outside the VA, told him, "*You are thoughtful and are aware of how you have changed. When others around you are stressed out, you think it's petty because of what you've been through. And thus you're less compassionate, and you're almost robotic when that happens.*" He remembers thinking that in some ways divorce is more difficult than war.

∼

Alpaugh went to several WWP events, including one that put him in a box seat at Giants stadium for a Bruce Springsteen concert. "That's what WWP does. They get people involved. My body, my limbs—those things heal. But I needed somebody who cared. I lost my network, but Wounded Warrior Project was always there. They were there through the rehabilitation of the physical injuries and the hell of dealing with the internal battles." He wanted to know how he could pay WWP back. "Al said, '*Just give us the next guy. So we can help.*' WWP became a way to help me see myself and to help others. Really," he wonders, "where's the algorithm in that process?"

Alpaugh describes how he helped a friend of a friend who worked on C-130 evacuation planes that transported soldiers with traumatic injuries from Bagdad to Landstuhl Medical Center in Germany. "I rode on one once and thought the guy next to me would die. You saw the destruction of war right in front of you." This affected Alpaugh and led to his sense of recluse and was the reason he struggled in his marriage. "I visited this guy and told him he wasn't alone. I brought him to Wounded Warrior Project. Al Giordano again was very helpful. He told me who to meet with to help this guy. I got him to go for help and went with him. The counselor explained what she did and I helped make it comfortable for him to open up. Over time, this changed him. And then he became a mentor at WWP. People who struggle with these things will never be 100 percent," Alpaugh says, "but he has succeeded in all parts of his life incredibly. Again, it was Wounded Warrior Project—but this time in my life it was to help me help someone else." And then, speaking of Giordano, Alpaugh says, "I know a ton of lives he's changed."

"Yes, there were exquisite black-tie, high-class events that WWP put on. There was Cipriani and the Waldorf," two top-tier New York locations where Wounded Warrior held fundraising affairs. "But every veteran felt important at those functions. I never saw any misappropriation. Every one of these events—we all thought they were important. It was so different from after Vietnam. WWP was always there, and they have raised the profile of veterans."

Alpaugh says he never had to call WWP, ever, referring to the Erick Millette allegations that the organization didn't reach out to people. "They called me." Now, though," he says—this was in 2017—"my calls don't get returned. I've tried. This kind of thing destroys not-for-profit capital.

People have stopped giving. All because someone misrepresented what happened. What Al did for my friends and me wasn't fake. I don't care what the media says."

Alpaugh says he can't imagine Giordano misallocating money. "I just can't. What I do know, for a fact, is that he changed my life and others'. To have someone so publicly destroyed . . .." Alpaugh drifts away for a moment in thought. Then he returns. In a world where it was widely publicized how disastrous and bureaucratic the VA is, and you can't argue otherwise, WWP—specifically Al Gordano—"changed the course of my life and others. That can't be taken back. He's a good man who did a lot—and got fired in five minutes. Doesn't he deserve a hug?"

~

By the fall of 2017, Alpaugh and Giordano hadn't seen each other for well over a year, and so when Alpaugh learned, almost too late, that Giordano was going to be in New York, close to where Alpaugh worked, he wanted to see him. "The reason I went to the Matt Modine event was to give Al a hug. Because of him, I have my sense of self-worth back and because of that, at least in part, I am a very happily married man. So here's the thing about that night. I always go home as early as I can—nothing is more important than my family—but that day I called my wife to say I'd be late. I had something really important to do. I knew he'd been through a lot," Alpaugh said, referring to Giordano's firing from WWP. [138]

• Matt Modine

Alpaugh's reunion with Al Giordano was at an event hosted by Matt Modine, who grew up watching the Vietnam War on television. The war entered his family's life when his oldest brother Mark, Jr. enlisted. "Now, the war had a different value," he says. "Walter Cronkite's evening reporting on casualties could mean my brother." Then, after his brother returned, Modine was witness to the treatment of the Vietnam veterans. "I chose to participate in three films about war: *Streamers* (the beginning of the Vietnam build up), *Birdy* (PTSD), and *Full Metal Jacket.* My research into the subject deepened my respect for veterans and the necessities to care for them after the many traumas they have endured." From Modine's perspective, Wounded Warrior Project "fit the bill."

Modine was so impressed with WWP he got involved with Soldier Ride. "It was a big ticket. I had my own not for profit, Bicycle For a Day, which was designed to empower individuals to do one thing that could have a positive impact on the environment. Most trips people make are within a few miles from their homes. Choosing to ride a bicycle for those short trips reduces one's carbon footprint and provides the rider with passive exercise (which is crucial in a country with an ever-increasing obesity and diabetes population). Merging BFAD with WWP was a terrific fit."

Modine took part in his first Soldier Ride in California. "My portion of the ride would be across the desert and end at the Pacific Ocean in Oceanside. It was during this ride that I got to know Steve Nardizzi." This was before Nardizzi became WWP's CEO. "Steve had driven the support vehicle across the United States and he was clearly the leader of the ride. His tough love and support were tempered by his incredible empathy for the wounded veterans. Many of the veteran riders were double amputees and needed very specific attention. It's hard for me to put into words the delicacy necessary in working with a young woman or man who has lost limbs. You need to give them their independence, as a matter of protecting their personal pride. You have to allow them to figure out how to solve problems on their own for those times when there won't be a support team to assist them during their private times of difficulty. And you have to be there to assist them when there's simply no other way than to pick up a person who's lost their legs or arms—and lift them into a vehicle or a chair. If anyone thinks that's easy, I invite you to participate in a Soldier Ride or volunteer at a hospital for veterans. I watched Steve balance his work with the veterans during the desert ride and the several subsequent rides I participated in. I was thrilled to see someone who had started from driving a support vehicle rise to become the president of the project because he had 'been in the shit' and understood, first hand, the needs of our veterans."

Seeing the work both Nardizzi and Giordano did to build Wounded Warrior Project left a mark on Modine. So did their departure. "When Steve and Al Giordano were dismissed, I began looking for a new organization to lend my support to. The decade plus that I worked with and supported the project was absolutely thrilling. The power of WWP, its outreach and wide national support was something I'd never witnessed with a charity. The support for WWP was the polar opposite of what we'd witnessed after the Vietnam War." Modine notes how veterans are being respected and celebrated these days, and that Wounded Warrior Project is a big reason why.

Modine says that Nardizzi and Giordano are two of the brightest, most passionate men he's ever met. "I want to make this clear: I never saw them spend money in any inappropriate fashion or way. They were always frugal. Having run BFAD, my own not-for-profit, I know you have to spend money to raise money. But you look at what those two guys raised, verses what was spent, and multiply that by an unprecedented support and awareness that the project provided for the veterans, and it is unmatched by any charity that I've ever seen. The free publicity that Al and Steve were able to solicit was simply unprecedented. They made WWP part of the consciousness of our country."

Modine says he was in a state of shock and disbelief after Nardizzi and Giordano were fired. "I'm thrilled that they've both been exonerated," he said, after a report[139] detailed how the allegations were either untrue or misleading. "But I'm infuriated that due process didn't protect them. It's horrible for everyone in a country that prides itself on a fair and just judicial system, that will allow a person to be simply accused of a crime, via a news reporter, and then be found guilty via the media, *before* all the facts can come into the light of truth."[140]

- **Harvey Naranjo**

"I get up early and I like staying busy," says Harvey Naranjo, a certified Occupational Therapy Assistant for one of our country's military medical facilities where he's worked since 2001.

Naranjo provides care for catastrophically wounded service members, "to begin," as he puts it, "the reintegration process." The process is not easy, by any stretch of the imagination. Just the magnitude alone: Naranjo estimates that he has personally cared for more than 2,000 soldiers and veterans in his roles.

Because of advancements in military medicine, service members were surviving injuries sustained in combat that they would have not survived in the past. Many hospitals in the United States were unprepared for the wounded who came home after the conflicts 9/11 spawned. "Not many medical providers were experienced in caring for polytrauma patients with blast injuries," says Naranjo. "People were saying, 'How would we be able to care for all these wounded warriors?'" Although the United States began bombing in Afghanistan in October 2001, the system—meaning the military hospitals—became overloaded in 2003 after the war in Iraq began. "No one really knew what to do," says Naranjo. "Luckily, people in the government then were open-minded enough to try new things" in an effort to care for the onslaught of the wounded "instead of letting the bureaucracy take over."

Naranjo feels fortunate to have been a part of the process of trying new things. In fact, when asked about how he feels about Wounded Warrior Project, he says, "This is what I want to say right off the bat: While I love Wounded Warrior Project and the other VSOs I work with, my loyalty from day one has been to the service members. Period. I see veterans and their struggles every day, and so I put them first—before any organization." He is also clear that he respects all VSOs, and in fact holds all organizations that help veterans in the highest esteem.

That said, he makes sure people know what he thinks of Wounded Warrior Project. "WWP is the organization, and has been from the beginning, that provided my patients direct access to make things happen." Many examples come immediately to his mind. "When a guy comes in and needs a computer. I would connect them to WWP. Done. Another one needs special adaptive equipment. I connect them with WWP. Done— whether it was a program a service member needed to enroll in, or whether it was something more simple, like getting a parent transported from the airport to the hospital." As an example, he explains, "Let's say you're lying in bed and your parents are coming from a small town somewhere in the United States, and they arrive at the airport and you're telling them to get to your bedside. How does that happen? The warrior could call WWP and tell them his or her family needs a ride, and they say, 'Sure, we'll make it happen and we'll pay for it.' Its little things like that that go a long way."

There was a hiccup, though, and it was a function of the rapid growth at Wounded Warrior Project. "This is my perspective," he begins, "and only mine. It was in the middle of the war, maybe around 2008 or so, when the direct access to the higher ups at WWP, which service members had become used to, began to decline." Also, other charities, other VSOs, began to clamor for their slice of loyalty. "Once a service member attaches to a VSO," Naranjo says, "it's difficult to change that loyalty."

Even in the nonprofit world, competition can be stiff.

Around this time, Wounded Warrior Project intensified its efforts to reach out to communities where veterans did not have easy access to either military hospitals or veterans' organizations. "That was the right thing to do," says Naranjo, "but in doing so WWP became less of a direct line for my patients. It became less intimate."

Even though WWP hired good people, they were overwhelmed. Naranjo can imagine that this hiccup might have played a role in the criticism the organization received. "There was no malicious intent on the part of WWP. It was just the desire to help every veteran. It was a passion to take care of those service members who needed help that had not yet been identified." But the charity caught up with its hiring needs and eventually regained its level of service as it better administered its growth.

Naranjo has met Tony Odierno, who would later become the board chair at Wounded Warrior Project, and is honored to have met him. "Tony was injured and came to the hospital," Naranjo says. "He was one of the first individuals I got to care for. This would be around 2004 or 2005. And you know what? I didn't know who he was until about four days into treating him. I didn't know whose son he was." WWP's website says, "Shortly after midnight on August 21, 2004, while leading three Humvees through southwest Baghdad to extract a team of snipers, U.S. Army First Lieutenant Anthony Odierno's vehicle was hit by a rocket-propelled grenade. The grenade took off a piece of his right arm, scraped across his chest, took off his left arm, and killed one of his fellow soldiers."[141] His father, retired United States Army General Raymond Odierno, served from 2011 to 2015 as the

38th Chief of Staff of the Army. Before then, he served as Commanding General of the United States Forces in Iraq. Odierno commanded the team that captured Saddam Hussein. Naranjo had a big deal on his hands, but the son never mentioned it.

"That was very meaningful to me," says Naranjo. "There were many important people who came through and when that happened, only the most senior personnel would be tasked to care for them. Naranjo was relatively young and inexperienced at the time. "When he saw me, he could very well have said he wanted someone else to care for him, someone more senior. But I went in there, to his room, and he treated me with as much respect as anyone else." Naranjo didn't actually realize who his patient was until "this general—and I knew he was a big deal—comes in to visit with Tony, and after he leaves I said to him that that general seems to like you a lot. He said, 'Well, I hope he likes me. He's my dad.' From that point on," Naranjo says, "I knew the type of family I was dealing with."

As far as Wounded Warrior Project is concerned, Naranjo says he just wants to see the organization get back to the way it was before the scandal. "I just want it to get back to the level where I can see where people really appreciated what they do, where people see the passion of WWP that shows they want to better service members' lives."[142]

- **Cindy Campbell**

"As I've gone through this journey," Cindy Campbell says, "I've had the opportunity to meet so many other sisters whose brothers died in the war and to hear their stories about the relationships they had with their brothers."

Campbell's brother Chris, a Navy SEAL, was killed, along with 29 other service members, in Afghanistan on August 6, 2011. They were aboard a CH-47 Chinook helicopter when it crashed, shot down by a rocket-propelled grenade launched from the shoulder of a Taliban fighter. Everyone died within a fraction of a second after the helicopter was hit. It was the greatest single-incident loss of American life in the war in Afghanistan, the deadliest moment in the history of SEAL Team 6 and the entirety of the Navy SEALs, and the deadliest single incident in the history of U.S. Special

Operations Command.[143] Altogether there were 38 people on board—30 Americans and eight Afghans—and one military canine. Twenty-two of the dead were Navy SEALs, including members of SEAL Team 6, Campbell's unit.[144]

Cindy found out about her brother's death as she glanced up to a television monitor while walking through a hotel lobby in San Antonio, Texas. "The media knew before I knew. My parents were trying to reach me, but my cell phone had been damaged earlier in the week," she says. Chris Campbell was in training or deployed for approximately 90 percent of the time while serving with SEAL Team 6. Still, finding out on television that her brother had been killed was beyond excruciating. "It was a gut punch. It was just horrible."

Campbell was slightly built: 5 feet seven inches tall and 140 pounds. "When kids come out for football for the first time," his high school football coach, Jack Baile, told the Associated Press, "the first thing you're worried about is, are they going to like to be hit, or want to be hit, and like to hit. That was not a problem with Chris. He had no fear with that." Baile remembers his reaction when he heard that Campbell had joined the SEALs. "That kind of fits Chris. He didn't have a lot of fear of things and I think he always wanted to try to prove to somebody that he could do things. He was an adventurous-type guy."[145]

Cindy was born into a military family. Her father, a retired Marine, served for almost 30 years. "When you think of war babies, you think of individuals who were in Vietnam or Cambodia or Africa or Bosnia or Syria. My father was in Vietnam before and after I was born," she says.

Chris didn't join the military because of his father. "He actually wanted to be a professional baseball player," Cindy says. "We grew up in North Carolina, near Camp Lejeune, near the water. He loved the water. He was like a fish. And then he began to watch videos of Navy SEALs. I thought, Oh, that can't be a good thing." She wasn't talking about service—"service is very valiant," she says—but more, "This is my baby brother. I know what happens when people sign up to go to war, and I don't want that to be him. He never became a professional baseball player, but joined a team that, in my opinion, is far more elite."

Cindy attributes a lot of her brother's positive qualities to their mother Diane. My mom instilled in us the desire to help people. He was so positive. He was a happy, good-natured person.

~

It was discovered a few days after Chris Campbell was killed that, if he was killed in the line of duty, he wanted donations in his memory to be sent to Wounded Warrior Project. In a phone call to her parents, Cindy learned that a handwritten note accompanied his will that said if something happened to him, he wanted 100,000 people to donate to Wounded Warrior Project.

To help spread the word, in May 2013 Cindy wrote 52 individualized letters to the editor to newspapers in all 50 capital cities, as well as to the *Wall Street Journal* and the *New York Times*, explaining Chris's wish. Four printed her letter. Also, WWP produced a mailing that included Chris's story and an appeal. But there was something else, something unique: inserted in the mailing was a small piece of fabric on which donors could write a short note to Chris or the family. The response was overwhelming. The fragments of fabric, after they were sent back, were sewn together into two large American flags.

"Meeting men and women who serve our country," Cindy says, "who have benefited from what my brother put out there, as his last request, is incredibly helpful." Supporters were able to identify with Chris's story and with what the family was going through. "There are no words—other than thank you—because we cannot carry on his legacy alone."

As for the news reports of January 2016 and their aftermath, Cindy is certain that her brother would be mortified. "I felt I had to stand up for WWP."[146]

So she did. In a letter to the *Daily News* of Jacksonville, North Carolina, she attacked the criticism Steve Nardizzi received for his salary. "As a business woman in corporate America, I am familiar with the salaries of those in key executive positions. I can assure you that saving lives is not on their agenda. Yet, their salary and bonus easily triples the salary Steve Nardizzi has been allotted. He and his employees work around the clock to help our nation's wounded. Perhaps those who continually bash the Wounded Warrior Project should apply for such a position or volunteer at an event and productively spend time talking with those who have benefited from their services."[147]

Cindy felt the *New York Times* story on January 27, 2016, was "inappropriate. It was like I got kicked in the gut and all the air went out of my stomach. It felt like a bully situation." So she wrote to Dave Philipps at the *Times*. After detailing Chris's story and death, she explained why she felt her brother wanted so many people to donate to Wounded Warrior Project and why she had positive feelings about the charity. "WWP has the potential to serve over 2 million military personnel who have been deployed to both Afghanistan and Iraq. For the civilian community, for those whose lives remain relatively untouched by the tragedies of war, it might be difficult to grasp that war forever changes a person. After serving our country for almost fifteen years and being on countless deployments, it became very evident that my brother would not escape unscathed. Unlike in the movies, the scenes in the theatre of the mind never end. One's life after war will never be the same!

"WWP was created after 9/11 to provide for the basic needs of our returning military men and women, literally meeting them in the hospital shortly after returning from the battlefield. Our country proudly rallied behind the organization because we were ashamed of the treatment our Vietnam Veterans unjustly received. Therein lies the vision upon which Wounded Warrior Project was founded: to foster the most successful, well-adjusted generation of wounded service members in our nation's history. Contributions soared, donors increased and the nonprofit grew. And, isn't that the point, especially when those you aim to help number in the millions? This cannot be done relying solely on unpaid volunteers. Why would anyone think that requiring a certain skill set, not to mention an emotional resilience and aptitude for working with our returning military to make a positive difference in their lives, should demand a salary less than that for a similar position in the corporate world where, a world where improving the bottom line is the only motive? Perhaps, if we changed our focus and paid people exceptionally well when they were involved in a profession that was interested in making the world a better place, we might actually begin to witness some remarkable changes in our society!"

Campbell was introspective about her passions. "If you have read this far, Dave, you are probably thinking that I cannot objectively comment on your article," she wrote. She had objectively legitimate questions, however. "What was the purpose of such slanderous accusations? Those employees who were fired provided no solutions. What was the duration of time they worked for WWP? The longer their employment, the less credible they become. If they truly had an issue with the way the organization was managed or how donations were distributed, a job change would have happened sooner rather than later. Disgruntled employees are always happy to share their negative experience, especially when they are corralled together by reporters who are more concerned with ratings in an attempt to feed the drama that more often than not drives our society."

Cindy would have done her brother proud as she completed her complaint on a positive note. "Rather than bashing an organization founded with the intent to do amazing things and who has been offering great programs and services to our wounded service members," she wrote, "let's rally behind them and be a part of their living logo. It is critical they continue to operate and receive donations to fund their work to pay it forward and help those service members who have sacrificed a great deal for our nation. I will continue to stand by Wounded Warrior Project, for the love of my brother. Although his physical loss from our family's life is heartbreaking, the legacy he left behind through his last request is enduring."[148]

Shortly after, Philipps responded. "While I don't appreciate you calling my reporting slanderous (i.e. false) you make a good point that the organization continues to exist and can change to better serve its mission. I would hope you would agree that increased transparency and accountability will help it do that."[149]

The following day, Campbell wrote back. "Of course, I agree that increased transparency and accountability for ANY organization is good business. Perhaps if our politicians, CEOs of 'for-profits', and reporters would practice such an approach, our world would not be in the condition in which we currently find it."[150]

- **Eric Edmundson**

"Eric was in theater for only six weeks when he got injured," Eric Edmundson's father Ed remembers. "I spoke with him by phone on September 30, 2005, and told him to stay safe and keep your head down. He said, 'Don't worry, dad. If anything happens, the Army will take care of me.'" That back-and-forth will always haunt Ed. Two days later his son's vehicle ran over an improvised explosive device in Iraq. Things changed in unimaginable ways after that.

Eric lived at Fort Wainwright in Fairbanks, Alaska, in the state's North Slope Borough, when he was deployed, and so his wife Stephanie and infant daughter Gracie had to fly from there to Walter Reed Medical Center in Washington, DC to see him when he returned from Iraq. His sister Anna Edmundson-Frese, a social worker and an Army veteran, traveled from North Carolina. "I can't speak for everyone," she says, "but when we got to Walter Reed, we knew nothing. I remember mom and dad showing up and none of us were military people. We had no idea what was going on."

Anna, who says she "went to the dark side by marrying a Marine," recalls that the family would be at Walter Reed for three months. "During that time, I saw a lot of families struggling and, unfortunately, dissolving. Eric's family was quite young—newly married with an eight-month old daughter." The family members, she said, "got together to do what was needed to support Eric and his family and sustain the relationship. Every family deals with trauma differently, but we were lucky because our parents have a background in medical care." Being a veteran helped, as well. "Not only does a family learn of an injury and then travel to whatever military institution, they also are entering a whole new culture. The military speaks a different language. They speak in acronyms. It's not just the stress of dealing with a loved one's trauma but being engulfed in a whole new bureaucracy you're not familiar with." Not every family is so fortunate to have had a care-giving or military background. "It takes a village," she says. "It not only impacts the individual, it impacts the family." Anna had also worked for Wounded Warrior Project for eight years as a family support coordinator.

Since then, it's been a journey, a journey well documented in the media, in part because Eric's story is so riveting and in part because the challenges are all too common. Through it all, however, Wounded Warrior Project was there. Eric's father says, "I think the Wounded Warrior Project, even in those early stages, had hired enough good people, good people who knew what to do, what to ask and how to give guidance. That helped a lot. They were in the trenches in the beginning. Actually they come into Walter Reed. There were other organizations that came into our room and gave phone cards, but the Wounded Warrior Project came in and they were interested in what was going on with everything." Ed remembers that the concerns went from the profound to the small. "The milkshake man came every Friday and gave out milkshakes," he says of WWP's efforts. "But you know, he was also listening. He said we might want to talk to one family or another to talk about what everyone was going through. Just knowing him was important. It opened a door."

Today, Eric communicates with the help of a computerized speech-generating device, much like the one Stephen Hawking used. In most situations where Eric and his caretakers can anticipate questions, they can take the time to essentially pre-program the responses. To a question about his service, after 15 seconds, with prompts from his mother in this discussion, his response through the computer was, "I was in the Army. I was a cavalry scout. I was stationed at Fort Wainwright, Alaska." He also later said, "I was injured by an IED in 2005. I have a traumatic brain injury as well as an anoxic brain injury. I am working hard to get my voice back." His mother says, "Eric's goal is to train his muscles to re-learn how to talk." And he is making progress. Asked where he grew up, he is able to physically say, although in a somewhat slurred manner, "Iowa."[151] For most people Eric Edmundson's life would be unbearable. But the way he lives it, similar to the way Hawking lived his, it's practically a celebration.

Wounded Warrior Project's Independence Program—the one designed for severely wounded warriors who rely on their families or other caregivers because of moderate to severe brain injury—plays a crucial role in the Edmundson family. "The beauty of that program is that it is flexible," says

Ed Edmundson. "Every Warrior's needs are different and every family's needs are different."

By accessing the program—a program that Eric's sister Anna helped develop during her time at Wounded Warrior Project—Eric has been able to continue in traditional therapy. You go and you work out in a therapeutic rec room with other individuals who are rehabbing." That's on the clinical level, Eric's father says. "But at the same time it's nice just to go to the gym as a guy and work out. He has a personal trainer. He goes to yoga and works out two or three times a week. The independence program assists in helping with the costs of the personal trainer, and that support allows Eric and his family to use those funds maybe for other things. Every family has different financial means and they want to be able to save for different things. I think the challenge for veterans is that, like Eric, they're on a fixed income." The VA doesn't cover the costs for this kind of care. "Plus," Edmundson points out, "the VA budget needs to be reauthorized every year."

That's one reason why WWP is so important to the Edmundsons. Ed says—this was in 2016—"Just a year or so ago, you know, the VA hadn't approved the budget, and Wounded Warrior project then said, 'Well, if they don't approve this budget, we'll send $500 out to every warrior alumnus and alumna in our system. So, for monetary means, programs like the independence program are helpful to just allow families to help save for the long term. No one had stepped in to provide this kind of care.

"The VA may provide the equipment and may provide the service and may provide the therapy," says Edmundson, "but Eric may need a piece of equipment or may need a service or therapy, but he has to wait months and months to get it. WWP can circumvent all that red tape and help provide that."

Eric says, "Wounded Warrior Project has been a part of my life since my injury. They have offered financial support, such as right now my gym membership but that is a small part of what they do and what they are. They have helped me become the man I am now. I can reach out to them with questions. I can hang out with other warriors. I can give back to others. With their support, I feel I have a friend. I hope they will continue to be a part of my life as well as my family's."

Eric Edmundson, like everyone else, celebrates his birthday. But each year he also celebrates, even more joyously, a day that only the wounded and their families can appreciate: "Alive Day." Every October 2nd, Eric celebrates the day he came close to, but defied, death.

CHAPTER 4

THE DAMAGE

Through January 2016, Wounded Warrior Project operated as a model for the modern charity, focused on a tangible social problem: the care of wounded veterans who returned home from war after 9/11. As it grew, the organization was in good shape and its unparalleled achievements were undeniable. That success, however, was seriously compromised after Nardizzi and Giordano were fired.

Immediate

- ### The Watch List

It was in early February, a few days after the allegations were reported, when WWP's board hired Simpson Thacher & Bartlett and FTI Consulting to perform an independent audit. During the five weeks while the audit was being conducted, the board prohibited Steve Nardizzi and Al Giordano from saying anything publicly about the news reports or about how the organization was doing.

On January 30, during the weekend after the initial stories, *CBS News* announcer Anthony Mason led his reporting with, "Charity Navigator, a national evaluator of charities, put the country's most prominent veterans' charity on its Watch List." When the meat of the story was handed over to Chip Reid, who had reported the original stories just days before, he essentially re-reported what had been aired the prior week: criticism of WWP's spending, an interview with a former IRS executive, the complaints that Nardizzi was paid too much, that WWP had donated money to another charity, and that it was sitting on too much money and not spending it for current purposes.[152]

What the report did *not* include—not one word, other than in Mason's introductory sentence—was anything about a "Watch List."

Ken Berger, the former CEO of Charity Navigator, acknowledged in the aftermath of the WWP crisis, "The Watch List is a function of media reports. The ratings are a very basic measure of performance, and there are complexities, nuances and circumstances that come up that you're not going to get from just looking at a website and a 990. These other sources of information can be very important." The news reports qualified to put WWP on a Watch List, as Berger explained the term, but the ominous tone that emerged strongly implied that Charity Navigator was now confirming all the bad things *CBS News* had reported earlier.

In reality, WWP was on the watchdog's Watch List solely because CBS and The *New York Times* aired the report to begin with. In effect, CBS was reporting that somebody took notice of its story, which then became its own story.[153] "It's a circular thing," said Berger. "A Watch List designation means we're watching the situation because some reputable media outlets have identified some problems that are being looked at."[154]

In September 2016 Charity Navigator discontinued its Watch List in favor of a more comprehensive Advisory System. According to its website, "Under the new system, charities are categorized into one of three designations: Low Concern, Moderate Concern and High Concern. These designations are objectively assigned based on a rigorous methodology that evaluates the ethical or legal issue the organization is facing."[155] The designations may be said to be objective, but any time the words "low," "high" and "moderate" are connected to the word "concern," the conclusion most likely is anything but objective. Furthermore, the methodology suggests a process and infrastructure that simply do not exist at Charity Navigator.

Al Giordano, WWP's former chief operating officer said, "The real chutzpah is when Charity Navigator put WWP on its Watch List because of all the press reports that *they* contributed to!"[156]

- **Reaction to the Story**

On January 30, the author of a letter to the editor at The *New York Times* wrote, "I was saddened to read of the wasteful spending at the Wounded

Warrior Project. Its television commercials with scenes of men, women and their families coping with deep emotional pain pull at the heart and purse strings. Now I wonder how employees can live lavishly off a large percentage of the contributions that should be serving people in need. According to CharityWatch," the letter continued, "the Wounded Warrior Project is, in fact, rated C. To stop donating to it is a response that makes sense. But what of the veterans in need? How do we help them?"[157]

The writer's sentiment can't be faulted. Anyone who had read or heard the story would naturally have the same negative reaction. The pull of putting everything that is donated to help a charity's beneficiaries, given that it derives from empathy, is extraordinarily strong. But at least she was able to parse the issue, separating what she thought about the work Wounded Warrior Project was performing from the alleged evils of those running the organization.

Two days later, on February 1, The Nonprofit Quarterly published "The Fundraising Factory Issue" in which the authors criticized the attention WWP paid to raising money. "This focus on expanding the fundraising base among individuals would, in fact, require capital well above what most organizations would spend, since acquiring new donors at a fast pace is an expensive endeavor, so there is a different 'model' at play here—a donor acquisition and growth model or a *fundraising factory*—but the fact that it appears to be funded by current donors without an acknowledgement of that is a very big problem. We also have no sense of when and if there will be a 'big enough' moment at which time we might expect a smaller fundraising cost."

The authors also called out Nardizzi for what they thought was his lack of transparency. "Of even greater concern is Nardizzi's record of fighting against financial transparency in nonprofits. Nardizzi is on the advisory board of the Charity Defense Council, an organization that advocates for less oversight in spending for nonprofits and promotes high fundraising costs and high salaries for nonprofit executives. Nardizzi himself makes $473,000 in compensation."

Nardizzi takes issue with the characterization that he was fighting against financial transparency. "That misrepresents my position and what the Charity Defense Council is all about," he says. "I personally advocated for increased and better charity oversight."[158]

The authors then compared Nardizzi to William Aramony, the disgraced former head of the United Way of America. Quoting from an archived NPQ article from 2011, they wrote, "Aramony is credited with making coherent and guiding the United Way network as it built from $787 million in fundraising proceeds to $3 billion. This growth fed directly into the coffers of UWA since the national hub took 1 percent of every dollar raised by every affiliate around the country. Aramony lived in high style while leading the network, however, with a salary that topped out at $460,000 and a number of perks later deemed criminal. The iconic image in his story was a UW-funded trip down the Nile with a teenage girlfriend."[159]

It has to be noted that, even if all of the allegations against Nardizzi were true—and they were not—comparing him with a convicted felon was unwarranted.

On March 3 CBS struck again, this time with the headline, "Top Wounded Warrior Donor Calls for CEO's Resignation." One of the first tangible pieces of evidence of financial damage to the organization resulting from the publicity, the report described the frustrations of Fred and Diane Kane. Fred Kane said Nardizzi should be fired. "Where is he? You lead from the front, good or bad. You don't hide," Kane said. "I don't understand how an organization that has many veterans who value honor and service and the chain of command can be led by a guy like that." Kane was so angry he cancelled the 2016 benefit golf tournament that he had sponsored for several years on behalf of WWP and started an online petition for a public audit; this, even though a forensic audit was already well underway. Kane said he wanted answers from WWP's board of directors and that he was "done" at WWP.

Also in that report, separate from Kane's complaints, was criticism of the board's own expenses "at five-star hotels, including the Beverly Wilshire Hotel in Los Angeles and the Waldorf Astoria in New York."

Reid reported, "When board members questioned spending decisions and executive salaries, their concerns were ignored," even though, moments earlier, he reported, "Sources with direct knowledge of the charity's operations said the board signs off on all of the charity's major spending, including expensive staff retreats." Reid then revealed that no one on the board would speak about the matter. [160]

While a news crew was descending on board members' homes—the clip in the report shows board chair Anthony Odierno scurrying from his front door to his car, clearly trying to avoid a reporter—one member of the board, Richard Jones, in what can only be imagined as a uniquely bizarre development, hid in his basement and called Steve Nardizzi in a panic to say he was "trapped" and asked him to call CBS to call off the dogs. In retrospect, Nardizzi thinks the story might have been fabricated. [161] It didn't pass the smell test for Al Giordano, either. "I called Jones back," he says, "and asked for his address so I could have a police friend do a drive-by. Jones gave me his address, but then immediately called me back to say there was no need to call the police as the news van had just left." [162]

In March 2016, *Fortune Magazine* named Steve Nardizzi and Al Giordano among the world's 19 most disappointing leaders. The article parroted the news accounts, saying, "A charity for veterans should be the last place that would "fritter away 40% of donations on salaries and overhead (including first-class air fare and lavish conferences) rather than using them to help grievously injured soldiers." Nardizzi and Giordano were in the company of people like Martin Winterkorn, the former CEO of Volkswagen; Martin Shkreli, founder and former CEO of Turing Pharmaceuticals; and Chris Christie, the former governor of New Jersey. [163]

The world did not take note when Nardizzi and Giordano responded, "The misreported facts are easily refuted." [164]

~

One voice, almost alone in its message, stood out from the others. On January 28, Sean Norris, the editor-in-chief of *NonProfit Pro* wrote an article entitled, "What CBS News Got Wrong."

Norris noted that it was fair enough to ask the question of where the money was going. "Wounded Warrior Project," he wrote, "has long been scrutinized for its spending habits, albeit in much smaller forums. Google 'Wounded Warrior Project controversy' and you'll find plenty of articles . . .

questioning the charity's actual contributions to veterans. Add in the recent allegations that Wounded Warrior Project is a bully in the nonprofit sector, and it becomes that much easier to question the charity's reputation."

Norris didn't dwell on the issue of the percent going to program and other costs—the main complaint in the news reports—because he thought something else was more important. "Convert those percentages to dollar figures," he said, "and they tell a different story." He noted the actual amount for programs at the three veterans' charities CBS cited: at the DAV Charitable Service Trust, it was $6.4 million; at Fisher House, it was $37.5 million; at Wounded Warrior Project, it was $148.6 million. "In other words," noted Norris, "Wounded Warrior Project spends three times more on veterans than those two organizations combined. Even if you factor out all other program expenses, Wounded Warrior Project still provided $42 million in grants and assistance to organizations and individuals in 2014, more than either Disabled American Veterans Charitable Service Trust or Fisher House spent on total program expenses."

He then took a swipe at the myopic attention the watchdogs, as well as the media, pay to overhead by quoting the blogger Richard Perry: "If you didn't have overhead, you wouldn't have anything. It is still mind-blowing to me to sit in a meeting with seemingly intelligent people and have them imply that overhead is bad. It must be pushed down to levels that make it impossible to run the organization and must be hidden in financial reports so ill-informed donors can't find or discern where it is or how much it is. This is truly comical." Still, Norris acknowledged, "With former and current employees lining up to file complaints about the organization's spending, it'd be foolish not to investigate further and push for greater accountability."

Norris noted that almost all of CBS's reporting depended on Erick Millette, who, he said, "diminishes the work the organization is doing—work that Millette has seen first-hand."[165]

Another moderating public voice was that of Jacob Harold, of GuideStar. In February following the news reports, he wrote that the criticism was "rooted in myths and misconceptions about nonprofit work." The media reports, he said, "fail to understand the reality of running a complex organization doing complex work in a complex world. These myths and misconceptions hurt other nonprofits, too."[166]

A private supporting voice came from a communications expert in the nonprofit world. "I've followed the recent news cycle about WWP with interest as a donor with a fair amount of professional experience in such situations. I wanted you to know how much I admire the way WWP has dealt with CBS's 'reporting'—with integrity, transparency, and courage. I'll continue to support WWP's mission with even greater commitment and confidence. And on behalf of those of us striving for a more contemporary and fair approach to charity ratings—keep up the good work!"[167]

Short Term

- **Reaction to the Firings**

On March 10, just hours after the board announced that Nardizzi and Giordano had been removed, *CBS News* led with the story. "We begin tonight with breaking news in our investigation of this country's largest veterans' charity," Scott Pelley announced. "The two top executives of the Wounded Warrior Project were fired today by the board of directors." What followed was a recap, again, of the network's earlier reporting of the accusations that the charity misspent donated money, including the now-infamous 2014 conference held at the Broadmoor in Colorado Springs.

Behind Pelley were two screens. On one, the word "dishonorably" appeared just above the WWP logo; to its right, on the other screen, were pictures of Nardizzi and Giordano with the word "discharged" superimposed.[168] They looked a lot like arrest photos—photos that may have been part of the reason that Nardizzi and Giordano, as well as their wives, received harassment comments and letters, and even death threats, from people too cowardly to identify themselves.

Erick Millette, when asked for his response to the firings, told *CBS News* in a report that aired the following evening that "it feels good" and that he was "guardedly optimistic" about WWP's future. Fred Kane was pleased as well, and said that the firings should be only a first step. "They need to change the culture. I think they can right the ship, but it's going to take a lot of effort to build up that goodwill again." Even family members of John Melia, whose backpack program led to the founding of WWP in 2003, weighed in. They accused "Nardizzi of going so far as to remove any mention of the Melia family from the WWP website" and said that "donors have every right to be angry about the lack of stewardship shown by the immediate past leadership."[169] The feeling conveyed by those CBS spoke with was that the worst was over and that a new day would soon dawn.

According to the board's news release that day, the independent audit concluded, "Certain allegations raised in media reports were inaccurate"; this, even though the *New York Times* said, incorrectly, that the review "confirmed many of the findings by the *Times* and CBS."[170]

The board's news release also stated that WWP "has already begun to strengthen its employee travel policies to more explicitly limit domestic air travel to economy class absent an exception for health or disability reasons. In addition, the Board has committed to other measures, including strengthening policies related to employee and director expenses, enhancing employee training on existing and new policies and procedures, and continuing to have its financial statements independently audited and available on the organization's Website. The Board will conduct an objective assessment of WWP's progress towards implementing these and other enhanced measures"[171]; this, even though many of the policy enhancements were already underway, the result of a normal and voluntary evaluation of businesses practices.[172]

The report was delivered only orally. Although the lawyers and the consultants presumably took extensive notes over the course of their one-month investigation, a physical report was never written. Despite being asked, no one at Simpson Thacher, FTI or WWP explained why.

The negative publicity instantly distorted what had been a highly regarded veterans service organization into a pariah of the nonprofit community.

The following day, in a story reflecting Fred Kane's account of the organization's fall from grace, the *Times* reported the "building pressure by donors, veterans and supporters of the organization that culminated

Thursday night in the abrupt firing of Mr. Nardizzi and his second in command, Al Giordano, who together earned nearly $1 million per year. By the
time the board met Thursday to dismiss the two men, contributions were
down and it had in hand an internal investigation that convinced it that top
management had to go."[173]

"Based on figures publicly reported by WWP," board members told
another news outlet, "the decline in fundraising began immediately after
exaggerated media reports and continued to accelerate as concerns sparked
by those reports continued to take hold among our donor base."[174]

That was not true. Contributions did not decline before the board met
to fire Nardizzi and Giordano. In fact, according to confidential monthly
fundraising reports, it was not until April, a month after the firings, that
donations began to suffer. It wasn't the awful publicity that ignited the erosion of donor support; it was the announcement of the firings.

～

A finger had to be pointed, and Nardizzi and Giordano found themselves
in the hot seat; after all, the scandalous extravagance and skyrocketing
spending—even though that narrative told a false story—took place on
their watch.

The optics weren't good either. Nardizzi was seen by some as brash
and confident to the point of coming off as arrogant. As Dave Philipps
explained in his NPR interview, "Steve Nardizzi made a habit of trying to
one-up his entrance from the year before. So he came in on a Segway, and
then the next year, he came in on a zip line." Once, he rode into the conference room on a horse. "In this one," Philipps said, referring to the opening
of the Broadmoor conference, "he repelled out of a tower down towards
the cheering crowd while there was a spotlight on him. I think he was trying to rev up his employees, but a lot of them saw it as absurd and a real
waste of money."[175]

Philipps's assessment was incorrect. In fact, the vast majority of
employees, including Erick Millette, said they thought the conference was
a valuable supplement to their work.

～

Even though there was noble purpose behind Nardizzi's dramatic entrances at the annual meetings, he accepted the criticism and has said he would not do it again. Optics—especially as smart phones make it possible for anything to be made permanently public—need to be considered in decisions people make.

The power of pictures compared to that of substance, however, isn't new. At least since television has been around, pictures have dominated. In 1984, Lesley Stahl, a CBS reporter, ran a critical story about Ronald Reagan. In her book, *Reporting Live,* Stahl described her thoughts as the piece went to air: "I knew the piece would have an impact, if only because it was so long: five minutes and 40 seconds, practically a documentary in *Evening News* terms. I worried that my sources at the White House would be angry enough to freeze me out." But that isn't what happened, she says. When the piece aired, Stahl wrote, Richard Darman, who was the White House Staff Secretary at the time, called her. "Way to go, kiddo," he said to Stahl. "What a great piece. We loved it." Stahl replied, "Didn't you hear what I said [in the broadcast]?" Darman answered, "Nobody heard what you said." "Come again?" she asked. "You guys in Televisionland," he responded, "haven't figured it out, have you? When the pictures are powerful and emotional, they override if not completely drown out the sound. I mean it, Lesley. Nobody heard you." Stahl's critical report about President Reagan had been accompanied by generally upbeat visuals. According to Darman's theory, the pictures registered more with viewers than anything Stahl had said.[176]

The damage in the visuals relating to Wounded Warrior Project wasn't in their existence—the board knew full well what was going on—but in the criticism of their existence *on television.*

~

On March 14, 2016, the week after the firings, Tony Odierno appeared on CBS This Morning. Charlie Rose,[177] the morning anchor, asked, "Why was it necessary for journalism to come in and point out something obvious to the Wounded Warrior Project?" Not everything, actually, was so obvious. "A lot of the allegations," Odierno said, "were not accurate," pointing to the faulty reports about the program budget and conference spending. When asked about how things got so "off track," he replied, "I wouldn't say it got severely off track." He then explained that any organization that conducts an evaluation of itself will find improvement opportunities.[178] Even though the interview began with a taste of confrontation, it soon devolved into a mutual statement of support for the nation's veterans. Odierno, a veteran amputee himself, seemed off-limits to any real grilling. No one seemed to notice that Odierno was implicitly criticizing CBS's journalism standards.

That same week, Odierno was also a guest on the Fox commentary show The O'Reilly Factor. He told Bill O'Reilly that the review conducted after the stories were aired in January concluded that the allegations were wrong. Odierno said, "Eighty percent [not the 60 percent that was alleged] of our spending did go to programs." Also, of the "$26 million that went to staff conferences, the audit showed that about 94 percent of that—$24.5 million—went to direct program expenses." As for the issue of expensive travel, he said, "Over 99 percent of the plane tickets were in accordance with . . ." At this point O'Reilly interrupted him. Odierno, if he was going to reference the actual financial accounting of expenses at WWP, was most likely going to reveal that only one percent of travel was at the first-class level, and that half of that was the result of using upgrade coupons that did not cost anything to WWP.[179]

The organization's board chair was asserting, stiffly but correctly, that an independent report concluded that, substantively, everything was fine.

And yet, he and his board fired the people most responsible for all the good work. O'Reilly asked why.

Odierno's stiffness continued, and to worse effect, saying the review was thorough, that it encompassed policies and cultural issues, and that after looking at the "totality" of things, "the board felt that a change was necessary." O'Reilly, after saying it seemed liked Nardizzi and Giordano were doing a good job—the news release basically acknowledged that they were—tried to drill down for specifics. "Why? You say the culture. What was the culture there?"

Again, Odierno began to wander, beginning to speak of "conversations" with advisors. But O'Reilly again interrupted him. "Tell me why, Captain." The reference to Captain was pejorative, apparently employed to say that although Odierno had been a military leader, what O'Reilly was hearing did not sound decisive. "Let's cut to the chase," said O'Reilly. "What were they doing—these two individuals who you fired—that disturbed you?"

"We reviewed judgment decisions that were made, the cultural aspects . . . these were all part of the briefings . . ."

O'Reilly: "But I don't know what 'cultural' things are. Give me an example." After Odierno said he would not provide specifics, O'Reilly asked if the donors weren't owed an explanation.

Still, other than something along the lines of how great an organization WWP was, Odierno said nothing specific.

O'Reilly asked one more time. After being told there were millions of viewers, including many WWP donors, tuned in, Odierno said, "The board is acting in the best interests of the organization, and this is what we felt, that a change was necessary to get the focus back on programs and serving and doing what we do." [180] That bland comment ended a frustrating interview.

- **Senator Charles Grassley Probes**

A few days later, on March 18, 2016, Senate Judiciary Committee Chairman Charles Grassley of Iowa wrote the first of two letters asking for detailed information about WWP's operations. He said, "Reports indicate a climate of hostility to employees who speak out against such lavish spending, many of whom are veterans themselves." He then warned, "If true, these allegations are a breach of faith with donors, taxpayers, and, more importantly, veterans." He gave WWP less than three weeks to respond. [181]

Simpson Thacher provided a point-by-point response to Grassley's questions. The letter said, "The claim that Wounded Warrior Project does not serve warriors and that 'Warriors call us, we don't call warriors' is false," and called attention to the 150,000 calls and the more than 100,000 emails sent to veterans and the growth of that outreach over the prior years. The letter also noted, "The claim in the media that the cost of the 2014 All-Hands Huddle at the Broadmoor Hotel in Colorado was $3 million is false. The cost was less than $1 million."

Simpson Thacher also affirmed that the charity was not, in fact, wasting its money. WWP "spends a substantial portion of donations on furthering its charitable mission, and will, under the stewardship of the interim Office of CEO and interim COO, continue doing so," and that "approximately 80.6 percent of donations were spent on program-related services for warriors and their caregivers." The letter then addressed the organization's vast outreach and services provided to veterans.[182]

Nothing Simpson Thacher said indicated anything was amiss and certainly there was no hint as to why the former CEO and COO had been fired.

Nardizzi and Giordano felt the reply was tepid. They said WWP should have confirmed "the great and measurable impact WWP makes. During our tenure at WWP the organization was a leader in impact measurement and reporting," and noted that there was a team dedicated to evaluating program effectiveness, setting measurable goals for both outputs and outcomes, and maintaining transparency. "At this point," they said, "it is beyond reasonable debate that WWP accurately reported on its 2014 audited financial statements, consistent with the requirements of generally accepted accounting principles, that 80.6% of its spending went towards program expenses."[183]

~

Simpson Thacher's response did not satisfy Senator Grassley. In a second letter, he said, "WWP has a tremendous responsibility to operate efficiently and to make the most out of the money it receives from the donating public. And as a tax exempt organization, it is able to take advantage of favorable tax treatment so as to ensure that our nation's wounded, and often times most vulnerable, are properly assisted with the help of the generosity of the American people. The trust WWP has engendered amongst the donating public requires it to be as transparent and open as possible with respect to its spending practices." Grassley then asked for a more detailed accounting of several categories of expenditures.[184]

- **A New Leader and His Challenges**

In June 2016, six months after the allegations were reported, Wounded Warrior Project chose Michael Linnington to be Steve Nardizzi's successor. From the day the firings took place, the goal was to find someone permanent, not to rely on Tony Odierno, who, although he assumed the role on an interim basis while heading the board of trustees, had a full-time job at JPMorgan Chase. Linnington arrived militarily credentialed. After attaining the rank of Lieutenant General, which carries three stars with it, and retiring from the Army, Linnington became the first permanent Director of the Defense POW/MIA Accounting Agency. He also served as the Military Deputy for Personnel and Readiness to the Under Secretary of Defense, and, before that, as Commanding General, Military District of Washington and Commander, Joint Force Headquarters-National Capital Region from 2011 to 2013."[185]

Wounded Warrior Project was serving tens of thousands of wounded warriors and their families with almost twenty programs. It was a major charitable entity with a great deal of administrative complexity. The question was whether Linnington's background was the right fit for WWP's needs. Even in a calm environment, however, a large nonprofit is most often best served by those with management experience. Reflecting the concern of many, one person said that Linnington "has never been outside the Department of Defense." Another wondered, "Is he prepared? The military prepares you to excel in leadership, focus, and passion. The nonprofit world is much different."[186] While leadership, focus and passion are in demand at nonprofits, as well as in the military, the military provides a well-defined structure; when a commander needs more money or personnel, he or she simply asks for it. It may not be provided, but that's another issue.

Furthermore, the military might not be the best place to find someone to oversee financial activities. "The United States Army's finances are so jumbled," according to an August 2016 Reuters news story, "it had to make trillions of dollars of improper accounting adjustments to create an illusion that its books are balanced. The Defense Department's Inspector General said in a June 2016 report the Army made $2.8 trillion in wrongful adjustments to accounting entries in one quarter alone in 2015, and $6.5 trillion for the year. Yet the Army lacked receipts and invoices to support those numbers or simply made them up."[187]

This may or may not be representative of the accounting in America's entire defense structure, but it is consistent with many peoples' concerns about the state of the government's budgeting process. In the nonprofit world fundraising needs determine almost everything, but raising money isn't part of the job description for Army officers and generals. Generating the revenue to ensure employees receive a paycheck on time is a task for which no one in the military is ever responsible.

Linnington's tasks were formidable. Much of his new role was generally uncharted territory for him, and Wounded Warrior Project was experiencing a uniquely tough period in its history.

Longer Term

Although the beginning of WWP's first fiscal year after Steve Nardizzi and Al Giordano were fired was hyped as filled with promise and additional growth, the year ended badly from a financial perspective.

• The Financial Damage

When he arrived in the summer of 2016, Michael Linnington promised to straighten things out. He told the *Military Times* that he was "firing half of their executives, closing nine offices and redirecting millions in spending to mental health care programs and partnerships as part of an organization overhaul in the wake of spending scandals." Linnington said he was optimistic, that the shake-up was not "an indictment of past practices at the charity, but a recognition of changes needed to keep the group relevant and providing the best resources possible to veterans." Some programs would continue but others would have to be stopped.[188]

The financial reports for that year did not paint a pretty picture. Although it was no fault of Linnington's—he arrived too late—fundraising dropped by $70 million, from $373 million in 2015 to $303 million in 2016—a decrease of almost 20 percent. In six months, WWP went from being the fastest financially growing charity in the country to the fastest financially declining charity.

Why six months? Nardizzi and Giordano were still running the place for almost the entire first half of that year and during that time fundraising results were higher by approximately $10 million than during the same period a year before. In the second half of the year, after the two men were gone, fundraising fell by slightly more that $80 million than during the same time the year before. Thus, the reason WWP's fundraising for the entire year of 2016 went down by *only* $70 million, was the increase of $10 million during the first half of the fiscal year when Nardizzi and Giordano were still there.

The following spring, Eric Miller, WWP's chief financial officer, said that the drop was to be expected. "Certainly it's all attributable to those events," he said, referring to the media accusations. Linnington, who by then had been in his position long enough to assert himself, said that the goal was to "cut deep, cut once, then restore whatever confidence was lost to quickly build programs. It was a tough time," he said. "I get a little emotional just thinking about it. Folks were very uncertain."

Linnington also announced some good news. "We have turned the corner, and donations over the last six months have exceeded the goal we set for ourselves," he said.[189] Miller echoed that sentiment, saying that, given the scandal, the drop in donations was actually in line with projections. "We made our adjustments, and everything has turned out okay because now we're growing," he said. "We're actually adding employees. In fact, some of the folks that we had to let go are coming back to us, which is always a great indication, so we're definitely in a growth mode. The American public has been extremely gracious and . . . we're making sure that we're optimizing" donations, "providing efficient programs that really help these men and women who deserve to be honored and empowered."

Miller even pointed out that WWP was "back in the good graces of the Better Business Bureau."[190] Similarly, Linnington said that he was "pleased to see the Better Business Bureau's report validating our impact and commitment."[191]

This was not true: a corner had not been turned by then and the Better Business Bureau said nothing at that point about the effectiveness of the new leadership.

- **The Evaluators Re-evaluate**

In late January 2017, one year after the allegations were reported, the BBB Wise Giving Alliance published the conclusions of its own investigation.

- Spending: "There was no evidence of lavish spending."

- Operations and Management Oversight: Based on data from 2011-2015 a "third party awarded WWP recognition as being one of the best nonprofit places to work."

- Joint Cost Allocation: "BBB WGA reviewed the organization's joint-cost allocated appeals against the reported joint-cost allocations in the organization's audited financial statements and found them to be in compliance with AICPA 98-2."

- Fundraising Practices: "BBB WGA found no evidence of inaccurate or misleading characterizations of the programs they were funding." Wounded Warrior Project "satisfactorily met all 20 of its accountability standards."[192]

Pretty much everything that was alleged to be wrong by *CBS News* and the *New York Times* a year earlier was found to be unsubstantiated by BBB's give.org.

After several meetings and much correspondence, Art Taylor, the head of give.org, said they didn't find the wrongdoing that was claimed, and the practices that could be improved were the kinds of things any charity could work on. The media allegations were off base, he thought. "We saw that an organization of sizeable scale had a conference. While the media reported that the amounts spent for the conference were unusual, and in some cases that they didn't support the mission of the organization, we found that WWP spent about $800 per person on a conference. Very few organizations that we know of can have a several-day off-site event and spend only $800 per person."

Taylor says he looked at the more sensational aspects of the story, too. Steve Nardizzi "rappelled himself down a wall, and I guess this was deemed to show that something improper was going on with the organization's funds. But we discovered that Nardizzi himself paid for that."

And there were other allegations that didn't hold water. "After we did our work, we couldn't find anything worthy of the high level of public negative sentiment" that WWP received, he says.

Taylor understands that some people were frustrated that give.org's positive assessment didn't come sooner. "We had to make sure we gathered all the facts," he says. And there are those who didn't agree with the assessment. "They might say, *Are you kidding me? How can you say that Wounded Warrior project meets all of your criteria?* Well, those people didn't investigate in detail the way we did. Maybe if they had, they'd come to a similar conclusion. Or maybe they don't understand the context within which nonprofits operate."[193]

A further acquittal came a week later, on February 1, 2017, when Charity Navigator, a major resource for the implications in the negative stories reported by *CBS News*, announced that Wounded Warrior Project had earned four stars, its top rating, with a score of 90.49 on a scale of one to 100. Its accountability and transparency scores were even better. The reason for the original poor assessment was Charity Navigator's unnecessarily contested issue of joint allocation costs, which Wounded Warrior Project both accurately and ethically reported.

~

Shortly after he was hired as the new CEO, Michael Linnington began advancing this narrative: Now that we have our troubles behind us, we're going to shape up and get leaner and meaner, and properly honor wounded warriors in the way they deserve. "Perceptions are reality," he said. "I regret the perception being out there that we've not shepherded the resources we (were) given to the maximum impact, and those reports are what's caused us to look at ourselves and what is focusing me to look at ourselves for how we can do better."[194]

Both Eric Miller's comment—he said WWP was *back* in the good graces of BBB's give.org—and Linnington's gave the impression that WWP turned things around after the crisis: he was "pleased to see the Better Business Bureau's report validating our impact and commitment." After all, the bad publicity took place at the beginning of 2016 and a year later charity evaluators gave the organization stellar grades.

Some of the people who commented on Charity Navigator's WWP page were happy: "Looks like Wounded Warrior Project is cleaning up its act for real" and, "Finally, WWP is overcoming its problems."[195] It would be only logical, as the comments indicate, for people to conclude: 1) bad things had been going on, 2) bad things were publicly reported, and 3) new leadership made it all better.

But that sequence was wrong. The exonerations of February 2017 were based on information from WWP's Form 990 for fiscal year 2015, which—and this is important—covered the period from October 1, 2014 through September 30, 2015, when Nardizzi and Giordano were still at the helm. The bad publicity led to bad evaluations, which should not have happened to begin with, but then a closer examination of the allegations showed them to be false and so the evaluations were revised.

In effect, Miller and Linnington were taking advantage of a confusing timeline—both men knew that BBB's positive report covered the time *before* the crisis, not after—to make it appear that they were correcting a problem when in fact, other than for inferior and sensational reporting, there was no problem. What took place after Nardizzi and Giordano were fired had nothing to do with the revised evaluations.

~

In 2016, while WWP was losing $70 million in fundraising revenues, total expenses for the year dropped by almost $50 million. The IRS asks charities to split their expenses into three categories: 1) programs, 2) management and general, and 3) fundraising. The total for the second category—basically, salaries and other operational overhead—dropped by $5 million, while those in the third—fundraising costs—increased by $5 million. Thus, since the change in expenses in those two combined categories was essentially a wash, WWP's work on behalf of wounded veterans took the big hit.[196]

The following language appears in notes attached to WWP's audited financial statement for fiscal year 2016: "Negative media stories in January 2016 regarding the organization prompted inquiries and requests for documents from Senator Grassley on behalf of the Committee on the Judiciary and from other parties. The organization responded to these inquiries and requests, and management does not believe they will have a material adverse effect on the organization's financial position, results of operations or cash flows."[197]

Fiscal year 2016 turned out to be a disaster, but what about 2017?

$\sim$

By the beginning of WWP's 2017 fiscal year, the board had developed a three-phase plan to go forward. Phase one was "Stop the Fire"; phase two was "Reframe Dialogue"; and phase three was "Path Forward."[198] The idea was to get ahead of the crisis and set a new tone with new leadership.

When Linnington made his comment—"We have turned the corner and donations over the last six months have exceeded the goal we set for ourselves"—in May 2017, about halfway through WWP's 2017 fiscal year, there was no way for anyone at that point to know how well or poorly WWP was doing to that point that year, partly because nothing official had been reported and partly because no one knew what the goal was.

Given the drop in 2016, it would not have been illogical to think that 2017 was going to be even worse. Some thought fundraising might decrease by an additional $100 million and dip below $200 million, which would mean a drop of approximately 50 percent over a two-year period.

In the summer of 2016, a few weeks before Linnington began his duties at WWP, he and Steve Nardizzi—the incoming and ousted CEOs—got together for a private, cordial meeting. Nardizzi reported that Linnington told him during that meeting that fundraising would probably drop badly, perhaps to $185 million by the end of 2017. Linnington denied this, or at least walked it back a little.

He said that projections were just that: projections. "It could be $185 [million]. It could be $155. It could be $355. I mean we haven't even started advertising. We haven't started the new process with the new organization," he said. "Wounded Warrior's fundraising could end up being much stronger than any such forecast."[199]

In addition to wobbling all over the place with his projections—and, remember, he knew the projection because the board established it by the end of the prior year—Linnington may have been a bit blithe, as he strongly implied that advertising, as if it were an easily controlled spigot, would save the day. But that's not how it works. Advertising was stopped and then, much later, resumed with more modest messaging. The cash flow from that source would be expected to diminish as the organization continued to spend less on advertising, and it would take a while after the advertising resumed to take effect.

Before the crisis, the projected goal for 2016, according to Al Giordano, had been $475 million. "We're talking a $300 million swing," he said, referring to the difference between $155 million and $475 million. No matter the final estimate, however, he knew fundraising results could be nowhere close to $355 million, as Linnington had implied. He said, "This is the most catastrophic decline of a charity in history."[200]

~

When it was released, the 2017 financial report showed that fundraising did not drop by $100 million; it dropped by only an additional $91 million. Total fundraising did not drop below $200 million; it dropped to only $211 million. It was later discovered that WWP—in what is called the Board Book, a summary of WWP activities presented exclusively and confidentially to the board—had lowered the goal for 2017 to $185 million.[201] This is most likely why Linnington used that number in his earlier interview.

The board knew all along, making a mockery of the notes accompanying the audited statement the prior year. It was such a low expectation that it permitted Linnington to technically claim, regardless of what he must have known to be sleight-of-hand messaging, that WWP had "exceeded the goal," at least for the first half of 2017.

WWP had not turned the corner. It had simply crawled over a newly revised and very low bar.

Then there were these details with regard to the claims that things were getting better:

- While WWP representatives repeatedly suggested that the organization was becoming more efficient, by any measure the organization was becoming less efficient. The 990s show that the percentage of total budget spent on administrative and fundraising costs increased significantly, from 20 cents in 2015 on the dollar to 25 cents on the dollar in 2017.

- An examination of full-time employee statistics showed that in 2015 there were 599 employees and that in 2017 there were 732 full time employees—not the cutbacks Linnington had said would be taking place. Put that in this context: In 2015 the budget was $352 million and in 2017 the budget was $231 million. This means that WWP employed 133 *more* people on a budget of about two-thirds.

- Wounded Warrior Project made much of the claim that executive salaries dropped significantly, but the 990s show otherwise. In 2015, executive salaries totaled $2.4 million. In 2017 that number was $2.3 million—an insignificant difference. Meanwhile, some "executives" were not in fact removed, but were simply subjected to a title change. A senior vice president might have morphed to be only a vice president—so he or she was no longer an executive—but that person was making the same or more a year later.

～

Figure 1. The revenue summary in the information returns for Wounded Warrior Project for fiscal years 2016, 2017, and 2018. Line 8 shows fundraising results.

Fiscal Year 2015—the year before Steve Nardizzi and Al Giordano were fired.

		Prior Year	Current Year
8	Contributions and grants (Part VIII, line 1h)	312,471,011.	372,546,396.
9	Program service revenue (Part VIII, line 2g)	0	0
10	Investment income (Part VIII, column (A), lines 3, 4, and 7d)	18,040,397.	13,351,364.
11	Other revenue (Part VIII, column (A), lines 5, 6d, 8c, 9c, 10c, and 11e)	11,554,706.	12,800,427.
12	Total revenue - add lines 8 through 11 (must equal Part VIII, column (A), line 12)	342,066,114.	398,698,187.

Fiscal Year 2016—the first full year after Steve Nardizzi and Al Giordano were fired.

		Prior Year	Current Year
8	Contributions and grants (Part VIII, line 1h)	372,546,396	302,707,725
9	Program service revenue (Part VIII, line 2g)	0	0
10	Investment income (Part VIII, column (A), lines 3, 4, and 7d)	13,351,364	7,201,279
11	Other revenue (Part VIII, column (A), lines 5, 6d, 8c, 9c, 10c, and 11e)	12,800,427	11,898,424
12	Total revenue—add lines 8 through 11 (must equal Part VIII, column (A), line 12)	398,698,187	321,807,428

Fiscal Year 2017—the second full year after Steve Nardizzi and Al Giordano were fired.

		Prior Year	Current Year
8	Contributions and grants (Part VIII, line 1h)	302,707,725	211,476,891
9	Program service revenue (Part VIII, line 2g)	0	0
10	Investment income (Part VIII, column (A), lines 3, 4, and 7d)	7,201,279	9,930,157
11	Other revenue (Part VIII, column (A), lines 5, 6d, 8c, 9c, 10c, and 11e)	11,898,424	5,357,390
12	Total revenue—add lines 8 through 11 (must equal Part VIII, column (A), line 12)	321,807,428	226,764,438

Fiscal Year 2018—the third full year after Steve Nardizzi and Al Giordano were fired.

		Prior Year	Current Year
8	Contributions and grants (Part VIII, line 1h)	211,476,891.	246,204,557.
9	Program service revenue (Part VIII, line 2g)	0.	0.
10	Investment income (Part VIII, column (A), lines 3, 4, and 7d)	9,930,157.	12,728,924.
11	Other revenue (Part VIII, column (A), lines 5, 6d, 8c, 9c, 10c, and 11e)	5,357,390.	4,829,215.
12	Total revenue - add lines 8 through 11 (must equal Part VIII, column (A), line 12)	226,764,438.	263,762,696.

During the first three years after Nardizzi and Giordano were fired, fundraising at Wounded Warrior Project declined dramatically. Even though 2018 was a better year than 2017, the organization still saw a decline of $125 million.

In that three-year period WWP raised $760 million. Had fundraising stayed the same as it was in 2015, a total of $1,116 million would have been raised during that time, which means the charity lost $356 million against not improving at all. Against Nardizzi's and Giordano's projections, which, based on WWP's fundraising history, were fairly modest—$414 million in in 2016, $475 million in 2017, and $515 million in 2018—Wounded Warrior Project lost $644 million.

In 2018 Wounded Warrior Project reported a total of $247 million in fundraising. This means that in the three years after 2015 when Nardizzi and Giordano were fired, the charity, compared to what could have been, lost a lot of money.

In that period WWP raised $760 million. Had fundraising stayed the same as it was in 2015, a total of $1.116 billion would have been raised during those three years, which means the charity lost $356 million against not improving at all. Against Nardizzi's and Giordano's projections, which, based on WWP's fundraising history, were fairly modest—$414 million in in 2016, $475 million in 2017, and $515 million in 2018—Wounded Warrior Project lost $644 million.

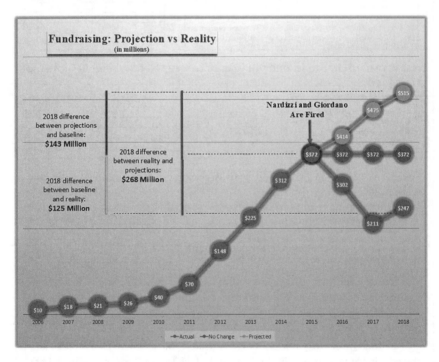

"Never before," Al Giordano noted, "have so few caused so much damage to so many veterans."[202]

A little more than a year after his initial, probing letters, Senator Charles Grassley delivered a 500-page report that bought into the verity of the allegations. The highlights of the criticism included: "The Wounded Warrior Project Inaccurately Reported Spending 80.6 Percent of Donor Funds on Program Services for Veterans"; "The Wounded Warrior Project Inaccurately Reported Spending $65.4 Million on Long-Term Support Programs for Veterans"; "WWP's Independent Review Disclosed Additional Inappropriate Use of Donor Funds"; "WWP's Use of Joint Cost Allocations are Questionable"; and "The WWP Alumni Program Lacks Proper Oversight and Requires Additional Changes to Ensure Efficiency."

Instead of parroting the allegations, Grassley could have reported that, as part of being well run, charities are challenged with complexities and nuances inherent in the nonprofit world, and while nonprofits should be held to very high ethical, as well as operational and legal, standards, the public needs to know the elbow grease that goes into establishing and maintaining such standards. He could have reported that he realized, contrary to what had been the developing narrative during the prior year and a half, that WWP would not soon simultaneously realize fewer costs and offer additional services, all the while experiencing an increase or more efficiency in fundraising.

But that wasn't what Grassley wrote. The bulk of his comments uncritically gulped in the media reports, and his concluding remarks were downright banal. "WWP is rightly focused on making changes, but more must be done. Charities serve an integral role in our society and have a tremendous responsibility to be a force for good. WWP should continue to strive to increase transparency and accountability to set a good example for others in the non-profit field."[203]

Left out of Grassley's report, possibly because it would upset the biased narrative that had been developed, was his response to his inquiry about WWP's whistleblower retaliation policy. Asked about it, as the topic of retaliation was a significant part of the news reports, a member of his staff said the senator "found no wrongdoing."[204]

∼

Of all the many terrible ways Wounded Warrior Project was diminished after the faux scandal, perhaps the most heartbreaking of all was the decision to discontinue funding the Long-Term Support Trust. In his August 2016 interview with the *Military Times* Michael Linnington said that a priority was boosting support for the trust initiative, as well as parts of the group's Warrior Care Network.[205] But that didn't happen.

Among the criticisms WWP received at the height of the frenzy was that the organization was sitting on too much money. Remember, Daniel Borochoff, the head of CharityWatch, said his biggest concern was that WWP was hoarding a $248 million surplus, and that not enough of it was being spent on veterans. "It would be helpful," he said, "if these hundreds of millions of dollars were being spent to help veterans in the shorter term in a year or two rather than being held for a longer term." According to *CBS News*, WWP said it had committed $100 million to a new mental health care initiative, and that the goal was to raise another $500 million for long-term care for severely wounded veterans. "But," Chip Reid then said, "it could be years before most of that money makes an impact on the lives of wounded service members."[206]

That concern is valid, no doubt, but it must be seen in light of a broader context: one of the fundamental purposes of a charity whose mission extends into the far and unknowable future. While all organizations need to be attentive to their short-term needs—and raise money for those purposes—many also need to do what they can to ensure their futures. Although there is healthy debate in the nonprofit world about the right amount of resources dedicated to future stability, this does not mean that charities are hoarding money that should be used for something else; it means instead that they take seriously their need to support future commitments.

The Long-Term Support Trust at WWP was intended to provide money for permanently injured veterans and their caregivers. Most of the wounds with which warriors return home don't heal quickly, and many will never heal. This meant that if WWP was to keep its promise—to honor and empower wounded veterans with the vision of fostering the most successful, well-adjusted generation of injured service members in our nation's history—then, to be serious about that promise, it would have to set aside some serious money, with a serious plan for prudently allocating it, for many years. The life expectancy of a 25-year old is about 60 years. Most likely, given the number of wounded that have returned to date, even the generous-sounding $500 million would be inadequate to do the job properly.

As it turns out, Wounded Warrior Project did not "boost" its funding for the long-term trust. The trust is a separate entity from Wounded Warrior Project, and so it cannot be abandoned, but the funding for it from WWP was essentially discontinued. In 2017 WWP gave $311,000 to the trust; the year before, it gave almost $55 million.[207] While the money is meant to be spent on long-term care for veterans and provide resources for caregivers, the vision behind the trust, at least in the aftermath of the firings, was dimmed. By April 2018, Linnington abandoned his enthusiasm for the trust. "There is no near-term intent," he said, "to increase contributions to the Long-Term Support Trust."[208]

~

Morale was significantly down after the news reports and the firings, and the writing was on the wall even before Linnington began his tenure at Wounded Warrior Project in the late summer of 2016. The staff knew programs would have to be reduced—that was the financial reality after fundraising had dropped so precipitously—but the resulting strategy slashed at the core of the organization's purpose. One employee wrote, "Abandoning our basic program delivery model" and "divorcing ourselves from our established relationships with warriors and family members is, in essence, divorcing ourselves from the very thing that led to our unparalleled success in the first place."

While the crisis had severe financial and programmatic implications, it also resonated on an individual level. After detailing the reductions in offices and employees, the person pointed out the importance of alumni teammates—those working closely with veterans and their families. Over 40,000 people were given what was called a "lifetime of commitment," a promise that had been recently reaffirmed in WWP's 10-year campaign. "Alumni teammates," the employee said, "very effectively triage, serve, and direct warriors and family support members to our programs and to the local external resources and networks they have established. Let's be clear, alumni teammates are in many cases the only source of light in these warriors' lives. As an alumni manager told me today, 'I had a family support member crying at a family dinner last night because she can't afford to do this for the family without us.'"

Yet, while its own revenues were dwindling, WWP continued to provide more money for other organizations. On its face, that's noble, but it meant that one promise—to fund its own programs, in whose names money had been raised—was being subsumed by another—to fund the programs of other organizations. "It feels fundamentally and ethically wrong," the person wrote, "to fund the growth of other organizations while simultaneously taking a hatchet to the very programs" donors' dollars were intended to fund. "I guess the question is, Will redirecting the extra" millions of dollars "better position us to restore the WWP brand and foster the most successful and well-adjusted generation of wounded warriors in our nation's history? In my opinion it does not."[209]

Several people shared the same existential questions concerning the future of Wounded Warrior Project.

• Peter Honerkamp Airs His Frustrations

Not only was Wounded Warrior Project falling financially and programmatically, there were no answers to questions about why things developed the way they had. Peter Honerkamp, the volunteer who was instrumental in conceiving Soldier Ride in 2004—and thus provided the thrust for the organization's spectacular financial and programmatic growth during the following decade—did not like what he saw and he was frustrated.

"In the aftermath of the scandal and the firings, staff at WWP were reluctant to talk to me," Honerkamp says. "People knew I was close to Steve and Al and they were worried that I might cause collateral damage by bringing attention to the baseless news reports, even though all Chris Carney and I were trying to do was refute them. I believe they were worried they might lose their jobs. As for the board, I'd always had close relationships there, but other than two meetings with Tony Odierno, the head of the board, no one on the board would respond to our inquiries. I believe the board wanted to ignore our criticism of their actions. You see, if there had been serious malfeasance justifying Al and Steve being fired, then surely the board was guilty of improper oversight. In fact, there was no serious malfeasance, but the board wanted them gone and here was the cover to do it."

Honerkamp explains that when he was at Soldier Rides, he would tell people that the media allegations were "bullshit." One of the people running one of the events asked Honerkamp to "not make a point of that," he said. "People were worried about their jobs and I was trying to exonerate Al and Steve. Look, I'm a founder. It was strange that instead of everyone screaming to the high heavens that we were wronged, everyone was muzzled."

He told those who asked that he not make a big deal out of the crisis, "I'm going to answer it. I don't want to hurt WWP, but I am going to be honest. But, having said that, how do you get the truth out without doing that? That's the elephant in the room." But some people reached out to Honerkamp. "*They* were bringing it up with me. The mantra from on high was that this was no big deal, that seven out of ten people hadn't heard of the crisis. But that wasn't true—not in my neck of the woods, anyway. I couldn't find anyone who *hadn't* heard about it."

In an effort to get to the bottom of things, Honerkamp met with Michael Linnington twice in 2016 and spoke to him by phone in 2017. He also met twice with Tony Odierno over that same time span.

"Linnington told me, 'We can't look in the rear-view mirror. What's done is done.' He didn't want to keep the 'negative focus' alive. And I told him that it's not just my two friends or the other people I know and like at WWP, some of whom have been let go and others who are afraid of being let go. It's all the programs that got destroyed, including the Long-Term Trust. And the problem is not merely that that occurred, but that the people who are driving the car that ran them over are still driving the car," he said with building passion. "I'm *never* going to let it go. And you can tell that to Tony Odierno when you see him again," he told Linnington. "He's not getting rid of me."

Honerkamp and Chris Carney later met with Odierno, who, Honerkamp thought, was "disingenuous." Odierno told them, "The firings of Nardizzi and Giordano had nothing to do with the media allegations. They occurred because the board felt the organization wouldn't grow without stronger contacts with the military. Odierno said this," Honerkamp says, "despite the fact that WWP worked closely with many other veterans service organizations."

Stronger contacts with the military? Honerkamp was upset. "Do you mean cooperating with Mullen"—Admiral Michael Mullen, the former Chairman of the Joint Chiefs of Staff and to whom Honerkamp was certain Odierno was referring when he said "military"—"who doesn't even know what our programs are, who's never even looked at the metrics of the website, who doesn't even know what the Long-Term Trust is? Who never looked at anything?" Honerkamp didn't let up. "You say *grow*? With Richard Jones on the board? I told Odierno that Jones is a traitor. Then I stood up and I shook his hand. Then I said that we are now adversaries."

Honerkamp says this is "incredible, but true. We cut our eyeteeth supporting our wounded warriors, and our board cost us hundreds of millions of dollars that hurt them all."

At another meeting with Linnington, after discussing the crisis and the follow-up, Honerkamp says, "Linnington wanted Chris and me to back off as he feared our continuing criticism of CBS, the *Times*, and the board's response would hurt WWP's reputation by association. I'm sure the board was pressuring him to shut us up, especially in light of our two contentious meetings with Odierno. I told Linnington that I understood why he was doing that. If I were in his position I'd probably do the same thing. But I was in my position and I couldn't. Things got a little heated. We were both passionate about protecting WWP. We just disagreed about how best to do it."

∼

Honerkamp and Chris Carney later wrote to the board of directors and the advisory board to explain why they were "horrified by the organization's failure to defend itself."[210]

A few months later, Honerkamp wrote an email to Linnington to remind him that the rides he and Chris Carney had started "raised over 10 million dollars at a time when WWP had raised under $10,000 and had one employee." Then, after recounting the challenges and successes of the early days, with supporting coverage for the rides on Fox News and CNN, he wrote, "They also revolutionized how we deal with our wounded soldiers. Instead of being relegated to their hospital beds, visited only by their relatives and doctors, they were getting out on bikes, empowering themselves and their fellow soldiers, setting the example for the incoming wounded and going into the communities they sacrificed so much for." Several, according to Honerkamp, "told us they would have committed suicide if not for WWP."

He wrote, "We were disgusted by the actions of our board last March. We were determined to both expose the baseless allegations made by the *New York Times* and CBS, and find out why our board fired the two men responsible for making WWP the largest veterans service organization in the country, introducing program after program that helped our wounded heroes—essentially filling the chasms that defined the response of the Veterans Administration and the Department of Defense.

"Over the last year," he continued, "we've spent time, energy, and money finding out what was behind it. We know a lot and we suspect a lot more. But no one who knows the whole truth is talking. Everyone on the board from last March wants us to go away. We're not. We just want the truth, and we are supported by many donors, many former and current staff, former board members, and many wounded warriors."

After saying that the board's "bizarre silence killed morale at WWP and cost the jobs of people who were dedicated to helping our heroes," Honerkamp finished: "The truth is easy—lies take time. Evasion takes even longer. WWP's board used an expensive investigation (cost unknown) as a cover to effectuate a plan that had nothing to do with CBS and the *New York Times*. The report revealed *nothing* that led to the firing of Nardizzi and Giordano. The board wanted an excuse for a takeover and they got it."[211]

PHOTOS

Courtesy of Steve Nardizzi

Courtesy of Al Giordano

Steve Nardizzi and Al Giordano, the former chief executive officer and chief operating officer of Wounded Warrior Project. The two men were fired on March 10, 2016 after allegations of misspending and misconduct were reported on CBS News and the New York Times. The allegations were largely untrue or misleading.

Courtesy of The Stephen Talkhouse

Where it all began: The Stephen Talkhouse in Amagansett, NY, the bar and club named after a Native American from eastern Long Island, is where, over a few drinks, the idea of Soldier Ride, an essential part of the Wounded Warrior Project's origin story, was born.

Courtesy of The Stephen Talkhouse

Stephen Talkhouse, the Montaukett American Indian who in the mid1800s made his living by regularly walking the 25 miles between Montauk and Bridgehampton, New York, to collect and deliver mail.

Photos by Matt Hindra

Peter Honerkamp, the owner of the Stephen Talkhouse, Nick Kraus and Chris Carney. The three men, among the founders of Wounded Warrior Project, originated Soldier Ride, one of WWP's most successful programs.

Photo by Matt Hindra

Heath Calhoun (left), Ryan Kelly (center) and Chris Carney (right), on May 22, 2005, just after touching their cycles' wheels in the Pacific Ocean as they depart on the 4,200-mile cross-country Soldier Ride, from Los Angeles, CA to Montauk, NY.

Photo by Matt Hindra

Ryan Kelly, Tony Snow, Chris Carney, and Heath Calhoun at Dodger Stadium in Los Angeles at the beginning of the 2005 Solider Ride. Veterans stopped at stadiums in Denver, Kansas City, Philadelphia, and New York to see the Mets, which aided the publicity for supporting veterans. Tony Snow, who at the time worked as a news reporter and host on Fox News and later as President George W. Bush's press secretary, was an early supporter and also generated publicity and interest.

Photo by Matt Hindra

On the way in 2005 . . . Soldier Ride participants stop at the White House to talk with President George W. Bush.

Photo by Matt Hindra

In this group photo of Soldier Ride participants in 2005, John Melia, one of the founders of Wounded Warrior Project, is on the far right, Al Giordano, another founder and WWP's chief operating officer, is on the far left, and President George W. Bush is in the center.

Photo by Matt Hindra

Ryan Kelly (back left) Heath Calhoun (front), and Chris Carney (right) in the Atlantic Ocean at Montauk, NY, on July 18, 2005, after completing the 4,200-mile cross-country Soldier Ride.

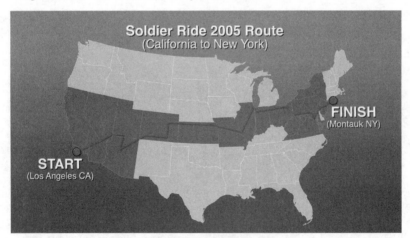

Map created by Matt Hindra

Soldier Ride 2005 traveled through 16 states plus the District of Columbia. Although Ryan Kelly, Heath Calhoun, and Chris Carney were the only ones to go the distance, hundreds of wounded warriors and other veterans, as well as many who were not veterans, joined in for parts of the ride.

Royal Photo Booth

From the June 2013 Board of Directors meeting. Several board members who were still on the board at the time of the CBS and New York Times reporting, including Tony Odierno (top left corner in hat), Roger Campbell (top row center, holding wine glass), Justin Constantine (top right, with fake glasses), and Guy McMichael (bottom left wearing leopard print hat). The board was fully aware of and involved in the culture at Wounded Warrior Project.

Eric Edmundson with wife Stephanie and their baby Gracie before deploying to Iraq in June 2005. Eric sustained serious injuries when, on Oct. 2, 2005, the Stryker vehicle he was driving hit an improvised explosive device. Eric suffered from shrapnel wounds to his abdomen. While awaiting transport to Germany, Eric went into cardiac arrest and was able to be revived, but sustained an anoxic brain injury.

Photos courtesy of the Edmundson family

While Eric Edmundson's body is somatically challenged, his life is vigorous and full.

CHAPTER 5

BEFORE THE FALL

The Buildup

Pointing out how misleading the news reports were was an exercise in futility because the fates of Steve Nardizzi and Al Giordano were determined well before late January 2016, which, as it turns out, was only a point in the continuum of a story pretty much already written.

Nardizzi and Giordano had for some time, largely because of their successes, been incensing important people connected to the government and those at other nonprofit organizations. This, mixed in with concerns about the style of their leadership, including the perception on the part of some board members that they were increasingly acting independently from the board, created an atmosphere in which, when Simpson Thacher delivered its assessment, it may have been easier than not for the board to fire the two leaders. But while some board members might have felt that it was the path of least resistance, at least one, it seems, had been orchestrating the result with purpose.

Why did the story break when it did? Although misdeeds were alleged, nothing timely or contemporaneous to the reports arose. Nothing new was discovered. The meat of the story was something that took place over a year before, and it all was already well known, publicized even.

$\sim$

The story in the *Times* was to be an in-depth look at one of America's great and growing charities. For several years, the *NonProfit Times* had included Wounded Warrior Project, which had grown to employ over 400 people, on its annually compiled "Best Nonprofits to Work For" list. In three of the five years prior to 2016, WWP was ranked among the top five organizations on that list.[212] Growth had been rapid and the numbers of veterans using WWP's services had been expanding at a fast rate.

But that growth, and the attention it drew, served to arouse suspicions that maybe things were moving along a little too quickly, that maybe WWP wasn't employing the same ethos, particularly in its fundraising, that the more established charities in the United States were adhering to, or claimed to be adhering to. As a result WWP was in the news several times before January 2016. While much of the reporting was not particularly flattering, no one was ever able to find anything wrong either, and when anyone looked beyond the concerns about aggressive fundraising, people found a charity on the move, using its fundraising results to good and efficient purpose as it dealt with critical and long-term issues that no other charities, or even the Department of Veterans Affairs, was trying to tackle.

Steve Nardizzi first learned of the newspaper's interest in the late summer of 2015. "We heard from several individuals," he said, "including a couple of warriors and former staff, that there was a reporter, Dave Philipps, from the *Times* asking questions." From what Nardizzi could tell, Philipps's tone, as relayed by those who had been contacted, did not sound negative. "The questions to the staff and to me, at least at the beginning, were open-ended," Nardizzi said. "When I asked why he was interested in us right now, he said that we were a large organization in the public eye. He said there are some negative perceptions around you and there are some positive things around you, and I think there's a story here." According to Nardizzi, Philipps told him, "I can't say you're going to be happy with everything that I write, but I think you're going to find it to be a fair and honest story about Wounded Warrior Project."[213]

At that time, Nardizzi didn't know there was more driving the story than WWP's place in the nonprofit pantheon. He didn't know that something had already been underfoot for a few months.

Philipps says he "was contacted in . . . June of 2015 by a small group of employees and former employees who felt like the leadership at WWP was going in the wrong direction. Their main concern was that good employees were getting fired for no reason. I was working on another big project at the time, so I slowly called around in [my] spare time, talking to members of the group as well as dozens of people I found on my own. It was important to me given the gravity of the story to reach out to all kinds of current and former employees, not just a small group that would be accused of being disgruntled. The type of reporting I was doing wasn't a 'scoop' but a deep survey of what was going on, so I wasn't worried about any competition. There just aren't that many reporters that do that kind of work. I finished the story in December but, because of its length, complexity, and vacation time for staff, it did not get read for a few weeks, and then, was waiting in line behind other more timely enterprise stories to run."[214]

In late November 2015 Philipps traveled to WWP's headquarters in Jacksonville, Florida to interview employees. "He was there for three days, maybe four," Nardizzi says, "and spent at least two full days in interviews." Philipps also went to a nearby Soldier Ride to see what that was all about. "He did my interview last, and he mainly asked how I would respond to critics of our fundraising, how much we spend on that. He asked me about our history and why John Melia left the organization, as well as about the value of our programs." At this point, there was no pressure and, although the unhappiness of some former employees was to be included in the story, the plan, Nardizzi thought, was to write an analysis of the largest veterans service organization in the country.

But then something happened. "Sometime in December both the *Wall Street Journal* and *60 Minutes* got onto the story," Philipps says. "I was notified by sources who had been contacted by them, but I don't know why they decided to start the story when they did—maybe it was a tipster, maybe it was zeitgeist. My feeling was that I was so far in front of them that it wouldn't really matter. They weren't going to get dozens of interviews before we printed."[215]

60 Minutes decided not to take on the story because there wasn't enough time to conduct the proper research to satisfy its standards. The *Wall Street Journal* gave it some thought, probably after some reporters there picked up some buzz from their contacts at CBS, but then decided not to go with anything, perhaps thinking that too much research would be required in too short a time.

But the CBS Evening News team did.

CBS "rushed their story," Philipps says, "figuring if they could do a scaled-down version, they could beat us. Turns out they were right." When asked if there was any coordination between *CBS News* and the *New York Times*, Philipps said no. Competition to get the story out first was the driving force. "I knew from sources that the story was coming in a day or two. I know to the news consumer it likely seemed like a coordinated one-two punch, but it was anything but."[216]

It wasn't until early January when Nardizzi learned that *CBS News* was also in the hunt. "We learned that CBS was on the story when we got access to the Facebook page," Nardizzi says, referring to the page that was created by unhappy former employees looking for a platform to vent their anger, to commiserate, and then to plot revenge. "We got outreach from CBS right after that, but their timeframe was much tighter. They got to us last minute with a litany of questions about misspending, about first-class jet travel, about a rumor that WWP was paying for an apartment for me. Ridiculous, but we answered all their questions."

As for why CBS was on the story at all, Nardizzi says he has no idea. "It's a mystery, especially the timing. The only thing we knew was that CBS started out very negative. And the *Times* then began to get negative."

In those final weeks before the stories were reported, it became clear that something wasn't right. Perhaps because Philipps felt boxed in by what he now knew was CBS's intentions to go negative, he got back to several WWP current and former employees with questions that were critical of the organization. He also stopped talking to Nardizzi and Giordano. "That the reporter at this point wasn't reaching out to us"—meaning top staff—"seemed odd," Nardizzi said, and quickly realized that the *Times* story was now being driven by several disgruntled former employees.

He then did what he could to get ahead of the story. "Some of the false stuff that we were told would be in the CBS story was pulled," Nardizzi said, "like the one about me getting an apartment in New York paid for by WWP. And another about someone who claimed he was fired because he was outspoken, when in fact he was fired because he hadn't been doing his outreach calls."

He also pushed back on the lies and inconsistencies. "At the very least, the fact that they knew that so much was untrue—and both the *Times* and CBS did know—they should have seen that as a red flag that called into question the sources themselves. We said CBS needed to vet their sources better, that we had evidence—actual evidence—that what they were going to say was untrue. "You would think," Nardizzi says, "that CBS would have questioned their sources after it became clear that a lot of what people were saying was shown not to be true."

There was nothing positive in the *Times* report either. Philipps did talk to many people—remember, he said: *"It was important to me given the gravity of the story to reach out to all kinds of current and former employees, not just a small group that would be accused of being disgruntled."* While that is true, he ended up using only the comments of the disgruntled. "The positive comments," Nardizzi says, "as well as all of the results of the on-site data Philipps gathered over the better part of a week when he visited WWP's headquarters in Jacksonville, wound up on the editing floor."[217]

~

Philipps must have sensed that at least some of what he was told by those disgruntled former employees was untrue because, just before publication, he offered the people who spoke to him a chance to change their story.

On January 23, 2016, the Saturday before the story came out, Ralph Ibson, a former WWP employee and a member of the Facebook page, included in his post an email message from Philipps:

> "Hi, Ralph. I gave Wounded Warrior Project a list of names of people included in the article who were fired and why they said they were fired. Here is Wounded Warrior's response. Essentially they are calling you guys all liars which is not surprising, and providing no details to back it up. However if anybody feels they were not honest with me about why they were fired they should probably tell me now. We are getting down to the wire."

It's that next-to-last sentence that might be interesting; journalists don't typically ask their sources if they were dishonest and if they might want to change their stories. The sentence before that might also be interesting; credible journalists don't typically openly side with their sources.

Connie Chapman, a former employee who started the Facebook group, said on her page, "I personally know my quotes are opinion; they are based on my experience but still are opinion. So, I want to discuss with him [Philipps] rephrasing my comments in ways that can be considered facts or inspire them to provide facts vs. opinion."

In addition, Amy Frelly, a former employee who expressed high regard for WWP before registering blistering complaints, addressed this matter on her Facebook page on January 23, 2016: "I know [someone] talked to him tonight and wanted to change some of her comments, and he was very willing to do so."[218]

That the Facebook group, consisting of like-minded ex-employees, existed, and perhaps still does, is not an issue in itself—and, according to at least one person who felt Nardizzi and Giordano were badly treated, "some in that group were honorable, hard-working people who legitimately felt they had been treated badly"[219]—but it is plausible to think that the 40 or so people whom *CBS News* claimed to interview essentially served as an echo chamber. Becky Melvin, a member of the group, wrote on November 12, 2015, "Strength in numbers by everyone saying the same thing about WWP!" Also, in an email written to WWP on January 22, 2016, *CBS News* producer Jennifer Janisch said, "*CBS News* has spoken with numerous former employees, at several levels of seniority, who have had strikingly similar stories to share about WWP." This alone should have served as a warning to the reporters that perhaps they didn't have both sides of the story or that the side they chose to promote was the one that was accompanied by far less credibility than the one they did not write about.

◁∽▷

In 2014, while he was at *The Gazette* in Colorado Springs, Dave Philipps won a Pulitzer Prize for his series "Other Than Honorable," which described the treatment of injured American soldiers being discharged without military benefits. He also was a finalist for the 2010 Pulitzer Prize, which cited "his painstaking stories on the spike in violence within the Band of Brothers, a battered combat brigade returning to Fort Carson after bloody deployments to Iraq, leading to increased mental health care for soldiers." In 2009 Philipps won the Livingston Award for his reporting on violence in infantry troops returning from Iraq. He has also written a book, *Lethal Warriors,* which chronicles how the 4th Brigade Combat Team of the 12th Infantry Regiment, stationed at Fort Carson, Colorado, produced a high number of murders after soldiers returned from unusually violent combat tours. [220] He is a graduate of the highly regarded Columbia Journalism School.

Chip Reid is no slouch either. He earned an undergraduate degree from Vassar, a graduate degree in public affairs from Princeton, and a law degree from Columbia, and has worked for more than 20 years in news at the highest levels for NBC and CBS.[221]

Philipps and Reid are both reporters with the kind of experience who, one might think, would meticulously and fairly write such a story about complaints at a charity with national impact. Yet both uncritically guzzled up a spoon-fed story, despite citing a good deal of research, that was a slam dunk for its audience because . . . well, as everyone knows, overspending, greed, and perfidy are the defining characteristics at charities today. While that is true at far too many charities, it's not true at most of them—and it wasn't true at Wounded Warrior Project.

Why were a seasoned *CBS News* team and a prize-winning *New York Times* reporter so shocked that former employees, almost all of whom were terminated for cause and dissatisfied, spoke poorly of Wounded Warrior Project's management? Why did these two news giants run the story as they did, even after they knew it was journalistically shaky? How could they not realize that, upon the most meager level of scrutiny, the stories would prove to be misleading?

Jack Murtha, at the time a Fellow at the prestigious Columbia Journalism Review, said the reporting "appears rock solid," that it was "a good day for journalism—and a hit in our book—when not one but two major news outlets use their resources to scrutinize what they say is the country's largest and fastest-growing veterans charity. The benefits to both vets and donors are clear." [222]

Were they? While an investigation into the bad practices at a charity is always a good thing, the authority of any investigation rests on the validity of the investigation's component parts. If the allegations are insupportable—if the bad practices are not, in fact, bad and if the offered evidence is just plain wrong—the conclusion is insupportable as well. Thus, it actually was not a good day for journalism and the results did not benefit either vets or donors. As Andrew Marantz wrote in *The New Yorker* magazine, "A journalist's first task is to gather information without fear or favor. The next task, which is equally crucial, is to scrutinize the data—to separate the facts from the fulsome bullshit."[223]

Murtha's article appeared on January 28, 2016, one day after the *Times* story and the completion of the *CBS News* series. Had he taken more time to react, perhaps Murtha could have reflected just a little more on what turned out to be stories built on fulsome bullshit. Peter Honerkamp reached out to Murtha demanding a retraction, but a retraction was not forthcoming.

∼

The public is used to being upset with the media. Most of the time, however, it's not that the facts are reported incorrectly but the way a story is written or placed—or even that it is, in the eyes of the editors, a story at all—that rankles the critics. This is a battle that reporters cannot win. At their finest, when it comes to making decisions, reporters bring to their journalism the best of their experience, discipline and judgment. In the end, developing a story—what's emphasized, what's discarded—is a subjective process. There's always going to be someone who thinks the thrust of a story is wrong.

But sometimes the media get the facts wrong, too. On March 30, 1981, at 5:10 p.m., a little more than two and a half hours after John Hinckley tried to assassinate President Reagan, Dan Rather, the CBS Evening News anchor, told the nation that James Brady, Reagan's press secretary, had died. Brady had been shot in the head and severely wounded, but he did not die.[224] CBS attributed "congressional sources." Both Rather and Frank Reynolds, the ABC anchor, delivered obituaries. Less than half an hour later, Larry Speakes, a White House spokesman, said that Mr. Brady was in "serious condition" but that he had not died.[225]

Contrast that with what Walter Cronkite put himself through on November 22, 1963 before reporting that President Kennedy had died. Cronkite's guiding principle was: "Get it first, but get it right." It took more than 90 minutes of grueling, chaotic back-and-forth with people on the ground to get the announcement of Kennedy's death on the air. Even when Dan Rather, who was in Dallas at the time, reported that a doctor and a priest had confirmed Kennedy's death—and even when CBS Radio reported Kennedy's death, on the basis of what two reporters in Dallas had said— despite what must have been an agonizing temptation, it was not enough for Walter Cronkite. He would not report Kennedy's death until there was official confirmation—and even then, he said, it was "*apparently* official"—from the White House. When Cronkite got that—and not before—he reported it on the air about twenty minutes before two o'clock in the afternoon on the east coast: "President Kennedy died at one p.m. Central Standard Time . . . two o'clock Eastern Standard Time . . . some 38 minutes ago."[226]

∼

Even though it is important and has far-reaching consequences, the Wounded Warrior Project story is not about anything as dramatic as a presidential assassination attempt. Even so, as a general rule, we should hope that journalistic integrity still demands getting the facts straight and the context right. Chip Reid and Dave Philipps could have done better than to rely on a group of disgruntled employees, speaking primarily through one man, Erick Millette, who was clearly upset.

The public can't be expected to know what is wrong when news reporting is inadequate. In the case of WWP, non-journalists might be able to discern that few people were quoted in the stories and that little from WWP's side was presented, but most people can't be expected to know, for example, about the limitations of Charity Navigator's process or that the IRS's Form 990 doesn't ask a question that WWP was accused of not answering. For that kind of knowledge, the public has a right to expect reporters to do their homework.

When a news organization identifies a story as an "investigation," it is claiming, even if the story is sensational or salacious, that it has conducted an extensive and thorough review of all the relevant facts and generated something it understands is fit for public consumption, with all the weight of honest judgment that obligation implies.

In its treatment of the Wounded Warrior Project allegations, *CBS News* and The *New York Times* lost the battle for a thorough and just accounting of what was important—the principal and complex portion of which, in this story, is the way charitable organizations are and should be operated, as well as what society should expect of them. This is no small matter because nonprofits and donors are playing an increasingly important and public role in humanity's quest to improve itself. At a time that increased inquiry has led the public to doubt the purity of charities, this story played into existing and growing biases. It simply felt right and, without the scrutiny of the journalism itself, not many people would have the motive to question the judgments. A worthy report would have included perspectives from both sides of the issue, especially as the side not very well represented was so much more credible.

For its criticism of accounting, for example, it would have relied on at least one accounting professional who knows the rules, and not only on a charity watchdog that doesn't follow those rules. But it seems that this was never going to be a report worthy of examination—instead, it was a conclusion backfilled with selected, out-of-context facts, which, in the end, generated the worst of what we hopefully call news: a version of events that seemed intended to bias viewers and readers. Allegations supported with cherry-picked facts—not proper context backed up and combined with relevant facts, a process worthy of real investigative reporting—drove the story.

The two news organizations did the public no favors with their inadequate and unnecessarily damaging journalism.

In this era, however, another battle is being lost. The difficulty for viewers and readers is not just one of interpreting the words of reporters filled with integrity trying to get the right balance in a story, but the perceived need on their part, and on that of their producers, to generate information as fast as possible. It might still be the "get it first, but get it right" philosophy, but it's without a Cronkite-like insistence on the more important of the two competing ingredients. America witnessed this rush during the presidential campaign of 2016. Responding to criticism of the media's intense and unprecedented interest in Donald Trump's most controversial statements, CBS president and CEO Leslie Moonves at the time said, "It may not be good for America, but it's damn good for CBS. The money's rolling in and this is fun."[227]

A lot has changed since the days of Walter Cronkite.

The Veterans Administration

Charitable organizations are independent organizations. They are not for-profit businesses and they are not part of the government. They form what has become known as the third sector of our society. In his majority opinion in the 1819 Dartmouth College case, *Trustees of Dartmouth College v. Woodward*—which is remembered mainly because it clarified the contracts clause in the Constitution and limited the power of states to interfere with private contracts—John Marshall, the Chief Justice of the United States, acknowledged the need for independent charities. "These eleemosynary institutions," he wrote, "do not fill the place which would otherwise be occupied by government, but that which would otherwise remain vacant."[228] Thanks to Daniel Webster's uniquely powerful and convincing oratory—some would say long-winded, as he spoke for four hours, without notes—Dartmouth won the case, as well as its independence from the state of New Hampshire.[229]

That understanding, put forth by the person many scholars think was the most revered chief justice in the history of the United States Supreme Court, has led to our current nonprofit structure where a vast network of privately run organizations, such as Wounded Warrior Project, tries to fill in the vacancies. This is not to say that charities don't work closely with government units. Even though this is not true of Wounded Warrior Project, as almost all of its revenues come from donations, many charities, including veterans' organizations, are supported in part by government grants.

Still, WWP doesn't work in a silo. It coordinates much of its work with the Veterans Administration.

Good thing, too. If there was ever an example of what Justice Marshall might have meant by "vacant" and the need for independent charities, the VA might be Exhibit A. To the confluence of a burgeoning demand, limited government resources, and inherent inefficiency comes the plethora of programs offered by Wounded Warrior Project. "Though the VA has come a long way from the 1970s, when many Vietnam veterans failed to reintegrate into society and became homeless and addicted to drugs," the *Huffington Post* wrote in 2011, "the department still has problems. The bureaucracy is notoriously difficult to navigate, and veterans are left to figure out on their own what benefits they are eligible for. As a result, many fall through the cracks—more than 720,000 veterans do not take advantage of VA benefits for which they are eligible."[230]

～

Although earlier we saw how the chief executive of one charity, Help Hospitalized Veterans, used donated money imprudently while claiming to help veterans, the Veterans Administration itself is often in the crosshairs. The *Washington Times* reported in 2016, that an employee in Puerto Rico was reinstated with back pay after she was fired upon being arrested for armed robbery. "She pleaded guilty," the newspaper reported, "but her union got her job back by arguing in a grievance that a VA manager at the facility is a registered sex offender. Another, a VA hospital manager, was once arrested for drunken driving and found in possession of pain pills."[231]

Long waits for veterans, however, has been the persistent problem. Two years after the scandal emerged over phony waiting lists for patients at the facility in Phoenix, the VA was still having severe problems. In its own audit, conducted in 2014, the VA acknowledged, "Meeting a 14-day wait-time performance target for new appointments was simply not attainable"; also, "In some cases, pressures were placed on schedulers to utilize inappropriate practices in order to make waiting times (based on desired date, and the waiting lists), appear more favorable."[232]

John Cooper, a spokesman for Concerned Veterans for America, said,

"The VA is still struggling with a lack of accountability, an inability to properly manage a budget rapidly approaching $200 billion, and a failure to provide veterans with timely access to care and benefits," he said. "The VA is broken, and if we want veterans to be assured of a VA that works, we need to systemically reform it."

The problem is part of a larger issue of leadership and goal setting. Research conducted by Harvard Business School argues, "the beneficial effects of goal-setting have been overstated and that systematic harm caused by goal setting has been largely ignored." The study identified an associated "rise in unethical behavior, distorted risk preferences, corrosion of organizational culture, and reduced intrinsic motivation."[233]

Lisa Ordonez, Vice Dean and professor at the University of Arizona, and one of the authors of the research, says, "Goals have a strong effect of causing tunnel vision, narrowly focusing people at the expense of seeing much else around them, including the potential consequences of compromised choices made to reach goals." Once people sense the risk of failure, they go into "loss prevention" mode, fearing the loss of job, status, or at-risk incentives.

An article in Forbes pointed out, "The Veterans Administration learned this lesson the hard way when trying to address the 115-day wait time in their Phoenix hospital. They set a new goal of reducing the wait to 14 days, which resulted in an alleged 24-day wait. But employees said they felt compelled to manipulate performance records to give the appearance of meeting these goals. As many as 40 veterans died waiting for care at the Phoenix center, some more than a year."[234]

Michael Mann, the leader of a surgical program at the San Francisco VA hospital between 2003 and 2011, contends that the VA's problems are far worse than waiting lists, which he says were normal, and that the VA misled the media, the public and Congress. "It's a system rooted in deep, increasingly malignant trouble."[235]

One veteran went into this stream of consciousness when he thought about the VA hospital in Indianapolis: "It was actually rat infested in the '70s . . . and the wait! A trick they now have: They'll make an appointment soon, sure, but then they call back to reschedule for much later. They call and wait—for one ring—and then they hang up. And the people taking blood, they look like they're on drugs—like they should not even have a job."[236]

~

While the increase in demand came after 9/11, the problems at the VA began well before. In 2014 CNN compiled the following:

- In 1921 Congress created the Veterans Bureau to administer assistance to World War I veterans, but it quickly devolved into corruption and was abolished nine years later under a cloud of scandal. In 1930 the Veterans Administration was established.

- In 1932 thousands of World War I veterans and their families marched on Washington to demand payment of promised war bonuses. In an embarrassing spectacle, federal troops forcibly removed veterans who refused to end their protest. Also that year, 10,000 World War I veterans, many unemployed, protested over pay.

- In 1945 President Harry Truman accepted the resignation of VA Administrator Frank Hines after a series of news reports detailing shoddy care in V.A.-run hospitals.

- In 1946 the American Legion led the charge seeking the ouster of VA Administrator General Omar Bradley, citing an ongoing lack of facilities, troubles faced by hundreds of thousands of veterans in getting services and a proposal to limit access to services for some combat veterans.

- In 1947 a government commission on reforming government uncovers enormous waste, duplication and inadequate care in the VA system and called for wholesale changes in the agency's structure.

- In 1955 a second government reform commission again found widespread instances of waste and poor care in the VA system.

- In the 1970s veterans grew increasingly frustrated with the VA for failing to better fund treatment and assistance programs, and later to recognize exposure to the herbicide Agent Orange by troops in Vietnam as the cause for numerous medical problems among veterans.

- In 1972 Vietnam veteran Ron Kovic, the subject of the book and movie, *Born on the Fourth of July,* interrupted Richard Nixon's GOP presidential nomination acceptance speech, saying, according to his biography, "I'm a Vietnam veteran. I gave America my all, and the leaders of this government threw me and others away to rot in their VA hospitals."

- In 1974 Kovic led a 19-day hunger strike at a federal building in Los Angeles to protest poor treatment of veterans in VA hospitals. He and fellow veterans demanded to meet with VA Director Donald Johnson. The embattled director eventually flew to California to meet with the activists, but left after they rejected his demand to meet in the VA's office in the building. The ensuing uproar resulted in widespread criticism of Johnson. A few weeks later, Johnson resigned after President Richard Nixon announced an investigation into VA operations.

- In 1976 a General Accounting Office investigation into Denver's VA hospital finds numerous shortcomings in patient care, including veterans whose surgical dressings were rarely changed. The GAO also looked at the New Orleans VA hospital, and found ever-increasing patient loads were contributing to a decline in the quality of care there, as well.

- In 1981 veterans camped out in front of the Wadsworth Veterans Medical Center in Los Angeles after the suicide of a former Marine who had rammed the hospital's lobby with his Jeep and fired shots into the wall after claiming the VA had failed to attend to his service-related disabilities.

- In 1982 controversial VA director Robert Nimmo, who once described symptoms of exposure to the herbicide Agent Orange during the Vietnam War as little more than "teenage acne," resigned under pressure from veterans' groups. Nimmo was criticized for wasteful spending, including use of a chauffeured car and an expensive office re-decorating project. The same year, the agency issued a report supporting veterans' claims that the VA had failed to provide them with enough information and assistance about Agent Orange exposure.

- In 1984 Congressional investigators found evidence that VA officials had diverted or refused to spend more than $40 million that Congress approved to help Vietnam veterans with readjustment problems.

- In 1986 the VA's Inspector General's office discovered that 93 physicians working for the agency had sanctions against their medical licenses, including suspensions and revocations.

- In 1989 President Ronald Reagan signed legislation elevating the Veterans Administration to Cabinet status, creating the Department of Veterans Affairs.

- In 1991 the *Chicago Tribune* reported that doctors at the VA's North Chicago hospital sometimes ignored test results, failed to treat patients in a timely manner and conducted unnecessary surgery. The agency later took responsibility for the deaths of eight patients, leading to the suspension of most surgery at the center.

- In 1993 VA Deputy Undersecretary of Benefits R. J. Vogel testified to Congress that a growing backlog of appeals from veterans denied benefits was due to a federal court established in 1988 to oversee the claims process. The VA, Vogel told the lawmakers, was "reeling under this judicial review thing."

- In 1999 lawmakers opened an investigation into widespread problems with clinical research procedures at the VA West Los Angeles Healthcare Center. The investigation followed years of problems at the hospital, including ethical violations by hospital researchers that included failing to get consent from some patients before conducting research involving them.

- In 2000 the GAO found "substantial problems" with the VA's handling of research trials involving human subjects.

- In 2001, despite a 1995 goal to reduce waiting times for primary care and specialty appointments to less than 30 days, the GAO found that veterans still often waited more than two months for appointments.

- In 2003 a commission appointed by President George W. Bush reported that as of January 2003, some 236,000 veterans had been waiting six months or more for initial or follow-up visits, "a clear indication," the commission said, "of lack of sufficient capacity or, at a minimum, a lack of adequate resources to provide the required care."

- In 2005 an anonymous tip led to revelations of "significant problems with the quality of care" for patients at the VA's Salisbury, North Carolina, hospital. One veteran who sought treatment for a toenail injury died of heart failure after doctors failed to take into account his enlarged heart.

- In 2006 sensitive records containing the names, Social Security numbers and birth dates of 26.5 million veterans were stolen from the home of a VA employee who did not have authority to take the materials.

- In 2007 outrage erupted after documents released to CNN showed some senior VA officials received bonuses of up to $33,000 despite a backlog of hundreds of thousands of benefits cases and an internal review that found numerous problems, some of them critical, at VA facilities across the nation.

- In 2009 the VA disclosed that more than 10,000 veterans who underwent colonoscopies in Tennessee, Georgia and Florida were exposed to potential viral infections due to poorly disinfected equipment. Thirty-seven tested positive for two forms of hepatitis and six tested positive for HIV. VA Director Eric Shinseki initiated disciplinary actions and required hospital directors to provide written verification of compliance with VA operating procedures. The head of the Miami VA hospital was removed as a result.

- In 2011 nine Ohio veterans tested positive for hepatitis after routine dental work at a VA clinic in Dayton, Ohio. A dentist at the VA medical center there acknowledged not washing his hands or even changing gloves between patients for 18 years. That same year an outbreak of Legionnaires' disease began at the VA hospital in Oakland, Pennsylvania. At least five veterans died of the disease over the next two years. Records showed evidence of widespread contamination of the facility dating back to 2007.

- In 2012 the VA found that the graves of at least 120 veterans in agency-run cemeteries had been misidentified. The audit came in the wake of a scandal at Arlington National Cemetery involving unmarked graves and incorrectly placed burials.

- In 2013 the former director of the VA facilities in Ohio, William Montague, was indicted on charges that he took bribes and kickbacks to steer VA contracts to a company that did business with the agency nationwide.

- In 2014 at least 40 veterans died while waiting for appointments to see a doctor at the Phoenix Veterans Affairs Health Care system. American Legion National Commander Daniel Dillinger said the deaths reported by CNN appear to be part of a "pattern of scandals that has infected the entire system." Also, as the scheduling scandal widened, a Cheyenne, Wyoming, VA employee was placed on administrative leave after an email surfaced in which the employee discussed "gaming the system a bit" to manipulate waiting times. The suspension comes a day after a scheduling clerk in San Antonio admitted to "cooking the books" to shorten apparent waiting times. Three days later, two employees in Durham, North Carolina, were placed on leave over similar allegations. Also, the chairman of the House Veteran Affairs Committee said his group had received information "that will make what has already come out look like kindergarten stuff." Finally, President Obama accepted Eric Shinseki's resignation.[237]

Unsurprisingly, the problems have continued past 2014.

There was the case of Mary Carstensen, who got tangled up in an ethics scandal. Before joining the VA in 2011 she created a company to assist nonprofits. The company had one client, an unidentified nonprofit, referred to in a 2016 memorandum from the VA's Assistant Inspector General for Investigations as "NPO." After she joined, she signed an ethics pledge "in which," according to the memo, " she vowed that for a period of two years from the date of her appointment, she would not participate in any particular matter involving specific parties that were directly and substantially related to her former employer or former clients." This she failed to do. The memo concluded that "Ms. Carstensen failed to fully disclose her prior employment with the NPO and her current relationship, which provided her compensation well in excess of the $5,000 reporting requirement." The Assistant Inspector General for Investigations made a criminal referral to the Department of Justice, but it declined to prosecute.[238]

There were revoked medical licenses. *USA Today* announced in December 2017 the results of an investigation that showed that the VA "allowed its hospitals across the country to hire health care providers with revoked medical licenses for at least 15 years in violation of federal law." The investigation found that "VA hospitals have knowingly hired other health care providers with past license discipline. In some cases, they have gone on to harm veterans."[239] Another newspaper, the *Washington Examiner*, in reporting the investigation's results, ran the headline, "The VA Standards Just Hit a New Low"; the article's author called for Congress "to free our veterans from this ineptitude." [240]

There was the case of the falsified email. In 2018, the *Washington Post* reported that, according to the VA's inspector general, the chief of staff for David Shulkin, the Secretary of Veterans Affairs, "doctored an email and made false statements to create a pretext for taxpayers to cover expenses for the secretary's wife on a 10-day trip to Europe" in the summer of 2017. "Vivieca Wright Simpson, VA's third-most-senior official, altered language in an email from an aide coordinating the trip to make it appear that Shulkin was receiving an award from the Danish government, then used the award to justify paying for his wife's travel. The VA paid more than $4,300 for her airfare."[241] Two days later, Simpson resigned from her post. In June 2017, at a bill-signing ceremony President Trump teased that Shulkin need never worry about hearing his "Apprentice"-era catchphrase, "You're fired." "We'll never have to use those words on our David," the president said. "We will never use those words on you, that's for sure."[242] On March 28, 2018, David Shulkin was fired.

There was the nursing-home saga. In June 2018 an investigation by reporters at *USA Today* and the *Boston Globe* revealed that VA nursing homes performed worse on several key measures than private nursing homes did. The measures included rates of anti-psychotic drug prescription and residents' deterioration. In some cases, the report said, "the VA ratings were only slightly worse" than what was measured at private-care facilities. "In others, such as the number of residents who are in pain, the VA nursing homes scored dramatically worse." A VA spokesman called the report "highly misleading to compare pain levels at the VA with those at private nursing homes because VA residents have "more challenging" medical conditions. Still, the VA's own internal quality tracking found that "VA nursing home residents were five times more likely to report being in pain than private nursing home residents."[243]

∿

While the national mood seems to be that government is full of waste and oppressive oversight, in fact government employees play a crucial role in the success of the republic. If there was ever an example of a government employee who wanted to use taxpayer dollars well and efficiently, but whose good intentions were hardly rewarded, it would be Rosye Cloud. After two decades of public service—working for the Department of Defense and NATO, and then assigned to the White House as the Director of Policy for Veterans, Wounded, and Military Families—in 2013 Cloud was selected as Senior Advisor for Economic Opportunities at the Department of Veterans Affairs.

She applied to multiple positions at the VA and made the final round of all of them; eventually she was offered two positions and had to choose. One was as a senior executive leading evaluation and analysis for VA headquarters; the other, in some ways not as alluring, was as a senior leader helping to advance economic opportunities for veterans. She chose the latter position, the less prestigious, primarily because after 20 years of service she felt it was time to roll up her sleeves and tackle an issue that she was both passionate about and that would help the largest number of veterans.

"My job at the VA," she says, "was to find innovative ways to help veterans increase their employment viability. The leadership was candid behind closed doors: the employees assigned to the work historically had poor performance and were transferred to the office as a means to remove them from work. I had employees—that's plural—who slept on their desk after lunch, boasted about online shopping the day away, or spent a good part of the day reading the newspaper. I wanted to improve the morale, but my first priority was supporting our veterans, improving operations, increasing accountability and reducing unnecessary costs, knowing that may mean eliminating duplicative or frivolous contracts." She describes her work positively, characterizing the VA as "the nation's covenant with those citizens who serve our country." She was candid about her firsthand knowledge of the poor care older veterans received in her own family, the fear the elderly have when navigating the bureaucratic system, and the thousands of military and veterans' cases she'd worked dealing with various crises. As a former military spouse and having experienced the loss of friends and family, her efforts felt personal.

Cloud's brand of fresh air, however, didn't serve her well. "I did not appreciate the regressive culture and inability and unwillingness to put veterans' needs first," she says. "My desire for innovation and change was completely counter to the thinking among those who grew up inside the VA. The VA has had more than its fair share—more than is found in other government agencies—of systemic issues and breakdowns over the years." And the infighting. "I didn't realize the antibodies that existed around what I was hired to do, especially when it came down to cancelling lucrative contracts and holding employees accountable." She describes "lifers at the VA who rose to positions of authority as compliance-based and rules-based, with little or no incentive to change things. Several employees bragged they were not interested in learning anything new. The hardest part of the job," she laments, "was hearing a veteran employee say things like this."

Cloud explains that she was "tasked to disrupt the status quo, be an innovator, improve operations, and think about how agencies could work better together. It was clear, after a full assessment of the economic opportunity landscape, that in order to make progress we had to have the courage to make both funding and personnel changes. In many cases we needed fewer people and a deliberate focus to hire personnel with critical skill sets. I discovered that a large amount of the monies earmarked to help transitioning military was used as a slush fund to fund overtime claims and technology projects outside of our organization—clearly, red flags that the strategy being touted to Congress was not fully supported."[244]

The bureaucratic details are convoluted, but the bottom line is that Cloud was caught in a swirl of entrenchment and jealousy, all the while exposing the waste of a major vendor and trying to overhaul a website to save, by her estimate, approximately $17 million a year.

After many failed efforts by government personnel at the Department of Defense, the Department of Labor, and the Veterans Administration, it was at the Veterans Administration where a jobs website was eventually established. Cloud asked that duplicative contracts within the VA be cancelled to assist in the unified adoption of the website. This seemingly obvious decision, however, was met with resistance. "DOD leaders," Cloud says, "were worried about the vendor backlash when they reduced their duplicative systems," but were more than happy to point to the VA and Cloud as the culprit for the inefficiencies. Vendors collaborated with one another and engaged staff on Capitol Hill to tarnish her reputation and question the validity of the tool. A former employee of one vendor told Cloud that his firm actively engaged in a behind-the-scenes amplification of negative rumors and stories about her so that she would be removed from the project. These vendors were fighting to keep millions of dollars flowing, and to keep Cloud from eliminating contracts.

~

Concurrently, while leading the efforts for the employment web portal, Cloud was tasked with designing a national outreach initiative to disseminate knowledge of earned veterans' benefits, such as the GI Bill, transition assistance program, and home loan and community services programs. Few communities could afford to hire veteran representatives, much less full-time ones, and this initiative created fully paid-for VA economic liaisons in communities with a high number of transitioning service members. For her efforts, however, Cloud was rewarded with an attack on her integrity.

Unbeknownst to her, in one of those communities, Norfolk, Virginia, the resources she was developing was creating friction and fear in one John Andrews, a Navy veteran, who was already having difficulties with his employer. Without knowing why, Cloud was suddenly being investigated for allegedly violating a conflict-of-interest rule and for allegedly getting Andrews, who worked as the first military liaison for Norfolk, fired.

Neither charge was true, but the investigation would have the desired effect: it provided vendors the fodder they needed to lobby VA officials and members of Congress to cancel the initiatives that were adding value to veterans—but not those that were adding to their profits.

~

Norfolk was chosen to be among several, and potentially a hub for, community-based—as intentionally distinct from Washington, DC-based—pilot programs to improve economic outcomes for veterans. The program was called VECI—the Veteran Economic Community Initiative. According to Cloud, the underlying rationale went like this: "Local communities are the best equipped to be the right connector to programs and services offered by the VA. Let's respect the DNA of the community, and, for the purposes of economic mobility, let's connect with the right players there. The VA isn't there telling them what to do and we're not there exercising the federal government's muscle. In fact, we're subordinating the government by asking, *How do we plug in to where you need us?*" The program was disruptive because, Cloud says, "It infused a resource that most communities can't grow organically, and at the same time, ideally, it was meeting a need."

It was in Norfolk where Cloud met John Andrews.

Andrews says he was fired because he pointed out a possible conflict of interest on Cloud's part. He claimed that "a man selling software to help veterans transition to new careers was married to a U.S. Department of Veterans Affairs official overseeing similar efforts."[245] The man linked to that software was Chad Cloud, Rosye Cloud's husband. But there might have been a more personal motive for the conflict-of-interest allegation.

Cloud acknowledged that she never felt comfortable around Andrews and went out of her way to not be alone with him. On multiple occasions, she says, "Andrews made negative comments about women, and in particular military spouses, going as far as referencing his recent divorce. Cloud says, "Andrews had very little private-sector experience, and claimed all veterans' issues to be his expertise—and his alone—which limited his ability to engage in expanded conversations about economic opportunities."

She spent minimal time with him. Andrews's supervisor, on the other hand, was more respectful and approachable. As well, he was also knowledgeable about policy matters and issues relating to community and economic opportunities.

Cloud knew Andrews was regularly in contact with VA leadership and the employees she was counseling for performance issues. He was determined to assist, however he could, she thought, in harming her personally. In one of many emails sent to her personal account, Andrews challenged Cloud by saying: "How dare you question my abilities?" He would also send her his insights on leadership and on ways she should conduct herself.

Cloud didn't respond to any of his emails, but did ask her leadership about flagging Andrews to the security office in the event he came to the office to harm her. The VA didn't do that, however, because, she was told, the threats did not specifically state he would hurt her physically.

Then there was Andrews's DUI. Her attorneys said, "Andrews believes, bizarrely so, that he was terminated because Ms. Cloud told his employer about a prior, undisclosed DUI conviction. This is flat-out false. Indeed, the City of Norfolk has made it clear that no one from the VA—including Ms. Cloud—had anything to do with Andrews's termination." Cloud says this was a "complete surprise" to her and that she "didn't know about any DUI, wouldn't care if he ever had a DUI, and that her only concern would be that, if he did, he sought help to address the problem that caused it."[246]

Cloud was told that the vendors lobbying to have her removed from the employment website tool met with Andrews in their offices and discussed ways to target her reputation. Eventually a partisan operative released a blog that would highlight how good sites were shut down due to Cloud. "The same operatives would post information about me on social media and went so far as to engage other operatives with ties to vendors to make false statements—like I purchased a three- million dollar house" says Cloud. "These operatives reached out to my supervisor and invited him to a private meeting at Sidecar, a local bar, so they could discuss the 'Cloud issue' personally. This dynamic got worse when I was detailed as the Director of Transition Assistance and began to uncover serious contracting and personnel mismanagement." The Andrews attacks provided cover for Cloud's reporting of improprieties to be dismissed or ignored.

"Andrews's delusional belief has fueled a significant bias against Ms. Cloud," her attorneys said. "This prejudice, for instance, can be seen in Andrews's post-complaint conduct—which can only be described as vindictive and obsessive. He has continually harassed Ms. Cloud through social media and threatening communications to Ms. Cloud and her colleagues. In doing so, Andrews has sought Ms. Cloud's expulsion from the VA, encouraged others to disseminate false information about her, and has gone as far as to say to VA officials that he will not rest until Ms. Cloud is 'destroyed.'"[247]

Cloud unearthed another problem, which, in turn, caused her problems. She had reason to believe, according to her attorneys, that Danny Pummill, Acting Under Secretary for Benefits at the Veterans Benefits Administration, used his position "to interfere with a $220 million contract and influence the issuance of subcontracts to benefit personal friends and perhaps himself." The attorneys said that Cloud asserted that Pummill applied pressure and assigned retaliatory work "to his subordinate employees to prevent the re-competition of a wasteful contract that awarded millions of dollars to contractors with whom he enjoyed a personal friendship." Her attorneys also said that Cloud believed Pummill created "shadow jobs as personal favors for individuals who either do not, or cannot, perform actual work, and his protection of those employees from review of their conduct or performance." In retaliation, Pummill, the letter stated, "threatened to 'bury' Ms. Cloud and reassign her outside of the organization."[248]

Pummill repeatedly told Cloud that it was "easy to fire federal employees if you audited timecards and travel." The threat was not lost on her. For years she had been raising concerns to her supervisor that his staff delayed making travel arrangements for her properly, that on multiple occasions anonymous people had canceled her hotel reservations while she was flying en route to a location, and that reimbursements were delayed for weeks, even months, so she would need to wait an unnecessarily long time after paying for trips out of her own funds. The staff often noted that if she didn't like things, she could do all of the work herself. "That was the VA way," she says. "Screw up repeatedly in hopes the work is removed from your plate and given to someone else."

Pummill, Cloud says, "tried to bribe me. He threatened me if I didn't steer a contract to a friend of his." It was a multi-million dollar contract "for a project that could be completed for a fraction of the cost." She went up the chain of command, but nothing was done. She went to the contracting officer, but again nothing was done. She asked for assistance from several senior VA officials, but they warned her that she was "breaking rank, going against the well-established 'Army officer brotherhood' inside VA," likely leading to her being targeted and disciplined. "The Department did not want negative attention on its senior leaders and Pummill and his friends were being vetted for promotions," she says.

"There were pressures and resistance from everywhere, and for each project I was executing. The resistance was coming from people who had something to gain—either financial gain or influence. This latticework of self-dealing and secrecy is at the heart of most system failures of the organization."

~

In the end, the pressure to shut down the employment website was too much. Within months of Cloud stepping away from the project, the use of the tool declined by 90 percent. Where millions of veterans and military had been conducting job searches, the numbers dropped to below 60,000 and then to only tens of thousands, according to Cloud. The community initiative was also sunset and disbanded, putting over 50 liaisons out of work and leaving over a hundred communities without the promised support.

Cloud says she exhausted every avenue to report her concerns. "I went all the way to the secretary's office and spoke to the chief of staff. I discussed my evidence and said this level of contract influence was not right. He said Pummill told him that I had sharp elbows. The chief of staff said it seemed that I had been humbled by the process sufficiently, and he said he believed that I believed what I was reporting was true."

Forging past what most might hear as a condescending comment, Cloud asked the chief of staff if she could bring him the evidence she had. "He said he didn't want to see it," she says, "and that if I felt that strongly about it, then I should go and report it to an official entity." Before she left the meeting she asked, "At what point did we, as leaders, stop solving problems?"[249]

Three months later, Danny Pummill left the Veterans Benefit Administration. The *Military Times* reported, "Pummill was suspended for two weeks in March for 'lack of oversight' in a relocation scandal involving two other high-ranking VA administrators, a reprimand that irritated some lawmakers who wanted harsher punishment for what appeared to be unwarranted promotions for longtime bureaucrats. But Pummill defended the promotions before Congress and accepted his suspension in an effort to move beyond the months-long controversy. He made no mention of the incident in his farewell note."[250]

∼

As for the conflict-of interest allegation, Cloud's husband was the sole owner of a software company that builds customer software solutions, often for government agencies. To avoid violating any rules—in fact, to follow them assiduously—Cloud wrote a letter to the Office of Economic Opportunity, in which she noted the potential conflict and recused herself from taking part in any matters the VA might have involving her husband's company.[251] Cloud's recusal followed guidelines and her letter was written in a timely fashion. Furthermore, she says, "My husband and I informed OGC"—the Office of General Counsel—"that he would never compete for any contract or work at the VA while I worked there. At no time did my husband compete for any work at the VA or seek to subcontract for work at the VA."[252]

John Andrews hung his complaint on an August 2014 meeting where Cloud's husband was to make a presentation before an advisory committee meeting on military and veterans education. He would demo the software program his company had developed for a client to help high school and college students along with career advancers and career changers.

Rosye was invited to the meeting but neither spouse knew the other would be there. Chad was scheduled to present later and wasn't in the room when everyone convened. It wasn't until an hour or so into the meeting that Rosye learned that her husband was to make a presentation. According to her attorney, "Cloud received a text message from her husband saying he was outside the meeting room waiting to be called in and thought he heard her voice. Ms. Cloud immediately confirmed Chad was, in fact, outside the meeting room." At that moment—prior to her husband's presentation—she excused herself and reported the incident to the VA's ethics personnel."[253]

The conflict was honorably avoided, or so a rational person would think. But no. Rosye was removed from her job. She believes she was scapegoated. Some higher-ups at the VA may have taken the Andrews allegations seriously, or may have wanted the allegations to look serious, because Cloud had been asking uncomfortable questions about Danny Pummill.

⁓

John Andrews sued the city of Norfolk because he said he was wrongly fired in November 2014. He said all he did was bring to the city's attention what he thought were ethical issues and the city paid no heed. He said he was "frustrated by Norfolk's lack of interest or inability to fully consider his concerns." U.S. District Judge Mark Davis didn't dismiss the lawsuit and said it could go to trial, but in January 2018 the city settled with Andrews for $157,500.

The settlement did not go over well with the Clouds. It was clear that Andrews and his employer had longstanding issues unrelated to them. Andrews repeatedly wrote about his disdain of his supervisor for not having served in the military, and yet asked him questions about his work. Chad Cloud conducted his own investigation and, through public-records requests, obtained government documents. Those documents, which were relayed to the VA's inspector general, told a very different story about Andrews and his personal agenda. They contained discussions between

Andrews and Cloud's VA employees in which they brainstormed how to engage the media and VSOs to help bring Cloud down. The emails also provided insight into the relationship between Andrews and the vendors selling technology tools. Cloud believes the emails show Andrews had plans to influence the state of Virginia to issue contracts to friends seeking federal and state contracts. If Cloud's projects were successful, that would mean no money would flow to vendors for these tech contracts.

On December 15, 2016, two years after the conflict-of-interest meeting that wasn't, the Clouds' attorney, Jonathan Lenzner, wrote, "The Department of Veterans Affairs, Office of Inspector General, has exonerated VA official Rosye Cloud, clearing her of any wrongdoing following an administrative investigation into baseless allegations of a conflict of interest with her husband Chad Cloud. After a nearly two-year taxpayer-funded investigation—in which Ms. Cloud fully cooperated with investigators—the OIG found no evidence of wrongdoing." Lenzner noted that Davis tossed out several of Andrews's claims, "further confirming that Andrews's accusations are meritless and nothing more than fantasy on Andrews's part."[254]

By 2018, Cloud was done. An OIG report, issued in early 2018, noted serious contract irregularities with the contract she had reported. No action was taken against anyone involved in the mismanagement of the contracts. Cloud found it "more than a little ironic" that the OIG never took the time to interview her prior to drafting its report.

"In the end," Cloud says, "the VA will never attract and retain leaders willing to put veterans and taxpayers first if they cannot create a values-based culture." I believe government should strive to be of value, seek efficiencies and continuously seek high-quality performance. Corruption should not be tolerated. Employees should never fear their employer will not support them if they identify wrongdoing. In over 23 years of service, I never experienced a culture as toxic as the one at VA. In no way does VA reflect all that is right with public service. Public service is critical to our nation. Veterans deserve better care and support by VA."[255] Still, before she left government service for good, she—and many others like her in government—must at times have wondered if fighting these antibodies was worth it.

~

It might be tempting to just get rid of the Department of Veterans Affairs. That's not going to happen, however, because, even with its persistent damaged environment and culture, the VA is simply too valuable to throw away. Still, if history and politics serve as any kind of guide, it will be a while before the VA gets its act together.

~

The VA has its supporters, and they have a case. Guy McMichael, who sat on WWP's board for several years, including when Steve Nardizzi and Al Giordano were fired, is an attorney who served as general counsel for both the VA and the U.S. Senate Committee on Veterans Affairs. He contends that the VA often gets a bad rap and, when he is asked about everything that has gone wrong, he is reminded, he says, of the old adage that "they can build you up just to take you down." He says his experience—"and this goes all the way back to 1971—is that the VA is both blessed and cursed by its mission. It's blessed because if veterans need something, typically you can make a case and get money a lot easier for veterans than other groups can with other agencies." In fact, he posits, "by and large a good, solid case can be made that the VA delivers care as well as or better than the private sector."

Others too feel positively about the VA. Phillip Longman wrote in Best Care Anywhere: Why VA Health Care Would Work Better For Everyone, "About a third of all health-care spending is pure waste, or worse, mostly in the form of unnecessary and often harmful care—amounting to some $700 billion a year," and then later puts forth something people don't often hear: "Medical errors are demonstrably less common in the VA than elsewhere in the health-care sector, and study after study demonstrates the VA's superior quality of care and high rates of patient satisfaction."[256]

Guy McMichael is not doe-eyed, however. "Unlike at a local hospital, a misadventure on the part of someone at a veterans' hospital makes the papers. Its problems come from over-demand," he says. "We've had a tremendous increase in requests for medical care and disability benefits," a demand that began not with post-9/11 conflicts but also with Vietnam veterans." Even if integrity could be found at every turn, the agency's task is so overwhelming that there certainly would be problems. McMichael himself says, "It is clear that the VA does not, and apparently cannot, help all veterans as envisioned by its motto."[257]

This is why veterans' organizations, like Wounded Warrior Project, are needed to help fill the gaps.

Challengers

Over the years, in addition to a growing number of supporters and an increasing donor base, WWP also attracted detractors. In 2014 The Daily Beast, wrote, "It's a broad but closely held sentiment within the veterans' advocacy community: grumbling and critiques about the fundraising behemoth WWP has become, and whether it has been as effective as it could be. In interviews, critical veterans' advocates and veterans charged that the Wounded Warrior Project cares more about its image than it does about helping veterans; that it makes public splashes by taking vets on dramatic skydiving trips but doesn't do enough to help the long-term wellbeing of those injured in combat. These criticisms come from a broad cross-section of veterans and their advocates, the vast majority of whom refused to speak on the record due to the sway the Wounded Warrior Project carries. They are such a big name within the veterans' community. 'I don't need to start a war in my backyard,' a double-amputee veteran who served in Iraq told The Daily Beast. But granted anonymity, the vet gave voice to what is at the very least a perception problem for the WWP: 'They're more worried about putting their label on everything than getting down to brass tacks. It's really frustrating.'"[258]

The feelings against the organization persisted. Art Taylor, the head of the BBBs give.org, says, carefully, that his sense is, "There was an element in the nonprofit sector, that saw Wounded Warrior Project's promotion of its successful fundraising practices as suggestive that *all charities should follow them. They're saying, We should essentially remove these artificial restrictions on how much money an organization should spend on fundraising because they are holding us back from growing and helping people.*"[259] Although it is true that there are no legal restrictions on how much money a charity can spend on fundraising, donors do not respond well when a charity is perceived as spending too much money on overhead. The definition of *too much* is hardly clear—and, of course, there is The Overhead Myth letter—but the idea is still so palpable that charities don't want to even be perceived as overspending on fundraising, and many felt that Wounded Warrior Project did, and got away with it.

∿

In 2015 Alex Graham, a veteran, claimed that WWP was a scam. "They're spending so much money on fundraising that there's nothing left for the veterans," he wrote on his website. One person replied, "I'm greatly concerned about all of the rumors and articles. I hate to say it, but I want to cancel my membership." While that was just an opinion, aggregated with others like it, it eventually worked against Graham.

Lawyers for Wounded Warrior Project were able to cite dozens of statements from social media sites where people criticized WWP and said they would not donate to it again. Graham gained so much negative attention that GuideStar, a nonprofit database, distanced itself from his characterizations of financial records he obtained from its website. Also, several national news organizations produced segments challenging Graham's depiction of the organization. In 2015, WWP sued Graham. "WWP has and will continue to suffer irreparable harm as a result of Graham's defamatory statements regarding WWP," the lawyers wrote in their complaint. [260]

Graham lost the case and was ordered to "personally remove all defamatory content regarding WWP, issue a retraction of his false statements, and "expressly state that the false, misleading and defamatory statements published therein are incorrect." He was also ordered to write a humbling apology on his and several third-party sites. [261]

That wasn't the only legal action that WWP pursued. In October 2014 WWP filed a lawsuit against Keystone Wounded Warriors in Pennsylvania, citing intentionally confusing similarities between Keystone's and WWP's logos. Even in this situation, however, WWP was painted the bad guy.

The *Nonprofit Quarterly* wrote a sympathetic article about Keystone in May 2015 with this headline: "Is Wounded Warrior Project a 'Neighborhood

Bully' Among Veterans' Groups?" The writer of a *Daily Beast* article in 2015 opined that WWP was, and quoted David Brog, the executive director of the Air Warrior Courage Foundation, as saying that WWP is "not looked upon very highly by [the veterans community]."[262]

Ruth McCambridge, the editor-in-chief of the *Nonprofit Quarterly*, wrote of "the attempt of a large, well-moneyed group to squash smaller nonprofits in the name of their mission 'brand.' Ugly. According to a number of smaller groups, the Wounded Warrior Project, with annual revenues of $235 million, has been spending a good deal of time and money suing other veteran-serving nonprofits on the basis that their names or logos constitute infringement on their brand." She also noted that another nonprofit executive said that WWP bullies smaller organizations.[263]

In 2007 WWP waged a battle with a nonprofit called Wounded Warriors Family Support, or WWFS. Its website was *woundedwarriors.org*. "If you were to look up the words *wounded warrior* on Charity Navigator's website," Steve Nardizzi told an audience in 2014, "you would find my organization, Wounded Warrior Project, and another organization called Wounded Warriors Family Support. Both organizations receive a three-star rating, which would suggest to potential donors that the two organizations are equally effective."

But they were not equally effective and, after the case was argued in court, a jury decided WWFS was a sham. A forensic accountant examined the financial records of WWFS and determined that some of the donations it received were explicitly payable to "Wounded Warrior Project," and some donors, in letters accompanying their donation to WWFS, referenced recent work by WWP.

The accountant also examined the amount of donations WWFS received both immediately before it began using the woundedwarriors.org website and after they closed it down, with the donations it received while that website was live. The bell-curve results were astounding. Before its website was created, WWFS averaged $1,337 per month in donations. After, donations spiked to almost $88,000 per month. Once the website was taken down, WWFS's donations dropped by more than 56 percent and WWP donations increased by 29 percent. "In 2007," Nardizzi said,

"Wounded Warrior Project sued Wounded Warriors Family Support to prevent that organization from deceiving the public and damaging the goodwill of our organization."[264]

The case went to court and at the conclusion of the trial in 2009 the jury found that WWFS intentionally confused the public, engaged in deceptive trade practices, and violated the consumer protection act. It awarded Wounded Warrior Project $1.7 million, including $1.2 million in misdirected funds donors intended for WWP and $500,000 in punitive damages.[265] On the WWFS home page, in red letters at the top, is this sentence: "This Site Is Not Affiliated With The Wounded Warrior Project."[266]

Provocateurs

- **Admiral Michael Mullen**

Criticism came not only from the media and other charities, but also from an influential former government official. Admiral Michael Mullen, the chairman of the Joint Chiefs of Staff from 2007 through 2011, was among WWP's most vocal critics. According to more than one person, who could not speak for the record, "It is no secret that Mullen, and even Donald Rumsfeld"—the former Secretary of Defense—"hate WWP."[267]

In 2010, Major John Copeland and Colonel David Sutherland authored a report entitled "The Sea of Goodwill." Sponsored by Mullen's office, it outlined the support America provides its wounded warriors. "Today," they wrote, "unlike any generation in history, citizens across the country are supportive in word and deed of the American Active Duty, Reserve, and National Guard Soldier, Sailor, Airman, Marine, and Coast Guardsman. Our nation is so full of support for our Service members it is difficult to illustrate all the organizations and individuals trying to do their part to support our veterans. Admiral Michael Mullen, the Chairman of the Joint Chiefs of Staff, calls this a 'Sea of Goodwill' of American support. He notes, 'The challenge...is how do you connect that sea of goodwill to the need?'"[268]

The paper essentially was a call for many organizations to work together to address the challenge of caring for veterans. Because of the growing jealousy among nonprofits, as well as Mullen's connection to some of them, Wounded Warrior Project began to be ostracized. Thus, the report also served as a rationale to spread money around. The thinking went: less money to WWP would mean more for other organizations. The sea would have more and better boats.

Chris Carney, who with Peter Honerkamp, began Soldier Ride, said, "If Admiral Mullen thought less money going to WWP would mean that the money would keep coming but would be spread among the other organizations, he was wrong. This is because WWP was raising money for its mission. The missions of WWP and those of other organizations don't overlap in many donors' minds. Also, because of WWP's size, many people took comfort in thinking the money was going to a good cause that was supported financially."[269]

Yet another person close to WWP's operations said, "It's not as if the lost money went to other veterans' service organizations. If WWP lost a hundred million, two hundred million, that was actually lost money to the veterans' cause. The other charities didn't step up to the plate and make their case."[270]

No one can calculate for certain if these sentiments are accurate, but they make sense. Even within the veterans' charity space, Wounded Warrior Project performs unique work and the sophistication of its operations is a magnet for thoughtful donors.

A big reason for the ostracism was the heavy television advertising campaign that Wounded Warrior Project conducted. Several people said they felt the ads that depicted the catastrophically wounded were the crucial problem, that too many people in the military and in other nonprofit organizations simply didn't like them—the military because its leaders complained they retarded recruitment efforts, and other nonprofits that served veterans because of their resentment of WWP's singular and historic growth.

As for the military, in February 2015 WWP held a five-year strategic planning meeting in Washington, DC. A little over a dozen people attended.

Among them was René Bardorf, then employed as the Deputy Assistant Secretary of Defense for Public Affairs in the Office of the Secretary of Defense. Bardorf said she heard at the Pentagon that the ads were negatively affecting force readiness—the measure of the military's ability to respond to national security needs.

Rosye Cloud, the former VA official, says, "There's universal, governmental sentiment that we want veterans to be seen as strong and we don't want recruitment to be hurt by portraying them as somehow broken. There's a self-serving element at times from the Department of Defense because they want to be able to say we build great people, that they are strong and steadfast. The reason a lot of the people who have such a visceral reaction about portraying a veteran as injured or vulnerable is that they themselves don't want to be seen that way." However, she says, "Many people know that we have to be honest about where there's a need and be willing to be transparent to the country about what it means to serve. Not all are hurt, but there is a very real possibility you may be called upon to sacrifice in ways that are life altering. Many people, especially the senior military officers, believe there's brand erosion when you have a veteran on TV who's really injured and hurt."

There's something strange in that. Who can deny that going to war risks the possibility of death and injury for many? "We have a national, cultural philosophy that every American is better off for having served," Cloud says, "and we market it that way to our youth, to our families, and anything that detracts from that value statement is at times resented."[271]

∼

Whether the WWP ads actually did negatively affect recruiting is up for some debate. The numbers are not clear, but according to a military research organization, the number of total active duty military personnel dropped between 2010, when the ads began, and 2014 by one half of one percent. Within that, the Army, which is where the majority of wounded veterans served, the drop was eight-tenths of one percent during those years.[272] "That's not a big drop," one person, who spoke on condition of anonymity, said, "especially since it's also true that fewer men and women were returning from war at that time than had been during the first decade of the new century. Clearly," the person said, "the WWP ads had no negative impact whatsoever on military recruitment."

Interestingly, something far more ominous than television ads poses a danger to the nation's military. In early 2018, the Heritage Foundation released a study called "The Looming National Security Crisis: Young Americans Unable to Serve in the Military," in which it concludes that "71 percent of young Americans between 17 and 24 are ineligible to serve in the United States military. Put another way: Over 24 million of the 34 million people of that age group cannot join the armed forces—even if they wanted to." Of those shown to be unable to serve, 32 percent is due to poor health, 27 percent is due to being physically unfit, 25 percent is due to a lack of education, and 10 percent have a disqualifying criminal background.[273]

Another participant at that planning meeting in February 2015, Pete Chiarelli, a highly decorated retired four-star Army general and former Vice Chief of Staff of the U.S. Army, said he had not heard of a decline in recruitment, and in fact strongly disagreed with the criticism of the ads. At a WWP advisory council meeting a few weeks later, Rick Tryon, a three-star Marine general and the former head of recruiting for the Marines, is reported to have said, "there was no way the WWP ads had an impact on force readiness." Another person close to the discussion said, "Those ads were 70 times more effective."[274] Even though—and possibly because—they portrayed the catastrophically injured, they raised more money than any other ads WWP aired.

The ads were expensive: $35 million in 2015. Charities can reach out to the public through direct mail, calls by staff members, calls from an outside telemarketing firm, or DRTV—direct response television. "By far," says Steve Nardizzi, "DRTV is the most expensive to buy into. Just to begin, for initial testing, you need between $2 and $3 million." But, he says, "It's actually the most efficient way to raise money, in large part because you retain donors better. The people who see the ads, and then decide to give, do so pro-actively. They aren't being coerced by someone on the other end of a telephone."[275] The ads were part of a fundraising program that raised almost $400 million that year. Of course, part of the reason any ad campaign succeeds is the quality of the messaging.

While the messaging proved to be effective for WWP, it was a problem not only for the organization's critics, but for its board as well. In one advertisement, a veteran said that, had he known how the government would treat him, he would not have joined. He wasn't saying he would not have sacrificed his life, but that he was unaware of how little the government cares, and that WWP saved his life. Because he was worried about how it would play at the Pentagon, WWP's board chairman Tony Odierno directed Steve Nardizzi to pull the veteran's sentiment from the video.

~

Not only did the ads separate Wounded Warrior Project from other veterans' service organizations, from the perspective of most other charities they also went off script. In his book *Uncharitable,* Dan Pallotta criticizes the notion that charities should be genteel in their messaging. "The decision about whether to buy advertising should be based strictly on a cost-benefit analysis, not on a pseudo-moral standard based on tradition, because a cost-benefit analysis will produce the most benefit for the needy. There is only one question that matters: is advertising likely to produce more value than it costs? This is a long-term question. If the answer is yes, there need not be further discussion."[276]

There is no doubt that the ads evoked wounds, physical, mental and emotional. One ad, about a warrior identified as "Dan," and narrated by Trace Adkins, the singer, went like this:

Dan: "We were heading out for a combat mission. My vehicle was sent six feet in the air in a ball of fire. I thought I was going to die."

Adkins: "Dan survived that terrible day, but paid a heavy price for his bravery."

Dan: "They've personally impacted my life, and they've personally impacted thousands of lives—not only the warrior but their family members."

Adkins: "The job of helping warriors rebuild their lives is massive and growing every day. Many of these service members suffered traumatic brain injury and post-traumatic stress disorder, and they'll need the help of Wounded Warrior Project for many years to come."

Dan: "Those warriors coming back today and tomorrow don't know what's ahead."[277]

Throughout, viewers heard a musical refrain: "Say a prayer for peace."

Another, narrated by the actor Dean Norris, highlighted the thoughts of the family of Eric Edmundson.

Norris: "Many of our warriors are returning from the battlefield, only to face a new war, as they struggle with devastating injuries."

Eric's Wife: "Some of the biggest challenges were, what's going to happen. Are we going to be able to stay together, keep the family together?"

Eric's Mother: "The soldiers need to know that when they're out there fighting for us that there are people back home if the worst happens.

Norris: "The greatest casualty is being forgotten."[278]

Yet another advertisement, this one with several male and female veterans—on camera but unidentified, and again with Trace Adkins, but with less narration—was also a story of hope in the wake of tragedy:

Warrior 1: "I heard a loud noise, and then everything went black."

Warrior 2: "I was set on fire. I couldn't breathe."

Warrior 3: "I saw the fireball. Everybody was panicking. I have never been so afraid in my life."

Warrior 4: "Everything changed after that."

Warrior 5: "The person who went to Iraq is by far not the same person who came back."

Warrior 6: "I was very isolated. I didn't want to talk to anybody."

Warrior 7: "I felt like there was no one there. There was no hope."

Warrior 3: "There's this feeling of brokenness; not being the person that I used to be. I had thoughts of ending my life."

Warrior 8: "When a person is scared and confused and alone, Wounded Warrior Project has been there to help them."

Warrior 9: "The needs aren't going away. Post Traumatic Stress Disorder is not going away.

Warrior 10: "The wounded warriors that are out there need help. They're going to be around for years to come."

Warrior 11: "I'm able to do a lot more now. I've come a long way."

Warrior 12: "There's so much emotional healing that . . . that goes on."

Warrior 13: "It's great to know there's an organization out there who's willing and able to help."

Announcer: "The job of helping thousands of wounded warriors rebuild their lives is massive."[279]

These and the other advertisements all have two compelling themes: one, in the words of the veterans themselves, we learn that the government isn't helping them to the degree they need help; and two, with much appreciation on the part of veterans, Wounded Warrior Project is making a significant effort to fill the gap. In all of them, the narrator asks for a monthly donation of $19.

"One of the really positive things in Eric's life," Eric Edmundson's mother Beth says, "was the opportunity to do a commercial for Wounded Warrior Project. It was a way to give back. A by-product of that experience, however, was that people now come up to him to tell him they've seen him on TV. That then prompts a conversation." Beth Edmundson says she remembers a housekeeper at a hotel who kept looking at Eric, "and then she just had to ask, 'Have you been on TV?' It's a positive. It's not a picture of 'poor me,' which is how an injury is often presented. Not at all. People say instead, 'You're just *doing* life.' It's just been a real positive opportunity."[280]

The ads stopped immediately after Nardizzi and Giordano were fired. Shortly after, a new advertising philosophy was developed with little of the bite the old ones portrayed.

~

After he kept hearing negative comments about WWP attributed to other veterans' organizations and military personnel, Nardizzi reached out to invite David Sutherland, the co-author of "Sea of Goodwill," to the WWP headquarters in Jacksonville, Florida. Nardizzi and other senior members of the WWP staff provided a full briefing for Sutherland, outlining the programs and the metrics used to gauge the effectiveness of those programs. According to Nardizzi, "Sutherland was unmoved. He came away from all that with the impression that we were good only at fundraising, and that we were using all the wrong metrics." Nardizzi told Sutherland that if he, Sutherland, could provide better metrics, then he would be interested in learning what they were. Sutherland never responded.

It is no small irony that the subject of much criticism of WWP—measuring the impact of its programs—was the very activity that WWP took so seriously. In fact, by any measurement, among all the charities in the United States, WWP was at the highest levels of assessing itself, as well as being transparent about it.

When Sutherland, who worked for Admiral Mullen, left government service in 2012, he began to heavily criticize WWP. Mullen, it was said by several people, relied on Sutherland's thinking on the topic of nonprofits serving veterans. In the years after he retired, Mullen met with several veterans' charities, a group collectively called "White Oak"—characterized by some as an "invitation-only cabal of nonprofits," where one participant said, "It was blood sport to bash Wounded Warrior Project." One source said that subsequent to the media allegations, Mullen called a meeting with other veterans' organizations to ask them not to work with WWP.

In particular, two charities—the Dixon Center for Military and Veterans Services at Easter Seals and the Institute for Veterans and Military Families (IVMF), a program at Syracuse University—were troublesome for WWP. After 2012, Sutherland served as the chairman and chief strategist for Dixon Center, and Deborah Mullen, Michael Mullen's spouse, was heavily involved with the Easter Seals chapter that serves the District of Columbia, Virginia and Maryland. In June 2013 WWP representatives met with the people at IVMF, who wanted WWP's financial support. At first, WWP agreed, but upon later discovering that IVMF had entered into an agreement with Dixon Center, WWP changed its mind—not because WWP didn't want other organizations to help veterans, but because it didn't want to potentially fund its own demise.

~

After tiring of the animosity, Steve Nardizzi wanted to meet with Mullen to hear first hand his criticisms, as well as his suggestions as to how WWP could improve. The meeting took place on February 8, 2013, at Mullen's office at the Naval Academy in Annapolis, Maryland.

Nardizzi and John Molino, the chief of staff for programs at WWP, represented WWP. Molino took extensive notes during the meeting and immediately after wrote a detailed summary of what was said, as well as of his impressions. When they arrived at the building where the meeting was to take place, they signed in and waited downstairs until they were told that the Admiral was ready to see them. The reception was cold: a handshake and a "come in." No smiles. Nothing about "it's good to meet you."

In addition to Mullen, Dave Sutherland, and Kimberly Mitchell, the president of Dixon Center, were in the office. Sally Donnelly, a special assistant to Mullen, joined a few minutes after the meeting started. Even though by then he knew Sutherland would be at the meeting, Nardizzi thought it was odd as Mullen hadn't said anything about it beforehand. Perhaps, he intuited, Mullen wanted to strengthen his forces.

The way those in the meeting configured themselves presaged the tension. Mullen sat in the first seat on the right side of the rectangular-shaped table. Nardizzi sat directly across from him. Molino sat at the head of the table. Mitchell was to Nardizzi's left, a chair between them. When Sally Donnelly arrived, she sat across from Mitchell and down the table a little from Mullen. But she was not actually at the table; she never moved her chair up, opting to sit slightly to Mullen's right rear. Dave Sutherland positioned himself between Mitchell and the opposite end of the table from Molino. Like Donnelly, Sutherland was also pushed back from the table. No one could be blamed for wondering if their body language sent the message that they were unengaged or thought this meeting was a waste of time.

In essence, there were two principal combatants; one brought three attendants; the other brought one.

Nardizzi began by thanking Mullen for agreeing to the meeting. He said that he wanted to meet because he had heard that Mullen had problems with Wounded Warrior Project and wanted to make sure that Mullen heard directly from the leadership about the organization's spending, metrics, and impact of the programs WWP offered.

To guide the conversation, Nardizzi began to distribute the physical pages from a PowerPoint slide deck, which explained the highlights of WWP's work. But Mullen, setting the tone for the meeting, leaned forward in his chair, elbows on the table, and said that he wanted to first say a few things. Nardizzi and Molino anticipated this interruption in their prep session.

Even though a clearly adversarial tone permeated the discussion, according to Molino, the meeting was polite and professional. "There were no raised voices and no finger-pointing," he wrote, "but there was no laughing, smiling or granting of the benefit of the doubt either."

Nardizzi remembers something a bit more contentious. "Mullen went on a rampage," Nardizzi says. "He began to immediately criticize WWP. He told us that we had no metrics, that we were not transparent, that our ads victimized warriors, and that we generally weren't doing good work." In the minutes that followed, according to Molino, Mullen said that "he continues to hear nothing good about WWP and that the reports are getting worse," that he'd heard from other organizations that they "don't deal with WWP," and that he'd heard that WWP was "unwilling to talk to Warriors until they 'sign up.'"

As the Chief of Naval Operations, his position before becoming the Chairman of the Joint Chiefs of Staff, Mullen liked what he saw when he visited WWP's headquarters in Jacksonville several years earlier. At this meeting, however, he said that he didn't like what he was hearing recently, that WWP was getting 'F' and 'D' grades from neutral sources. This was a reference to the appraisals charity evaluators had provided.

Nardizzi explained, "We discount and disregard the ratios because they measure the wrong things, and we willingly accept the grades we receive. We could easily get a top rating if we decided to accept government money, but we made the decision not to do so in order to be able to forecast accurately our future programs." Nardizzi explained how accepting government money can actually manipulate the ratios and offered the back-of-the-envelope analysis he did on Easter Seals, the USO, and another organization showing how, if government grants are extracted from those organizations' financials, the ratio of money each spends to bring in a dollar is comparable to—and in some cases less favorable than—WWP's. Molino then wrote in his after-meeting notes, "It is purely my impression, but I concluded Admiral Mullen did not like being schooled on this topic and was not pleased that Steve had an understanding of the subject that was far deeper than his own."

~

Mullen, according to Molino, said he was a "program guy and output-driven," and that he hadn't seen any metrics for WWP. He also accused WWP of "a lack of transparency."

Both Nardizzi and Molino were stunned. At the very least, as the sign-in register showed that Dave Sutherland arrived about 30 minutes prior to Nardizzi and Molino, the two assumed that Sutherland had been prepping him—WWP's numbers being one aspect of that preparation—in the time they were together before going into Mullen's office.

To the criticism that WWP had "a lack of transparency," Nardizzi referred Mullen back to the website and 'the plethora of information contained therein to include information few, if any, other organizations willingly make available."

To the implied criticism that metrics were absent at WWP, Nardizzi was initially reluctant to put Mullen on the spot, but, after a brief back-and-forth during which Mullen maintained that he would have to "see numbers to believe" that our programs are so effective, he said, "Admiral, I'm afraid I have to ask: Have you ever visited WWP's website?" "To his credit," Molino recalls, "Admiral Mullen did not BS us. He answered, 'No. I have not.'" Nardizzi then said, "That's too bad because it's all there. We strive for the best in transparency, and all our work, all our metrics are right there for anyone to see." Mullen then said, according to Nardizzi, that he would defer to Sutherland. At that point there was total silence and Molino took note of Mullen's body language. Molino wrote, "He removed his elbows from the tabletop, sat back in his chair, and let his shoulders slump slightly, but noticeably."

After the awkward moment passed, Nardizzi offered to add any other metrics Mullen thought would be valuable to measure the effectiveness of our programs. Mullen said he would have to take a look before he could comment further. Sutherland added, 'Maybe you're measuring the wrong things.' Steve countered that Dave should suggest better metrics for our consideration."[281]

∼

About Mullen hearing nothing good about WWP, Nardizzi countered, "We're hearing just the opposite from Warriors in our annual survey, which has a remarkably high response rate and is subject to outside analysis. We are not hearing such negativity in the reviews after each program event we hold; nor are we hearing this on our annual phone calls to every registered warrior."

Nardizzi offered Mullen a copy of WWP's annual alumni survey. "Do you expect me to read this?" Mullen asked when he saw the thick document. Nardizzi said that he brought it as a reference document for him or his staff.

As for the assertion that other nonprofit organizations "don't deal with WWP," Nardizzi cited the many grants WWP had made, as well as the formal partnerships with other major charities, including the American Red Cross, Give an Hour, and Operation Homefront.

As for WWP's decision to put money aside to fund a long-term trust to help with lifetime disabilities and the home-based caregivers needed to deal with them, a topic that Mullen also brought up, Mullen acknowledged the benefit of looking years into the future, but said there needs to be a sense of urgency because "in 24 months, America is going to forget about us. About 20 organizations are going out of business each month," he said, and "WWP is going to be alone in this space in two years. WWP should step up and take responsibility for the effort."

Then Dave Sutherland said, "WWP has a huge voice," to which Mullen then added, "Yes, positive and negative." Mullen, according to Molino, then said that although WWP "had placed 500 warriors the previous year in careers through Warriors to Work," that number is "a drop in the bucket." He added, "Walmart has said it is willing to hire any veteran who applies."

Molino responded to this. "The Walmart hires are routinely part-time, without benefits, and without the likelihood of a career." Nardizzi added, "Ours are quality placements and that, while 500 may not be the largest number, it is one of 18 programs we offer to warriors." Mullen asked, "Why don't I know about these things?" Nardizzi said he couldn't answer that question.

∾

Above all, it seemed, was Mullen's dislike of WWP's television ads depicting the catastrophically wounded. According to Molino, he said, "I am appalled at the advertising"; "I've heard that warriors feel as though they are being used"; "WWP is sending absolutely the wrong message"; "A WWP ad is not where I would want to be." Mullen said he thought "the ads were demoralizing and singularly focused on raising money," and that the advertising "broad-brushes the entire population, stigmatizing everybody." He thought the Trace Adkins ad in particular victimized wounded warriors.

Nardizzi disputed all of that, saying the ads were not demoralizing and that they stigmatized no one. "Our ads are extremely effective," he said. "Every warrior and every family in our ads has volunteered to participate."

At this point, Molino wrote, "Nardizzi offered his phone to Mullen so that he could read a recent text message he received from a veteran's spouse praising the ads and asking when her family might be able to appear in one. Mullen refused to take the phone, so Nardizzi read excerpts from the text." Molino added, "It would be wrong to consider the visual impact of the ads without listening to the narrative because it is routinely positive and talks about what the warrior has been able to achieve despite his or her injuries." Mullen responded that, if that is the message, it isn't coming through. Nardizzi pointed out that this is a population that most charities don't serve well, and that it was important to get the word out so that the public could help support the catastrophically wounded.

"In fact," Nardizzi said, "we have a waiting list of people who want to be in our ads, and we have no intention of discontinuing them. These are real warriors and I'm not going to silence their voices simply to satisfy the Department of Defense."

~

The one area where Mullen seemed not to take issue with WWP was that of Nardizzi's salary. "I don't care about your salary," Mullen said. "It's none of my business. That's between you and your board."

The meeting ended on this note and, Nardizzi thinks, with Mullen unconvinced that the WWP ads did any good, "but that he might have a more difficult time trashing us at cocktail parties now that he has been exposed to the truth."[282]

After reading the essentials of this account, when asked if he could be interviewed about it, Mullen replied simply, "I have nothing else to add."[283]

- **Erick Millette**

Two months after the meeting between Mullen and Nardizzi, Erick Millette joined the Warriors Speak Program at Wounded Warrior Project. When Solider Ride came through Washington, DC in April 2013, Millette was in the audience at the White House when President Obama said, "During two tours in Iraq, Erick survived 17 IED [improvised explosive device] attacks. They left him with the kind of injuries that you can't always see: head trauma, brain injury, PTSD. Erick's military career was cut short but he's taken on a new mission, and that's sharing his story with audiences across the country. He spreads the message that it's okay to talk about these unseen wounds of war. It's okay to seek out help, to seek out support. Erick says that the Wounded Warrior Project literally saved his life, and now through his work he's helping save even more lives. So, Erick, thank you so much."[284]

During the ceremony, a camera panned the audience where Millette could be seen basking, appropriately, in the thanks of a grateful president and, through him, a grateful nation.

Later that year, he told a reporter for WBZ, a Boston television station, "I don't think I'd be sitting here having this conversation or be able to present my story, my troubles or how I overcame them without the Wounded Warrior Project. I was one drink away and one bullet away from suicide just last November, and Wounded Warrior Project pulled me into their program and said *you're not alone, we're going to take care of you*."[285]

The following year, Millette wrote on Facebook, "The words I speak reach so many ears. I often wonder who listens to those words. Tonight I'm reminded of those that do. A few months ago I received a call from a Warrior in hysterics. She only spoke of another Warrior who was on a bridge ready to become another statistic. He was about to become one of 22 veterans a day that take their own life. With the help of Mark Cubbedge and many others at Wounded Warrior Project, we were able to talk him off that bridge. Wounded Warrior Project not only impacted his life, WWP saved his life."[286]

In September 2014—seven months after the retreat at the Broadmoor Hotel—Millette, on a radio interview, spoke glowingly of Project Odyssey, one of Wounded Warrior Project's programs. WWP had recently conducted its annual survey to obtain background information from veterans using WWP's services relating to physical and mental well being, and economic empowerment. Comments from veterans included, "I went to a foreign country and when I came back, this was the foreign country. I am lost and scared and don't know what to do to make it better." And, "Coping with my emotional disconnect has been most difficult." And "I have nothing to do in life that matters." And many more.[287] Specifically, the issue was how veterans, after they return home, deal with having seen their fellow warriors or civilians being wounded or killed. The interviewer noted that almost 80 percent of those surveyed were dealing with one or both of these traumas.

Millette said the best answer to working through the problems is peer support. "I've tried counseling with people who have never been in the military, who have never been in combat, and it was very ineffective." When he went to Project Odyssey in 2012, he interacted with a group of other Iraq and Afghanistan veterans. "It was that week when Wounded Warrior Project not only impacted my life so much, but Wounded Warrior Project clearly saved my life. I should say that before I went there, I was putting a gun in my mouth more than a spoon or a fork. I was drinking so heavily to self-medicate, to get rid of these images, these memories, and I was slowly killing myself, whether it was going to be with a gun or with a bottle. And Wounded Warrior Project took those things away from me in just one week, and turned my life around one hundred eighty degrees because they introduced me to 14 young men who were experiencing the same things, which let me know I wasn't alone." Later, Millette said, "Impacting and changing lives, and saving lives is what we're doing."[288]

Over the next several months, something changed. Millette became bitter and began to work against the interests of WWP. The turnaround was breathtaking.

~

Sometime in 2015, around when he quit his job, Millette began to feel outrage over the cost of the Broadmoor event in February 2014 and the nature of the activities, claiming that the conference was the breaking point that led him to become a whistleblower. That outrage must have come as a surprise to many people who had heard him praise Wounded Warrior Project, including board member Justin Constantine, who attended that conference and said, "Have you ever attended a conference with 450 people super excited about their jobs who just want to keep doing great things for those they support? I just did at the Wounded Warrior Project's annual All-Hands Huddle, and am walking away very proud of the energy every employee puts into taking care of our wounded warriors and their families."[289]

Millette told the *New York Times* that he quit after growing disillusioned about his work with Warrior Speak. "I wasn't speaking anywhere unless I was collecting a check," he said. "They wanted me to say WWP saved my life. Well, they didn't. They just took me to a Red Sox game and on a weekend retreat."[290] This directly contradicted what he said in the WBZ interview a year earlier.

There was more. On his Facebook page in January 2016: "I cannot wait for the day that WWP fails"; on *CBS News* later in January 2016, "I began to see how an organization that rakes in hundreds of millions of dollars a year is not helping my brothers and my sisters"; On WJAX in Jacksonville in March 2016, "They had been lying to the board and lying to donors, to veterans. They've been lying to the American public"; and on *CBS News*, also in March 2016, "It feels good. It really does. And I didn't do it for me. I did it for all the veterans that Wounded Warrior Project claims to serve."

The change of heart might generously be explained by considering that Millette might *never* have had good feelings about Wounded Warrior Project, that he lied to WBZ and, presumably, in an act of honest desperation came clean to the public; that is, Millette could have been the shill he later essentially claimed he had been. That possibility, of course, would raise questions about Millette's integrity and honor, the values most associated with those who have served in the military.

But while we don't know why he made false and contradictory statements,[291] his express purpose seems to have been to harm the organization.

∿

Mike Landrum has a unique insight into Wounded Warrior Project because he advised and coached participants in Warriors Speak, the program where Millette was employed. Organizations, such as Rotary Clubs and other civic groups that wanted to actively support veterans, would call WWP and ask for speakers. During Landrum's three-year tenure, he trained over two-dozen veterans to tell their stories. He says the idea was in part about recruiting others who needed the services of Wounded Warrior Project. "Some of the most important students in the program," he says, referring to those who were being trained to speak publicly, "were mothers and spouses of wounded veterans. They had incredible stories to tell. They served WWP and all the veterans with their speaking skills and their ideas. They were quite impressive."

One extraordinary speaker was a woman named Donna who had suffered sexual abuse from her fellow soldiers. "Active military personnel can be wounded in many ways," Landrum says. "I'm afraid it's much more common than we think. You have to think that if Harvey Weinstein could violate so many, then, with all of the women serving in the military, a lot of them are fending off the men." But this woman speaking, Landrum says, was an example of the work Wounded Warrior Project does. "She was able to tell her story and shine some light on a problem that the rest of the military is pretty hush-hush about."

As for Wounded Warrior Project, he says, "I think it's equivalent to many companies in terms of professionalism and high morale. WWP wanted to be known as the military organization after the military. One of the problems veterans have is that they miss their unit. This group understood that endemically, and they provided a kind of unity for them so that belonging to Wounded Warrior Project was a source of pride for the veterans. The speakers I trained and worked with were extremely proud of their connection to the organization.

"Except for Mr. Millette."

Landrum was aware when Millette was "gung-ho about WWP. That was the training we were doing for him. He should have been proud." Landrum explains the WWP logo, which depicts a soldier carrying a wounded soldier on his back. "Everyone comes into the organization as the soldier being carried. Then, once you get into WWP, you become the carrier." Landrum remembers a speaker in the program named Adam Poppenhouse. "He lost both his legs. He had sticks for legs. He was driving a Stryker, a 40-ton vehicle, when it hit a mine that blew the vehicle off the road and blew him a hundred yards or more out of the vehicle, and took his legs." Despite that, Adam maintained a sense of humor. "In his speeches," Landrum remembers, "he'd begin by standing up and saying, *Hopscotch anyone?* Then he'd say, *I may not have my legs but I can still carry my buddies off the battlefield.* He could say this because he was doing what he was doing, making speeches so others would know what happened and how Wounded Warrior Project could help them."

And this: "Norbert Lara—Norbie to his friends—a company sergeant with an MP company in Bagdad was on patrol in a Humvee one night when an enemy rocket was fired in front of the vehicle. The rocket took his right arm off at the shoulder and continued through the vehicle to also take the right arm of the female lieutenant sitting behind him. Both survived. The lieutenant also became an important person in WWP."

In his talks Norbie would ask his audience, "Have you ever heard someone say, 'I'd give my right arm to know my purpose in life'? Well I did. And I found my purpose at Wounded Warrior Project. So they would all link it back to the logo. It was very moving to work with these people—because they meant it. And the whole organization from top to bottom meant it." Landrum pauses. "Norbie, by the way, is a scratch golfer—hits a drive, with his left, his only, arm over 200 yards."

Landrum's job was to help these men and women tell their story. They were able to move an audience and tell the story of the logo—and find the rest of the veterans, because they're killing themselves at a rate of 22 a day. There are millions of veterans in this country, and there's help for them.

"And that," Landrum says emphatically, "was entirely due to Al Giordano and Steve Nardizzi. They are men of great honor. They have great imagination and terrific organizational skills. They made it apparent to the public how necessary Wounded Warrior Project was. They were filling a role that the government had dropped." Landrum then says, "The Veterans Administration is completely overwhelmed." Another pause. Even so, "In their wisdom," he says, referring to Nardizzi and Giordano, "they knew they had to work out a way to work with the Veterans Administration. And they did."

Landrum remembers how the Wounded Warrior Law, signed into law by President Bush in 2005, came about. "Most moving to me is the story of two guys in Walter Reed Hospital. One of them is on the phone with his grandmother, and he's saying to her, '*I wish I had gotten killed because then there would be a $500,000 insurance policy for my family. As it stands now, my wife has had to give up her job to come here to Walter Reed to* *help nurse me, and she's not going to be able to work or earn anymore. And there's no insurance."* Ryan Kelly, the man's roommate, overheard that call, and, because of the man's predicament, he later worked with Wounded Warrior Project to help create and then pass legislation into law where the wounded, not just the deceased, can have insurance. "That phone call," says Landrum, "was the stimulus."

～

Landrum's observations—and those of thousands of others—of the good work and meaning of Wounded Warrior Project sharply contrast with the story Erick Millette began to tell. He had been a part of the Warriors Speak program before he became inexplicably disgruntled, although there might have been an early hint of what was to come. "He was about the weakest in the class," Landrum says. "I thought this guy was not going to be a speaker. He was a troublemaker and a malcontent. A complainer; always complaining."[292]

Despite his claims that the Broadmoor event led him to become a whistleblower, Millette remained employed at WWP for another year, and even pursued other positions within the organization. In fact, he wrote to Maryanne Scales, the Process and Personnel Manager at WWP, "I wanted to reach out to you to see if we were doing Operation Outreach again this year? If we are I would like to volunteer my time with it. I have a few ideas I would love to share with you to try and get the staff more involved."[293]

- **Richard Jones**

During the month that followed the February 2013 meeting with Admiral Michael Mullen and Steve Nardizzi, Richard Jones, who was a senior executive at CBS, began his service on the Wounded Warrior Project board. According to Nardizzi, Jones approached him about becoming a board member.

Jones was the person Peter Honerkamp was upset about in his September 2016 meeting with Tony Odierno.

In a few of the *CBS News* reports about Wounded Warrior Project, the announcers pointed this out: "Full disclosure, a CBS Corporate executive serves on that board."[294] Perhaps the disclosures would have been more full had they identified Jones, whose position at CBS was Executive Vice President, General Tax Counsel, and Chief Veteran Officer, and that his position on the WWP board was chairman of the audit committee, in which capacity he oversaw the completion of the audited financial report and the 990, which was an important and controversial subject in the CBS story.

Gayle King, the co-host of *CBS Morning News,* received an email from a top advisor to CBS, which said, "The deputy General Counsel, chief tax attorney, AND chief veteran officer (a corporate officer) of CBS is one of only six board members of WWP. HE is THE board member specifically who signs off on audit and organization finances and expenditures and who was never called by CBS reporters prior to the story airing."[295]

That's right: one of the pillars of CBS's scathing critique was aimed at a function of the operation that one of the network's own senior executives was overseeing in his capacity as a board member at Wounded Warrior Project.

∿

Just prior to Jones coming to WWP, and just a week after that meeting between Nardizzi and Mullen, CBS ran a public service announcement on behalf of WWP during the Super Bowl, a close game in which the Baltimore Ravens beat the San Francisco 49ers. The ad was short but effective: "Without the sacrifice of our military and their families, there'd be no Super Bowl. Let's unite to show our appreciation. Text $10 to Wounded Warrior Project that shows our heroes we stand by them, as they stand by us. CBS cares."

As it happens, Jones also served on the boards of both Dixon Center for Military and Veterans Services and the Institute for Veterans and Military Families. That is, in what was surely a conflict of interest, Jones served on the boards of two organizations that openly disliked WWP, while at the same time serving on the board of WWP. This raises the question of why Jones came to be accepted on the WWP board, and why he wanted to be on the WWP board. Jones's service on the Dixon Center board began in

January 2010 and his service on the IVMF board began in January 2011; his board service at WWP began in March 2013.

When WWP board members interviewed him, Jones did not fully disclose his close relationships with the two other organizations. Some were not pleased when they learned this afterward. It was relevant information that would have factored into their decision. But it is also true that the board did not perform its own due diligence. After all, it was all right there on his publicly accessible LinkedIn profile. Jones's connections to the other charities went undisclosed for some time and by the time the allegations were made he had risen to a position of substantial authority on the board.

John Loosen, who served on the board for nine years, from 2006 through 2014, said, "The board at the time vetted all of the applicants for board openings, and I know we vetted him. At the time, as I recall, we all thought this is great. What an asset he would be to the board given his background as an attorney and as an accountant. Did we do our job vetting him properly? I don't know. What role did he have in the CBS story? If he did, we didn't do our due diligence."

If *CBS News* really had all those urgent and controversial questions about WWP's finances, as was reported, one might wonder why someone was unable to simply ask Jones what was going on. The stock answer to that question is that the news division and the corporate division don't charge into each other's territory, but that's a weak response in this case, especially since a central element of the story hinged on factual information—found on WWP's IRS Form 990, the completion of which Jones oversaw. It would have informed, not suppressed or prejudiced, the story.

CBS claimed that WWP denied repeated requests for comment from Nardizzi. This is not true. In a letter written the day after the network aired the first story, WWP said, "We are outraged to see that CBS chose to run the story despite our ongoing efforts to set the record straight. We can only deduce that CBS willfully set aside the information WWP provided in favor of the false statements made by a handful of former, disgruntled employees." WWP then accused CBS of "willfully" setting aside important information provided by WWP and of failing to contact the charity through readily available channels. "At a minimum," it said, "prior to running the story, CBS could have contacted one of its own senior executives . . . by calling him at extension 2978. You are fully aware that Mr. Jones is a Wounded Warrior Project board member and Wounded Warrior Project's audit committee chair, and has the ability and insight to provide you with accurate and truthful information regarding Wounded Warrior Project's financial documents."

The letter demanded that "CBS immediately correct the record, issue a retraction of the false statements, and issue an apology to the public and the tens of thousands of wounded veterans and their families who have been offended by these false statements."[296]

That did not happen.

Nor, oddly, did the letter remain on WWP's website for very long. It was as if WWP had second thoughts and wanted, for some reason, to placate CBS.

Also, it seems odd that Jones, as the chair of WWP's audit committee, didn't come to the rescue when the organization was criticized for its accounting procedures. After all, he oversaw the process and his training and experience made him an expert—far more of one than anybody who worked at a charity watchdog group—in the area of financial accountability.

In addition to questions concerning his motivation to become a WWP board member and his conflict of interest as the CBS story developed, Jones also had a conflict in its aftermath. He actively participated in the interviews of employees Simpson Thacher conducted concerning the media stories; that is, he was a party to investigating his own actions. "Should he have recused himself of any vote on Steve and Al?" asked a former board member. "I think at a minimum, yes, he should have recused himself."

This conflict is why Al Giordano said that Jones should not even have been in the room as the board chair informed him he was being fired.

One former board member implored Tony Odierno to ensure that the financial review would be impartial. "I think you need to assure it is indeed independent. We all know how 'independent' reviews can be tailored to the client's desired outcome. You get someone that is beyond reproach and has not worked for WWP in the past."[297] The board member was assured the review would be impartial, even though Richard Jones, hardly an impartial player in the drama, effectively oversaw the review.

Another former board member, who spoke on the condition of anonymity, asked this: "Should he have resigned?" Probably. I think if he had any real high standards of ethics, when CBS was doing the research on this he should have resigned at that time. If it would have been me, I would have resigned—particularly if I knew what CBS was doing. In my mind, CBS made a decision and they were setting out to prove what they wanted to prove so that they could be justified in doing the story. The producer of CBS contacted me several times. She wanted to have a call with me after the story aired and I stiff bombed her a few times. I never did talk to her because they came out with the news story before I had a chance to talk to anybody."

Yet another former board member, who also spoke on the condition of anonymity, said, "Richard Jones seems to be the key person in this whole story."

Rebuked for Success

- ### The Board Evaluates

A few former board members said they thought the current board might have had issues with Steve Nardizzi.[298]

The most prominent complaint was that he was moving too fast and not communicating well with the board. "There was considerable dissatisfaction with Nardizzi well before the CBS and *New York Times* stories," according to at least one person familiar with matter. The gist was that there was a lot going on at Wounded Warrior Project and that Nardizzi needed to do a better job of consulting with the board.

Another issue was that neither Nardizzi nor Giordano had signed his employment contract. One person said that Nardizzi felt that, by not signing, the board had more to lose than he did. Basically, according to another person, the board felt that Nardizzi wanted, "arrogantly," to be in a position to leave whenever he wanted and to take the top staff with him. John Loosen, the former board member, said, "It was our responsibility. Nardizzi and Giordano were our employees, and we needed both to sign their employment contract or suffer the consequences. But it was not hard to fix, and the board and I should take responsibility for that. Not signing the employment contract was negligent, Loosen admits, "but this was not considered a priority to me based on the continuous and rapid objectives they both presented to us for providing ingenious ways to better serve those in need. They were both always on the mark in implementing new programs that we supported almost always. The problems were small compared to the benefits Steve and Al brought to WWP. We always doubted Steve with his big ideas, but we eventually did almost everything he wanted, and it was always successful."[299] Still, the contract issue did not get resolved.

There were those on the board who thought, even though there was no evidence, that Wounded Warrior Project was "sucking up" all the veterans' money; that is, as others had alleged, the success of the ads was detrimental to other organizations that were not raising much money. Still, WWP was making grants to some of those organizations that were providing services that WWP didn't. It was said, however, "Nardizzi didn't like this and tried to sabotage the effort."

Some board members felt that since Nardizzi "had a string of successes," as he did over the years, that "it's easy to think it's all about you, and not about the organization." One said, "Most of the board felt that the organization was growing too fast."

The board decided to hold a meeting in March to discuss Nardizzi and Giordano's leadership. Even then, though—this was prior to the devastating news reports of late January 2016—there was no discussion of firing either of the two men. That meeting, however, never took place.

To be clear, a nonprofit board has every right to hire and fire its executive director, as well as other senior leadership, and, lacking a contract that says otherwise, it doesn't need a reason. Regardless of the real damage the firings created and the evidence that more was at work than an honest assessment of the two men's abilities, the WWP board was legally within its rights.

~

As for the organization's growth and whether the board bought into it, and how the board felt he was brash in pushing forward, Nardizzi says, "You have to remember that the board had the final say on the budget. During the growth years" before he was fired, "we were trying to get ahead of a curve with warriors who needed help. Our revenue would come in, always over projection, and I'd explain how I'd like to spend that money on new programs." On that, Nardizzi says, "I never heard a peep from anyone; no suggestion that we didn't want to grow. There was never a dynamic of push-pull where I'm running roughshod over the board on growth."

As far as being against helping other charities, Nardizzi adamantly disagrees. "That's the first I heard of this. To be clear, I came up with the idea of making grants to other organizations. In fact, I had to fight the board to get them to start a grant program."

Nardizzi explained how two programs—the Independence Program and the Long-Term Support Trust—came into being where there was much "healthy discussion," as he characterized it. This was huge and involved raising an additional half billion dollars, with the goal of raising a billion dollars to help warriors and their caregivers over a period of many decades. "That's a monumental task and we had many meetings during and between several board meetings on whether or not we could accomplish it." He described how the money would be raised and the types of services that would be offered. "I gave the board aggregate numbers and compelling stories about the gaps in services." By "gaps in services," Nardizzi meant the services the VA was not providing or not providing robustly for veterans.

To launch the Warrior Care Network—a partnership with leading academic medical centers that connect warriors and their families with world-class, evidence-based mental health care—Nardizzi described an intricate process by which research would be conducted, reports would be issued, discussions would take place, and then all those steps would be repeated and refined.

"By the time a finished proposal was ready to be presented, the cumulative result of a collaborative, collegial process," Nardizzi says, "there were still some board members with concerns." One was Tony Principi, a former secretary of the VA, who wondered whether WWP would be encouraging the VA to abdicate its responsibilities. "He thought one of the VA's primary responsibilities was providing health care, and that we should not supplant that. We could do clinical work, yes, but more? He wondered if we should be undertaking so much, or whether we should push back to have the VA do more. As I say, healthy dialogue." In the end, the program was established, with the board agreeing because, even though health care is the job of the VA, the VA wasn't doing enough.

Another concern was whether hospitals that would be part of the WWP network would double bill: they could bill the VA, get reimbursement, and then bill WWP. "That was a very fair concern," says Nardizzi. "So we ended up revising the project plan to include specific protections that would permit WWP to audit the hospitals to ensure that our funds were being used for patients who weren't getting reimbursed through the VA. It was another good dialogue." Nardizzi says he also instituted measures to confirm effectiveness and efficiency.

Finally, regarding the complaints about growing too fast, Nardizzi said, "Ironically, after we budgeted for the Warrior Care Network, I wanted to grow *less* fast." It was the first time that he went to the board to not approve a massive increase in budget and to not plan for a massive increase in revenue because he thought WWP needed a year to level set and catch up on staffing to operate the programs well. "I actually had to push the idea," he says, "that we not grow as quickly." He says "some board members said that they thought we were growing too fast and that I was pursuing growth they weren't aligned with, but I only heard of these fabricated concerns after I was fired. No board member ever suggested that we should grow less quickly. If they were truly unhappy with the pace of growth, why make more growth an annual goal for me?"[300]

As for the meeting scheduled for later in March, Nardizzi was unaware that anyone was unhappy and was told the meeting would involve a normal agenda. "I mean, when I was reviewed, the whole board clapped—they were happy with my performance."[301]

~

There is a "they said-he said" feel to these differences, but the performance review Nardizzi received just a few months before he was fired provides tangible evidence of what the board really felt about Nardizzi. An outside, professional firm guided the process with the board. The review covered several priority goals and an assessment of his core leadership competencies.

As for the competencies, not one board member rated Nardizzi below "highly successful" or "successful." The majority of scores were at the highest level. As for the priority goals, almost all the ratings went the same way. In fact, in one category—participation in the Independence Program—Nardizzi discovered that he rated himself below what the board rated him. While he wasn't perfect, he was not delusional either. "If you recall," he says, " some of the media reports included allegations from disgruntled employees suggesting we 'padded' our participation numbers or sacrificed quality service to generate numbers. As you can see, I didn't even do that when it impacted my own evaluation and bonus."[302]

Board comments on the goal of increasing job placements included, "Congratulations—nothing is more rewarding to a warrior than a job. I hope this program gains much more momentum going forward." On establishing strategic direction, a typical board comment was, "Steve is an excellent leader of WWP." In the category of passion and results, one board member said, "I would rank Steve a number higher than his rating from what I see and observe." On revenue growth, a typical comment was, "The fundraising continues to be amazing."[303]

Al Giordano adds, "The board held us accountable for revenue growth in our annual evaluations. Roger Campbell—a long-term board member and a former compliance officer on Wall Street, whose wife has worked for VA helping veterans for over twenty years—was very frequently heard to say this about WWP: 'It's a great American success story.'"[304]

As for Nardizzi's evaluation on "Board Relations," a typical board-member comment was, "I am very satisfied with my relationship with Steve and his team, as well as with all of the Board members."

The board felt similarly about Giordano. He too was evaluated at the same time on essentially the same criteria as Nardizzi was, and the vast majority of the board agreed that Giordano had met the target goals. Comments were favorable and supportive: "Al is a good people person and networker"; "Al has demonstrated to me clear and unwavering courage";

"Al has demonstrated that he is not afraid to make the call"; "I think this is very good on all fronts"; "Al and team did an outstanding job this year, and year over year. Given the need, I hope they continue to grow over 20 percent per year."

Giordano's entire review is read with this overt affirmation.[305]

There was no brew of dissatisfaction in the reviews. In fact, the board authorized substantial bonuses for Nardizzi and Giordano.

• Simpson Thacher Evaluates

In late 2011, four years before the Wounded Warrior Project board hired Simpson Thacher & Bartlett to review its financial activities, another non-profit, the William J. Clinton Foundation, hired the same firm to conduct a review of the foundation's governance and relationships with its affiliates.[306] Almost everyone interviewed, according to the report, "stressed the need for a stronger board and stronger management; stressed the need for the board and the managers to meet, lead and manage; called for strategic planning; called for sustainability planning; and called on the Foundation to develop the infrastructure of a best-in-class charity." Those interviewed rated the effectiveness and efficiency of the foundation's operations in the range of seven to eight, but those same people rated the efficiency of the foundation itself far lower, between one and four.

The report, which was 22 pages long, found several problems. They included the management structure and favoritism. "The current Foundation Board is very small and is comprised solely of 'insiders,'" it said.

Also, while the foundation had a conflict-of-interest policy—actually two, one for directors, officers and key employees, and another for other employees—the report noted, "It appears that neither policy has been implemented, and the Board Conflict Policy may need revision to address the issues raised by interviewees. That is, it appears that conflicts are not timely disclosed. In addition, when staff becomes aware of conflicts, they are unsure how to raise and clear these conflicts. Finally, Board members do not appear to be following the policy when they become aware of conflicts."

In the area of financial oversight, the report stated, "Numerous interviewees commented that they believe that the Board needs to take a more active role in overseeing and managing the Foundation and its finances, programs, and activities."

As for transparency, an important component, both from a management perspective and an ethical one at a nonprofit, the report said, "Numerous interviewees reported confusion and a lack of transparency between Clinton Foundation roles and responsibilities and outside roles and responsibilities of a variety of individuals. Interviewees also mentioned instances in which gifts and other payments received by staff had not been properly disclosed."[307]

Although the report was written in bland corporate prose, the essence was a damning operational indictment for an organization with $187 million in assets and unparalleled international influence.

One person, Charles Ortel, a Wall Street analyst who often publicly weighs in on philanthropy issues—and, it should be noted, an unrelenting critic of Hillary Clinton—said of the Clinton Foundation's activities, "This was bright line illegal. This is a rogue charity that was out of control for years. And the trustees elected to not correct them. We're not talking about people with no knowledge of the laws. These are people who can't claim ignorance."[308]

The Simpson Thacher report was conducted before Hillary Clinton was a presidential candidate, and thus before the severe pay-for-play and influence peddling allegations began to dog her campaign. As one political commentator said about the foundation in the late stages of the campaign, "What worries me is that many—but not all—in my business are spending so much time shaming Trump voters, that they seem to have forgotten some important features of political corruption: what it is, what it looks like, what it sounds like and what it smells like. Particularly when it comes to Mrs. Clinton, her husband Bill, and the pungency of the influence-peddling scandal involving the multibillion-dollar Clinton Foundation."[309]

But even those who think that comment, as well as those of Charles Ortel, represents only conservative stridency against a Democrat, the concern was real, as well as broad and measured. After acknowledging that the

Clinton Foundation broke no laws, Richard Painter, the former chief White House ethics lawyer for President George W. Bush, wrote for the *New York Times*, "The problem is that it does not matter that no laws were broken, or that the Clinton Foundation is principally about doing good deeds. It does not matter that favoritism is inescapable in the federal government and that the Clinton Foundation stories are really nothing new. The appearances surrounding the foundation are problematic, and it is and will be an albatross around Mrs. Clinton's neck."[310]

Now, let's juxtapose that with Simpson Thacher's evaluation of Wounded Warrior Project.

~

The first thing to note about the Simpson Thacher report on Wounded Warrior Project is that it was, at the board's request, not delivered in a written format. The reason given was that it is not typical for such a report to be written, that an oral accounting was all that was needed. But it isn't typical. After all, if an organization with assets of $187 million was important enough to warrant 22 written and publicly accessible pages, it would seem logical to think that an organization with assets of over $300 million, which affects the lives of over 100,000 veterans and their families, would merit more than the scant 385 words in the oral summary the WWP board released on March 10, 2016, when, at the same time, it also announced that its two top executives had been fired.

But that was just the first signal that things about the decision weren't going to add up. Thanks to the Grassley report, released over a year after the firings, we know that, in response to Grassley's earlier inquiries, the attorneys at Simpson Thacher actually did provide a 10-page written letter describing their findings at WWP. It was just never made public until Grassley included it in his own report.

Compared to the picture painted of the Clinton Foundation, WWP looked pretty good.

"WWP performs substantial services in furtherance of its mission," wrote Simpson Thacher. "The claim that WWP does not serve warriors and that 'warriors call us; we don't call warriors' is false." Furthermore,

Simpson Thacher said, "Key aspects of the January 2016 media reports are demonstrably false or exaggerated," and confirmed that the claim of a $3 million All-Hands Huddle, the one at the Broadmoor in Colorado, was not true. It also confirmed that conference spending was "mischaracterized," as more than 90 percent of those expenses was related to programming.

As for the issue of paying for first-class transportation, after examining travel information for the five-and-a-half year period between August 3, 2010 and March 23, 2016, Simpson Thacher wrote, "A very small percentage of paid domestic flights were booked in first class and domestic business class. The overwhelming majority of these flights have been in economy class. Less than one percent of the total number of these flights appears to have been for travel by employees. Of 406 first class flights," it noted, "138 appear to have been booked for warriors or their caregivers, as warriors sometimes require first-class travel to accommodate physical disabilities." Furthermore, the vast majority within that one percent involved complimentary upgrades.

The accounting also criticized the unfair assessment from Charity Navigator, which CBS News used to launch its story. "The difference between WWP's 80 percent figure for the portion of donations spent on programming and Charity Navigator's 60 percent figure is largely attributable to Charity Navigator's disregard of recognized joint cost allocation principles." It then described how a third-party contractor, Gary Ellis, performed a detailed, line-by-line analysis of the content of the organization's emails, direct mail pieces and Direct Response Television scripts. "Overall," the report said, "we found that the joint cost allocation process was transparent, well-documented and fully disclosed. Furthermore, we did not find any indication of bad faith, either on the part of WWP or Mr. Ellis, and Mr. Ellis informed us during his interview that he has never been pressured by anyone at WWP to deliver certain results in his cost allocation."[311]

It should be noted that a number of highly regarded charities, including Planned Parenthood, Food for the Poor, the NRA Foundation, World Vision, the Natural Resources Defense Council, and the United States Olympic Committee, along with many others, have reported jointly allocated expenses.[312]

One of the criticisms of WWP was that Steve Nardizzi was paid too much money. In 2014 he was paid $496,415. *CBS News* reported that it was "in line with similar-sized charities, but former employees told us they thought it was too much."[313] Simpson Thacher wrote, "Based on data from independent executive compensation studies, WWP's senior executive compensation is not out of line with acceptable practices in the nonprofit space. In fact, Nardizzi's salary was between the median and the 75th percentile of chief executive officers at comparable charities."

A dart thrown with a blindfold can be thrown on any 990 and the results would be similar at many charities. One such dart might land on, say, Vassar College. In 2015 the president of Vassar, Katherine Bond Hill, earned approximately $1.9 million—four times as much as Nardizzi. Vassar's operating budget was $250 million, about two thirds of what it took to run Wounded Warrior Project. Its fundraising totaled approximately $22 million, while WWP raised close to $400 million. Vassar's fundraising budget that year was about $10 million, an efficiency percentage well below that of Wounded Warrior Project's fundraising efficiency.[314] No one has complained about Vassar's financials, not even CBS's Chip Reid, an alumnus.

At its core, the Simpson Thacher report recommended simply that WWP improve its travel and spending policies, reevaluate conference locales, but with no specific suggestions, and strengthen the processes related to joint cost allocation. The truth is that there's not an organization in the world—for-profit or nonprofit—that couldn't improve at least some of its operations. To be told that travel, spending, or accounting policies should be tightened is pretty milquetoast when it comes to reviews like this.

~

Two Simpson Thacher observations were mildly critical. "WWP's general approach to policies and procedures," the report said, "has become inadequate for an organization of its current size. While WWP had some written policies, WWP's governing philosophy was often to trust employees to act reasonably, responsibly and professionally. The lack of a full complement of easily understandable written policies was no longer appropriate for an organization of WWP's size and exposes the organization to risk."

The other less-than-positive observation related to conferences. "Whatever the operational and strategic value of bringing all employees together once a year, the overall and per-person costs of All-Hands Huddles has substantially increased over the last five years." This came after, the report conceded, "Most employees insisted that these events were very important for team building and strategic development and for enabling employees across the country to get together face-to-face. The WWP leadership also told us that discontinuing the events would significantly impact the organization by curtailing strategic planning and development efforts."

Simpson Thacher said it "did not see evidence of any fraud, embezzlement, or misappropriation of funds."

It also said, "There is ample basis"—although none was shown—"to terminate Messrs. Nardizzi and Giordano. During the course of our review, we encountered instances in which Messrs. Nardizzi and Giordano showed"—although none was produced—"poor judgment and professionalism, particularly given WWP's mission."

~

Steve Nardizzi is convinced that the board directed Simpson Thacher's conclusion, that the decision to fire him and Al Giordano was made well before the review was completed, and that the comments about the two men's failings were a dishonest attempt at retrofitting.

"How could it have been otherwise?" Nardizzi wonders while pondering the sequence of events. "Their first interview with me, conducted in the first week of February 2016, was filled with broad-based questions. The second interview, conducted in the second half of February, was filled with fishing-expedition questions, with the most bizarre allegations. For example, they asked if I had an apartment in New York paid for by WWP." Simpson Thacher also wanted to know how often Nardizzi traveled to New York City, if any of that travel was personal and, if so, whether Wounded Warrior Project paid for any of it. "Ninety five percent of my travel to New York was on business—many of my meetings with board members were there—and the records showed that I personally paid for the other five percent," Nardizzi said. "This was weird because they already had access to all my financial records."

That first interview took place before *CBS News* ran its damaging report, on March 3, 2016, about the board's expenses. The second interview took place after. Nardizzi concludes that the more pointed, almost antagonistic questions in that second interview were born of board members telling Simpson Thacher they had already decided to fire him and needed evidence to back it up. "Well," says Nardizzi, "they didn't get anything." An outside law firm, Arnold & Porter Kaye Scholer LLP, which was engaged by WWP, reviewed what went to Simpson Thacher and, according to Nardizzi, the attorneys said, "We often do the types of assessments that Simpson Thacher is doing, and we see no major problems, nothing of any concern."

Nardizzi points out that Simpson Thacher's only criticism of his and Giordano's work was that some policies, procedures and controls hadn't kept pace with the rapid growth and were in need of strengthening. "In fact, our policies had grown exponentially over the years, and they were reviewed by outside auditors, outside law firms, in-house council, and our in-house accounting staff—and, of course, the board. From a policies and procedures standpoint, we were solid."

Nardizzi also cited the Simpson Thacher review of the Clinton Foundation. "They found very detailed and challenging conflicts of interest for everyone from board members to senior staff, and Simpson Thacher did not recommend terminating anyone. But, in our case, that minor tweaks to a travel policy were needed, they somehow came to the conclusion that the organization that I had grown from $18 million a year to almost $400 million, with almost a hundred thousand warriors being helped—and never even a whiff of malfeasance—I needed to go."

Nardizzi doesn't think that anyone at the Clinton Foundation necessarily should have been fired, but he wonders about the disparity. "The things they found in the Clinton report," he says—"specific allegations, including conflicts of interest—were much more egregious than anything that's been remotely suggested that went on at Wounded Warrior Project. Simpson Thacher came to the conclusion the board told them to come to."[315]

Al Giordano says, "Simpson Thacher examined more than $1.2 billion of expenses covering a period of six years—approximately one and a quarter billion dollars with nothing out of place. They couldn't find *one penny* that was misspent."[316] Why six years? That was the period of time defined by the statute of limitations in Florida after which no legal action could be taken for fraudulent financial misconduct. Presumably, however, given that there was nothing wrong in the financial records of what was examined, there would be no reason to think anything amiss took place earlier either. It would be unlikely that any other charity, especially one the size of Wounded Warrior Project, would emerge wholly unscathed from such a granular financial audit that covered the same amount of time.

- **The Nexus**

There was a curious nexus: Admiral Michael Mullen (someone close to the government), the Dixon Center and IVMF (charities hostile to WWP), *CBS News* (the media), and the influential Richard Jones (a WWP board member and a senior executive at CBS).

Dave Philipps of the *New York Times* initiated work for a story, but, it appears Jones got wind of it and– as when the timer for an already-built bomb's detonator is activated—he led his company's news division to accomplish a goal that aligned with that of organizations and people who simply didn't like the successes of Wounded Warrior Project. Then, as the allegations created doubts, the board caved. Philipps, when he realized the tack *CBS News* was taking—a much more salacious one than in his originally planned thesis—decided to play out the same slant.

CBS reported some allegations that were untrue and others that were misleading. The reporting led to an investigation. The expectation was that much wrongdoing would be found. But nothing was.

While *CBS News* chose to highlight what it thought was a pattern of thriftless spending decisions made by WWP's senior staff, the Simpson Thacher investigation not only found no misspending on the part of the staff, it did find—and this was not made public—that the board spent a lot of money on itself. "The highest expenditures we ever had," says Al Giordano," were board expenditures. I'm not saying they were flagrant or out of bounds, but the highest booze bills were at board meetings. The highest-cost hotels we used as an organization were at board meetings."[317] CBS had to try to cover its tracks, which led to its March 3, 2016 report on board spending. It was after this became known that the tone of Simpson Thacher's questions for Nardizzi and Giordano became antagonistic.

Certainly, over a period of six years, something would be found to incriminate Nardizzi and Giordano. Right? Having aired its reports, *CBS News* now had a major interest in finding perfidy at WWP: the credibility for its decision to highlight problems at the organization was at stake. But an exhaustive investigation found nothing. If the thinking is that Richard Jones pulled the strings to get *CBS News* interested enough to do a story, it's likely that he then began to feel some heat from his employer. Something had to be found, or else he had just sent a highly regarded news organization down an embarrassing rabbit hole. And why?

The available evidence points to the nexus.

The writing was on the wall for Steve Nardizzi and Al Giordano for a long time before they were fired.

CHAPTER 6

BOLD PERSPECTIVES

NO ONE SPEECH, ARTICLE, PAPER, or, even, book can address all the challenges to be found in the nonprofit sector or those that concern donors. The sector is too unwieldy. In it reside many causes: education, arts and culture, the environment, animal protection, human services, foreign aid, and religion, as well as hundreds of their subsets. It's as if the nonprofit sector isn't even a discrete idea, so vast is its reach. Even though we call it society's third sector, in many ways the activities of charity bleed into business and government activities. Think how the American Civil Liberties Union or the National Rifle Association affects our discussion and policies in government. Think of people who claim that if only business principles were transported into the boardrooms of charities more problems could be solved; let the free market drive the research into a cure for cancer and cancer would be cured. Or so the thinking goes. Furthermore, the ideals charities espouse often contradict one another. Two examples, of thousands: Planned Parenthood and National Right to Life pursue opposite agendas; The National Rifle Association and the Brady Campaign to Prevent Violence pursue opposite agendas.

Activities and policies outside of the charitable world influence how we view the role of charities, and activities and policies within the charitable world make the sector itself difficult to fully understand.

∼

It's not a stretch to think that there is not one human being alive in the United States today who has not been positively affected by charity. Born in a hospital? Occupied a bed at a homeless shelter? Attended a house of worship? Played at camp? Boy Scout? Girl Scout? Taken home a pet from the local animal shelter? Played basketball at the local Y? Gone to college? Listened to a story on NPR? Watched a program on PBS? Visited a museum? Thought of committing suicide and called a hotline? Learned how to shoot a gun? Walked in a park? Breathed clean air? Gone fishing? Returned from war? We kid ourselves if we think we're only bystanders or donors, and not recipients.

The organizations that perform the work of bettering society are of many sizes. Some have revenues of hundreds of dollars, or less, while others generate billions. Some are run by volunteers who are paid nothing, while others are run by professionals who are paid millions. Some can hardly scrape up the funds for a computer, while others rival the technological capacity of our most sophisticated for-profit companies. The marketing programs of some are at their best when a friend tells a friend, while others show up in an ad during the Super Bowl.

According to the World Bank, if the global nonprofit sector were a country, it would have the sixteenth largest economy in the world. In the United States, the nonprofit sector contributed $878 billion to the economy in 2012, or about 5.4 percent of our nation's GDP.[318]

How can something of that diversity and size be captured into a single idea? The only thing that the more than one million charities in the United States have in common is that none of them has a shareholder. No one has purchased the right to own a piece of the revenues and capital growth of the organization. That's because, in a very real manner of speaking, the organization is owned by all of us. Instead of shareholders, the public owns the activities of a charity. And the public entrusts those activities to trustees, today's momentary guardians of the future. Thus, one way to at least begin to capture the place charities have in today's society is to look through the prism of public accountability. Another is to look more granularly, at the charity's mission.

The public is more curious—and skeptical—than ever before, which has led to a growing number of questions about the role, management and governance of nonprofits. This in turn has led to greater criticism. If we're not careful, the criticism will morph, particularly for those uneducated about charities, into cynicism: *Just one more overpaid executive frivolously spending too much when people in need go wanting.* Enough of that, and it may seem as though there's really no place for organizations that say they do the work of angels, but don't. Enough of that, and some people might ask why charities even exist.

~

One of the more contentious problems facing charities today is their relationship with the government. To get a sense of the tension and its origins, we might benefit by reaching back to George Washington. It could be argued that Washington didn't want charities to exert much influence on public policy. In his Farewell Address, written in a letter to the public in 1796, he said, "The very idea of the power and the right of the people to establish government presupposes the duty of every individual to obey the established government. All obstructions to the execution of the laws, all combinations and associations, under whatever plausible character, with the real design to direct, control, counteract, or awe the regular deliberation and action of the constituted authorities, are destructive of this fundamental principle, and of fatal tendency." By "associations," Washington meant it the way Tocqueville did—the kind of organizations that we today call charities.

Even though the vast numbers of people who work at charities think of themselves as bursting with plausible character, Washington still wouldn't give them license to interfere with the government's work.

But while Washington saw the dangers of associations to be that their agendas had the potential to contradict the will of the people, as voiced through legislation passed by their representatives in Congress, in today's world another, competing concern has developed: federal, state and local governments are pressured to reduce their funding of charities. If it were not for the lack of adequate support from the Veterans Administration, there would be no need for a Wounded Warrior Project, or any other association designed to help veterans. (Of course, whether it is the government's job to provide for veterans—or to engage in any of the numerous other social causes the government has supported in the past—is a separate, deeply divisive question.) Washington's plea came at a time when the government wasn't involved in any such matters. What persists, and grows, is the tension created when the goals of charities are expanding at a time when many people want government to shrink.

The juxtaposition between that and the concern that charities are usurping the role of government policy, as expressed by the citizenry, puts the charitable world in a tenuous, confusing place.

~

In that space of tenuousness and confusion are many challenges. Dark money is one. Dark money is money given to nonprofit organizations, primarily those defined in section 501(c)(4) of the Internal Revenue Code, that can receive unlimited donations to influence elections. A key component of that support is that donations are almost always anonymous. Over the past several years, dark money has grown dramatically. The Center for Responsive Politics reports that "spending by organizations that do not disclose their donors has increased from less than $5.2 million in 2006 to well over $300 million in the 2012 presidential cycle and more than $174 million in the 2014 midterms."[319] While this may not seem like a direct challenge to the nonprofit sector, it is a challenge to our democracy—money, and not a majority of human voices and ideas, determine our government's priorities—and when people begin in earnest to correct the problem, they may very well look to throw the baby (nonprofits) out with the bathwater (dark money).

Challenges to the nonprofit world also come from places other than the government. The donating public is getting more concerned about where the money goes and how it is spent. From the relatively small donations to the Red Cross in the immediate aftermath of 9/11 to a multi-million dollar donation to Princeton University, charities are experiencing donor resentment when they don't do as the donors wanted and as the charities said they would do. Running a fundraising operation at a charity today involves more than accepting the money; it's also about making sure donors are kept abreast of how their money is being used, and that it is used correctly. Attention to this matter will become more important as wealthy donors, with their ever-larger gifts, make up the lion's share of all donation amounts. As a percentage, less philanthropy is coming from small gifts, and, frankly, large charities, which get most of the large donations, are putting smaller charities at risk. As Marc Gunther wrote in *Vox* in 2017, "You can think of this as the nonprofit sector's inequality problem. The rich get richer: Well-established, brand-name organizations see spikes in donations, especially during crises. Smaller groups, including those that are deemed to be more effective than their better-known peers, and especially those serving the extreme poor, are left to muddle along. The upshot is that charitable giving doesn't do nearly as much good as it could."[320]

Speaking of poor charities, one in eight community-based organizations—small charities that work to improve the social well being of people in their neighborhoods—are insolvent; this, even though, according to a report conducted by the Nonprofit Alliance, "The human services sector impacts the lives of an estimated one in every five Americans; human services CBOs [community-based organizations] employ more than three million Americans and generate in excess of $200 billion per year in economic activity."[321] It is not a stretch to think that thousands of charities in other sectors are also in bad enough financial shape to be declared structurally insolvent.

With pressure from government, pressure from wealthy donors, small charities that will run out of money, and a changing public perspective in what charities do and how they report on their work, it is quite possible that in the next generation the charitable landscape will be far different from what it is today.

～

While the utter simplicity of the methodologies employed by organizations that purport to evaluate charities fails the public, the question not only remains but is placed into sharp relief: How can we better understand the value of a charity? It is the responsibility of us all to better understand what organizations do and how they affect society. It stands to reason that if people are going to give away money, they will have an intense interest in making certain it is used well.

Following are the perspectives of five people who have thought extensively about the role and value of charities. Theirs are not the only, or perhaps even the best, views on the question, but they are insightful, as well thought provoking, and should be included in a larger discussion about society's plight as we await the arrival of the next generation.

- **Thomas Brown: Specificity of Ambition**

The world of nonprofits is fundamentally changing. Given the de-democratization of philanthropy—fewer donors responsible for more of the philanthropic take[322]—given the modern donor's need to see change in his or her lifetime, and given the growing drive for accountability at nonprofits, charities need to change the way they interact with society: expectations need to be set and then met.

Thomas Brown, who advises businesses and families on important matters, including on their philanthropy, uses a different vernacular from that of most fundraisers and other charity executives when he speaks of goals. "All business happens in conversation," he says. "After the idea is born, there's a conversation between the originator and others. Say, for example, that two people agree to set up a lemonade stand. One says she'll put up a million dollars if the other goes out and buys a bunch of lemons and hires some people, so that together they'll make lemonade. This all happens in conversation." A general understanding is arrived at and all is good. But of course, when broad ideas collide with the details of actual activity, things don't always go as well as hoped. And that, says Brown, is often because the goals weren't identified clearly or with enough precision at the outset.

"There is usually plenty of blame—one person didn't do enough work, the lemonades were bad, whatever—but," Brown says, "I focus on what the expected outcomes were at the beginning," which need to be specific and known. "What one person might want is be to be seen as the lemonade king and what the other might want is to make $100,000. Absent specificity, the two partners are not aligned in their expectations. But, worse, neither outcome is likely." Brown uses the phrase *specificity of ambition*. "Ambition, he says, "is a commitment to cause a specific outcome. And that includes a horizon of time, the more specific the better. If you don't define a specific outcome, you are doomed, in my view, to have uncoordinated conversations and actions."

He says, "Many studies show unequivocally that the more that organizations commit to specific outcomes, and do so publicly, they achieve more than they would otherwise, even if they fail. This is partly because of the accountability inherent in the public announcement, which leads to more scrutiny." This fights with the idea, Brown says, that it seems to be human nature to avoid being put in the position where one's actions are scrutinized, especially publicly.

This is a challenge at all enterprises, but it is particularly a thorny issue at charities. Very few charities define their goals specifically, and with a time horizon. An exception for that, Brown posits, is the Michael J. Fox Foundation, which he supports because he is familiar with the organization's management, operations and business strategy. "Their ambition," says Brown, "is to find a cure for Parkinson's disease in our lifetime." He says the word *cure* is specific and that people can agree on what that means, and he says that the phrase *in our lifetime* is also fairly specific, even though we don't know whose lifetime is being referenced. "In that sense, it could be more specific, but what's important is that the organization has coordinated its actions to that outcome. Its actions would be quite different if they were being conducted absent that specific ambition." Brown says, however, that most nonprofits are reluctant to be specific in the way the Michael J. Fox Foundation is.

❧

One reason for reluctance to set time-specific goals is the fear of failure. If, for example, the American Cancer Society committed to curing cancer by, say, 2030, he thinks that there would be an overwhelming fear of failure. "If 2030 rolled around and cancer wasn't cured, the people at ACA might think they failed." In one sense they'd be right, but in another, far more important and profound sense, they very well could be wrong. "The pressure is enormous and the scrutiny is intense." But Brown says, "It is precisely that fear of failure that gives birth to innovation."

So many nonprofits do not set specific goals and hold themselves accountable that Brown, who is not mired in the nonprofit vernacular, wonders how we got here. How has society allowed it to happen that charities exempt themselves from accountability? "If you write a check for $1 million as an investment in a small for-profit company and the management executives didn't have any outcomes to which they'd committed themselves, and then published the results as required but not the underlying metrics behind the results, and then sort of shrugged and said *here it is* . . . well, no one would tolerate that. It wouldn't come close to acceptability."

What's more baffling to Brown is that many for-profit companies outdo charities at measuring the good work they perform. Nicholas Kristoff, the *New York Times* columnist, says that the best industries for doing good "are held accountable by metrics."[323] "But we routinely accept a lack of specificity and accountability with nonprofits," says Brown. And he sees no refuge in the more opaque missions. "Even with homelessness," he says, "you can agree on what the goals are. The measurement process is a sticky problem, but you can agree on the metrics and the goals."

Brown speculates that the lack of public accountability at charities became acceptable because, broadly speaking, wealthy people divide their money basically into two piles. The larger one is for personal needs and the family, and the other is to be used for good deeds. "It's a smaller pile of money, and it's dependent on the larger pile of money, but it's different and there are different criteria for the deployment of each pile. For the one pile, the person is crisp and focused, but for the pile of money intended for charitable purposes, the person has a much more lax set of criteria."[324] That makes sense. Donors, most of whom rigorously manage the money they use for themselves, their families and their businesses, don't as rigorously oversee their donations.

But that is changing, and charities that engage their donors in their specificity will benefit.

• Richard Feiner: Profits at Nonprofits

We have a lot of problems, and no one sector of society has all of the resources or tools to fully confront them. Increased collaboration with both government and business is inevitable. While at present it's subtle, the growth of for-profit and nonprofit partnerships is inexorable. Therefore, in addressing long-term social goals, we must ask whether good intentions can be consistent with good business.

Richard Feiner, a fundraiser and a teacher of a course on innovations in the charitable sector at Columbia University, thinks that all sectors will need to work more closely together in the future. "The 20th Century model—grant-based, philanthropic-based—has accomplished a great deal," he says, "but the globalization of the world right now is such that the problems have been magnified. Whether it is on what Wounded Warrior Project is doing or in dealing with other social problems, such as climate change or social services for the homeless, the problems are spinning out of control in such a way that the nonprofit sector can't address it completely. At the same time, the for-profit sector is finding new opportunities for growth by adopting a social impact ethos into their business models. General Electric, for one, has come up with new products that specifically address energy usage, while appealing to the millennials who make a social commitment by the commercial products they buy. When making a light bulb, GE will source the materials from socially minded businesses. They are investing in the communities that create those products. And that is happening all along the value chain."

While this mindset drives CSR—*corporate social responsibility*—Feiner says for-profits are taking it a step further, to CSV—*creating shared value*. "Rather than taking a CSR approach, which is a nice-to-have, or which is an expense, the concept is flipped and becomes a profit-generating unit. It's also an investment in the community."

According to business strategists Michael Porter and Mark Kramer, who first introduced the concept of CSV in an article they wrote for the *Harvard Business Review* in 2006, "Shared Value is not social responsibility, philanthropy, or sustainability, but a new way for companies to achieve economic success." It's an idea that has been adopted by a wide spectrum of companies and industries around the world and is currently a business-driven, sustainable model pervading global business and capital. Although General Electric was one of the first to take on the "do well by doing good" corporate mantra in 2005 with its initiative, Ecomagination, other successful companies doing similar work include Nestle, PepsiCo, and Becton Dickinson.

The Corporate Social Responsibility and Creating Shared Value movements are alive and gaining traction.

∽

But it's a difficult and confusing path. Over the past several years, something called the B-Corporation has been gaining traction. A B-Corporation is a for-profit company. Some are certified by the B Lab, a nonprofit, to show they meet rigorous standards of social and environmental performance, accountability, and transparency. A B-Corporation's by-laws include the company's commitment to social good, which indemnifies the company from any legal action brought by shareholders for not pursuing the highest profit for them. Think of it this way: A B-Lab certification is to business (a B-Corporation) what the Fair Trade certification is to coffee or USDA Organic certification is to milk.

Etsy, an e-commerce website focused on unusual handmade products, was a B-Corporation. It "held itself up as a paragon of righteous business practices," according to a 2017 *New York Times* article. "Etsy's founders believed its business model—helping mostly female entrepreneurs make a living online—was inherently just."

But as it tried to grow, it failed in keeping its originating values dominant. The once-robust mission statement—which included a commitment "to reimagine commerce in ways that build a more fulfilling and lasting world"—was reduced to just three words, "Keep commerce human," accompanied by a spreadsheet outlining its goals for economic, social and ecological impact. "Etsy had the potential to be one of the truly great ones," said Matt Stinchcomb, an early Etsy employee. But he thinks the company cut anything that wasn't essential to the business. "This is a cautionary tale of capitalism," he said. The 'Values-Aligned Business' team, which oversaw the company's social and environmental efforts, was dismantled. A new focus on profitability sapped many employees of their enthusiasm.

Etsy is no longer a B Corp. Josh Silverman, the new CEO as of the end of 2017, said, "The company had the best of intentions, but wasn't great at tying that to impact. Being good doesn't cut the mustard."[325]

But although the Etsy story shows that efforts to marry goodness and greed are fragile, and indeed may not be sustainable, it's clear that society's most difficult challenges are not going to be solved only by nonprofits. And there are people who won't give up on the idea. The *Times* columnist Nicholas Kristoff has spoken to the shortcomings of charity. In Kenya, Christie Peacock, who used to work in the aid world, says she got disillusioned with the NGO model. (NGO, non-governmental agency, is the term used for charities in many countries around the world.) She left her nonprofit to found Sidai, a for-profit founded with start-up capital from the Bill and Melinda Gates Foundation, and, in her view, better addresses her goal of serving Kenyan farmers. "That's the advantage of a business approach," Kristoff writes. "It is often more sustainable and scalable than a charity."

Kristoff notes that business leaders are often cynical. "Tycoons always claim to cherish ordinary people's best interests even as they rip them off. American tobacco executives have killed more people than Stalin managed to, and pharma executives recklessly peddling opioids may have killed as many people as Colombian drug lords, yet these business leaders sometimes seem to get moist-eyed describing the work they do."[326] Frank Bruni, another *New York Times* columnist, agrees. The primary concern of companies "isn't public welfare. It's the bottom line. I say that not to besmirch them but to state the obvious. Their actions will never deviate too far from their proprietary interests, and while tapping their genius and money is essential, outsourcing too much to them is an abdication of government's singular role."[327]

But, according to Kristoff, there is more talk, at least, of change, and, to a growing degree, actions behind the talk. "What's driving the rethink isn't a tingling of the tycoon conscience but brutal self-interest," he says. "Millennials want to work for ethical companies, patronize brands that make them feel good and invest in socially responsible companies. Some of this is shallow and some is deep, but it's authentic: Doing good is no longer a matter of writing a few checks at the end of the year, as it was for my generation; for many young people, it's an ethos that governs where they work, shop and invest."[328]

~

"The nonprofit sector all along has pursued social good, social mission," says Richard Feiner, "from a philanthropic point of view. Now, the for-profit world is finding ways to re-orient itself toward social good from the profit motive." He also notes the growth of social finance on Wall Street. "This is orchestrating new products, such as social impact bonds. The government sector, in its commitment to servicing society, is strapped for funds and is tapping into both the nonprofit and the for-profit sectors to make sure that government fulfills its social contract."

How might this relate to Wounded Warrior Project? "WWP could be a partner in a social impact bond that is helping the government redefine its VA hospital system" (a good example since we've seen how messed up the VA hospital system is). A social impact bond is an innovative agreement intended to promote private investment in social causes, as well as incite innovation and increase accountability. Private investors fund an intervention through an intermediary organization. The government repays the funder only if the program achieves certain goals, which are specified at the outset of the initiative and assessed by an independent evaluator.

Feiner says, "A social impact bond can often be put together by a social finance unit of a financial institution—such as JPMorgan Chase, Deutsche Bank or Bank of America—which receives its money from within or from its own institutional investors that align themselves for social good." Private equity companies and pension funds, as well as sizable charitable endowments that can devote a portion of its asset mix to this purpose, are players in the impact bond world. "In this scenario" says Feiner, "the social finance unit of the commercial entity enters into a contract with the government that is running the VA hospitals"—in the case of the hypothetical Wounded Warrior Project scenario—"or a governmental agency." From there, the nonprofit sector is engaged as the actual provider of services. "The charity would be the program implementer." It is common for the players engaged in establishing the SIB to select an external, neutral entity, often itself a nonprofit, to evaluate the progress based on the agreed-upon metrics by which success or failure is to be measured. "As well," Feiner says, "there can be an external guarantor to provide a loan guarantee against that external funding." Here, he cites Bloomberg Philanthropies, which provided most of the guarantee for the Rikers Island Project, which was the first program in the United States to be supported using a social impact bond funding structure.

∾

Rikers Island, as anyone who has ever watched "Law and Order" knows, is New York City's notorious jail complex, and in 2012 the city launched a program designed to break the cycle of re-incarceration, or recidivism, for adolescents between 16 and 18 years old in the jail. The formal name of the project was the Adolescent Behavioral Learning Experience (ABLE) program.

The for-profit entity was Goldman Sachs's Urban Investment Group, which, via its clients, invested $9.6 million with a loan to MDRC,[329] (Manpower Demonstration Research Corporation, an education and social policy research organization), which then acted as the intermediary by overseeing the component activities—such as setting up the financial arrangements, selecting the intervention and service provider, and training staff, as well as other tangible components—of the program. Bloomberg Philanthropies agreed to offer $7.2 million—75 percent of the Goldman Sachs loan—which Goldman's Urban Investment Group could access as a guarantee—as a way to incentivize and de-risk the investments—to make this social impact bond more attractive to Goldman's clients.

The organization that actually delivered the intervention to the young people in jail was the nonprofit Osborne Association and Friends of Island Academy.[330] The Vera Institute of Justice, whose mission is all about improving the justice system, served as the program's independent evaluator.

The following schematic shows how all the pieces fit together:

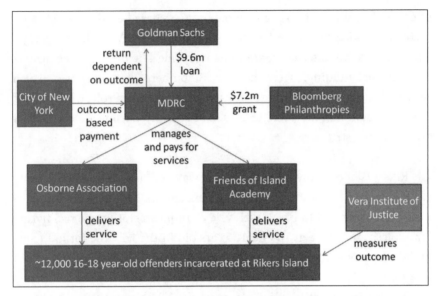

https://emmatomkinson.files.wordpress.com/2012/08/ny-sib.png

If the set-up looks confusing, that's because it is. When we think of using our donations to help society through single-charity efforts, such as a homeless shelter, for example, we think of the money being given directly to the organization, which then uses it to buy the blankets, pillows, and cots that the homeless can use to sleep at night, as well as the food. And the same is true about many organizations that are a lot larger and more layered. But the dive into the structural details here is useful because it illustrates the way governments, businesses, and nonprofits can work together. If complex problems with overwhelming, even unknowable, price tags are going to be addressed, the solutions, at least at first, will also be complex.

The goal of the Rikers Island Project was to reduce recidivism among the youths by 10 percent or more. If the program succeeded, MDRC would receive a payment from New York City and would reimburse Goldman Sachs. Also, MDRC would work with Bloomberg Philanthropies to repurpose the $7.2 million for future experiments. If the program failed, MDRC would use the $7.2 million from Bloomberg to repay Goldman Sachs.

The project failed. The Vera Institute reported, "Vera determined that the program did not lead to reductions in recidivism for participants. The change in recidivism for the eligible 16- to 18-year-olds, adjusted for external factors, was not statistically significant when compared to the matched historical comparison group. Furthermore, the 19-year-olds and the study group (16- to 18-year-olds) displayed similar trends in rates of recidivism over time, indicating that any shifts were the result of factors other than the ABLE program. The program did not reduce recidivism and therefore did not meet the pre-defined threshold of success of a 10 percent reduction in recidivism bed days."[331] Feiner's take was more nuanced and optimistic. "My understanding," he says, "is that some reductions in recidivism were achieved, but not at the level pre-determined by all SIB participants."

While some saw a silver lining in the failure—no taxpayer dollars were spent—the critics of the program were pessimistic. "The failure of the Rikers experiment to achieve the project's intended outcomes," wrote Donald Cohen and Jennifer Zelnick for the *Nonprofit Quarterly,* "raises more questions than answers, particularly with regard to the potential of SIBs [social impact bonds] to address complex social problems and serve vulnerable communities."

In science, they wrote, "failure can still be deemed a kind of success, since data can be helpful in revising or shelving a working hypothesis. But did the Rikers SIB experiment provide that kind of clarity? The claims of success at Rikers hinge on the assertion that the program cost taxpayers nothing. Indeed, the city isn't on the hook for any repayment, but we don't know the true cost of the intervention. According to MDRC, 'the arrangement required considerable in-kind support from city government leaders and staff.' These are real costs—paid with taxpayer dollars—and should be part of the accounting equation."

But worse, they contended, "When SIBs fail, social problems persist: Taxpayers avoided paying some costs for the program, but the underlying problems that contribute to recidivism remain." Also, "The scope of SIBs is limited by the demand for short-term results: Most social problems are complex and require comprehensive programs and policies that stay the course. A bias toward programs that produce quick, measurable results narrows the public dialogue and waters down findings."

Furthermore, the authors wrote, the investments could be used differently. "Philanthropy plays an important role in funding social interventions. In light of the failure of this first-in-the-nation SIB-funded intervention, philanthropic organizations may be asked to bear more of the risk to keep SIBs attractive to investors. A 2013 report by MDRC notes that it 'may be necessary for benevolent funders to step in to "smooth the curve" for traditional investors.' Not only does this undermine a key claim of SIBs, that they shift responsibility to the private sector alone, but it suggests that philanthropic dollars might be diverted from directly funding other innovative programs, shouldering risk for private investors instead." Feiner, however, questions that the shift is total. "My understanding is that the SIB model shares responsibility between public and private entities. It does not shift responsibility solely to benevolent private sector funders," he says.

"The range of factors needed to create meaningful change in the lives of young people who face multiple social and economic challenges is beyond the control of any one social intervention," they wrote. "There are far too many questions remaining to conclude that SIBs are an effective vehicle for funding social programs. Other approaches, such as reducing misdemeanor arrests, disrupting the school-to-prison pipeline, changes to the bail system, and raising the age of criminal responsibility would have significant impact on the numbers who cycle through Rikers. If the goal is to solve social problems, not privatize the public sector, we should consider a simpler solution—public investment in schools, jobs, social programs and innovative criminal justice."[332]

While Cohen and Zelnick's assessment of the Rikers Island Project was damning and pessimistic, it should be noted that we are just beginning on the path to figuring out how businesses and governments can fit into the larger picture with philanthropy, and the social impact bond seems to be a harbinger for future efforts to address some of society's more intractable problems. Also, it should not be lost in the criticism that the goal was, as Thomas Brown champions, measurable and specific. While that generates the real possibility of failure, it also provides urgency and clarity, often the precursors of success. Besides, not everyone felt so doubtful. James Anderson, who led the Government Innovation portfolio at Bloomberg Philanthropies in New York City, and Andrea Phillips, a Vice President in the Urban Investment Group at Goldman Sachs—two of the key players in the project—said, "Still, we're encouraged that the innovative public-private partnership that allowed all of us to try to help these young people in need and do something new—called a social impact bond—worked." In their explanation of what they admitted was a "counterintuitive" conclusion, they said the program shifted risk from taxpayers, distinguished good data and good intentions to help show what works and what doesn't work, and explored a new approach.[333]

∽

One of the important variables in this complex equation is the definition of success. Feiner says, "The whole idea of these public-private partnerships is that they bring all these different players together to the table while the project is in formation. It's not as if Deutsche Bank and a pension investment fund come together to say we want to do a project and we'll go find implementers."

This means that nonprofits are still very much quarterbacking the process. "But they don't feel comfortable in this space," says Feiner. "Most nonprofits have a limited view of the problems that our sector can solve and our role in how they can be solved. They need to see the broader and greater good."

Feiner says there are other platforms, in addition to social impact bonds, other tools that the nonprofit sector has been reluctant to take up, and that one of the reasons that charities have not been more experimental in trying other ways to raise money is that traditional efforts have been so successful. Still, he thinks the social impact bond idea, along with others, can be a game changer in society. "There could be," he says, "a change in what we consider to be philanthropy."[334]

• Dan Pallotta: Unshackle Charities

Dan Pallotta, the author and philanthropy activist, is perhaps the most vocal critic of Charity Navigator's business model, which, as he sees it, is all about gathering data on the cheap. "They look at the 990s, look at revenue, look at program expense, then do a simple division and come up with an overhead ratio," Pallotta says. "That information was free to them, and it would take an analyst all of seven minutes to consolidate it and put it up on their website. So, as the discussion over the past years has evolved into one of impact, they just don't have a business model that can support that or do anything substantive. All they can do," he says, "is process simple data."

That identifies the problem, at least in part, as one of having the resources to do the right job. As of 2017, GuideStar's budget is in the $12 million range and Charity Navigator's budget is a little more than $3 million.

But, of course, it goes well past economics, Pallotta says. He asks an interesting question: How do you create good information in a market-place where you're not the consumer of the product? Many donors to a charity are not in fact its clients or beneficiaries, and so a valid consumer rating is hard to come by. "One way," he says, "is to create a massive data-base where a lot of information on a lot of charities is stored and people can access it to make their own decisions based on the data." Another is to "conduct a prolonged education campaign so that donors do the work. Go to the charity and do your own research. In that situation, you're respon-sible. It's on you." A third way is to create and scale up legitimate vetting organizations for different sectors of the charitable world. "We know the organizations that deal with cancer, for example, so we could have a place where sector-specific evaluations are conducted."

Regardless of the delivery system of the evaluation, however, the right questions need to be asked. Pallotta notes that many charities currently fly under the radar. "When you say 90 percent is going to programming, nobody asks what impact you have. In the case of Wounded Warrior Project," he says, referring to numbers and impact, "they were doing both things well. They had customer-satisfaction surveys for all their programs. Measuring impact is difficult and if you wanted to take a first step, that's a great first step. If your own customers aren't satisfied, that means you're not having an impact." But if they are, donors will take note."

Pallotta points out that, as of 2015, Wounded Warrior Project repre-sented 40 percent of private fundraising for veterans' services. Yet the char-ity didn't exist 15 years earlier. "It was just nothing," he says. "How did they go from nothing to this? In 2005 they spent $1.5 million in fundraising and generated $10 million in revenue with 43 percent overhead. If you were a watchdog you'd say that's shameful, that you have to focus on one thing and that's lowering your overhead."

But, Pallotta says, WWP asked different questions: "How many veterans are there who don't have services? How large do we need to be to provide them all with services? How much money would we have to raise to be that big? How much do we need to spend on fundraising to get that much money?" Pallotta pauses here as if the essence of the answers should be obvious to everyone, and he is perplexed that no one seems to see it. By the time Steve Nardizzi and Al Giordano were fired in March 2016, "they ended up spending $74 million on fundraising and generating $400 million revenue, with $250 million going to veterans. There is no way to get to the town called $400 million without first going through the town called $74 million. There is no way to do it." Could it be done differently? "Yes," Pallotta says, "you could find a donor who gives you $400 million every year." Or take more time with more modest growth. "Yes, you could be willing to take a hundred years with a traditional program and low costs. But if you wanted to do it right, the only way is with this kind of scale—and if you're dealing with life and death issues that you don't have a hundred years to wait to address, you need to scale now. And for that the media will crucify you."

Pallotta says that because charities are held down. "Everything is miniature against the scale of the problem. People are petrified to go into that kind of aggressive fundraising—because of the cost of it."

And there's no ability to fight back, Pallotta says. The nonprofit sector doesn't have any of the fundamental tools of grassroots organizing that every community has. "There's no alternative point of view in the media saying there's a different way to think about this. The gay community has an anti-defamation force. The Jewish community has an anti-defamation force. The disabled community, the Mexican American community—they do, too."

Pallotta says this inability to fight back has allowed the media to unfairly criticize charities. In 2012 CNN, for example, "destroyed Roxanne

Spillett at the Boys & Girls Clubs of America because she makes $800,000 a year."[335]

Following is the transcript of the network's story about Spillett and the charity. It's clear why the story is sensational, but impact—not just expenses—is important.

Wolf Blitzer: A CEO's million-dollar salary and bonuses, millions spent on travel, conventions, lobbying fees, all are raising eyebrows among U.S. senators. This time it's not corporate executives and their sites, but rather executives of a very popular and long-standing charity. CNN's Lisa Sylvester is here in The Situation Room working this story for us. It's the Boys & Girls Clubs of America that do important work, but what is going on here?

Lisa Sylvester: Wolf, as you well know, the Boys & Girls Clubs of America has done a lot of great work over the years helping underprivileged kids. Last summer President Obama visited one of their clubs, reading to the kids. But now the group's executives are coming under fire. Four Republican senators want to know more about the national group's finances, and we'll start here with their 2008 tax records. The president of the nonprofit organization has a base salary of $360,000, a performance bonus of an additional $150,000, and then, on top of that, an annual benefits package, including contributions to a retirement fund, totaling more than $477,000. Total annual compensation for the president: $988,591. Other expenses the senators are inquiring about? In 2008, the group spent a little more than $4 million on travel, more than $500,000 on lobbying and more than $1 million on conferences and meetings. This is all coming at a time when boys and girls clubs have had to close because of a lack of funding.

(Beginning of Video Clip Content)

Senator Charles Grassley: Is it legitimate to be siphoning off a lot of money, taxpayers' money, to high salaries and travel and lobbying efforts when we have needs for keeping the Boys and Girls Clubs open because they serve such a useful purpose, and particularly in poverty-stricken, low-income areas of the country?

(*End of Video Clip Content*)

Sylvester: So, the reason why Senate lawmakers are looking into all of this is because it's taxpayer dollars that are involved here. About 40 percent of the Boys and Girls revenue comes from federal funds and they're seeking a reauthorization now, $425 million over the next five years.

Blitzer: What do the Boys & Girls Club, the leadership, what do they have to say about this?

Sylvester: Well, the group is, in fact, defending it expenses. The $4 million in travel, well they say that covers 350 national staff members who are often visiting local clubs. And they say their CEO—Roxanne Spillett's—pay is comparable to other charitable groups.

(*Beginning of Video Clip Content*)

Evan McElroy (Chief Communications Officer of the Boys & Girls Clubs of America): Our CEO's compensation, our executive compensation, is totally in line with similar nonprofit organizations. If you look at the lists that are published online about the nonprofit sector, you would even find that her salary and overall compensation is lower than many comparable executives.

(*End of Video Clip Content*)

Blitzer: I know you've been doing some checking. Is that true, is her salary in line with other comparable charity groups?

Sylvester: Well, what we did is we took a look online and there's a group, it's called Charity Navigator. And what they do is they track nonprofit charities and they say that the average CEO salary for 2009 for groups in 100 million or more in expenses, is $462,000. The president of the Boys & Girls Club annual salary and bonus, if you tally it up, is about 550,000. So it is, Wolf, actually higher than the average.

Blitzer: But if you bring in another $400,000 and retirement, annual retirement, that brings it up to close to a million dollars a year.

Sylvester: Yeah, we're talking a lot of money, here. And again, keep in mind, this is at a time when the Boys & Girls Clubs—well, some of these clubs are having to close because they don't have the funding and the resources.

Blitzer: Stay on top of this for us, because the sad thing is that a lot of little boys and girls could be hurt if people stop making contributions because they're upset about a million dollars a year going to the president and CEO of this charitable organization.[336]

Pallotta argues that the entire piece was born of misconceptions. "Not once was there a mention of what the organization accomplishes," he says. "It's only about overhead."

The Charity Defense Council, a nonprofit that Pallotta leads, has a rebuttal: billboards. "There's one we put up that says, *Don't ask if a charity has low overhead. Ask if it has big impact.* Another, which shows the faces of people who work at charities, has the words, *I'm Overhead* on it. It's important to show how the people—the overhead—are essential to the cause and not separate from the cause."

Beyond Pallotta's own efforts, which are small compared to the way he identifies the need, he imagines an ad with Bill Gates and Warren Buffet. "They look at the camera and say, *We've given more money to charity than anybody in history. And over the course of doing it, we've learned a few things. We've learned that we've been taught to do it wrong. You shouldn't look at things like overhead. You should look at things like impact.* If we could get leadership at that level to start talking to the public, I think that would change the public's mind very quickly."

Pallotta says, "As a sector, we have to have a powerful, long-term, public case, and we need to campaign if we're ever going to change the way the public thinks about these things. So whether in ten years from now the public will be enlightened on the overhead question depends on how successful our efforts are."

Altogether, accounting for donations, fees, and the revenues generated through the taxes employees pay, estimates are that the nonprofit sector generates a trillion dollars of economic activity. "The health and human services portion of that is approximately $180 billion," Pallotta says, "and never once have they taken out a full-page ad in the *New York Times* to talk to the public about what it does for America. America has never seen an ad that says, *We're your nonprofit sector. Here's what we do.* Nothing like that."

⁓

Pallotta feels that joining forces would help. "You could get as much impact out of consolidating the sector as you could by growing the sector, but there's no financial incentive for merger and acquisition activity. Since you've stripped profit and money out of the sector, all people have are their egos, and their pride, and the organization they've created. In fact, there's a huge disincentive. *I'm going to lose all my psychic benefit. I have no money already. I've given that up, so now you want me to merge with you and I'm going to lose my legacy too?* Until we introduce some kind of financial incentive . . . " he says without finishing the thought, possibly because another thought is crystallizing in his mind.

"What if you could provide the incentive in the form of a tax credit? What if you work at a nonprofit and you've been there five years? Maybe," he speculates, "you could get a tax credit equivalent to three years of your salary. That would make somebody think. *If I make $90,000 a year, that would be $270,000.* I don't know. But something has to happen to introduce a financial incentive. Otherwise," he says of the future of those who work at charities and the success of the charitable sector, "it looks pretty much the same."

Pallotta notes, "There was no outrage over the losses Wounded Warrior Project suffered because of the crisis. Some journalists mistake their certainty for knowledge, and—as we saw in the *CBS News* and *New York Times* reports—if they're not certain about the facts, they're certain about their point of view. If this were the gay community and someone had done that to a gay person, there would have been an uprising in the gay community. The sector has a profound inability to get pissed off."

Pallotta is not saying charities should act more like businesses. "Give charities the same big league freedoms we actually give to business. Stop giving the business sector the tools of capitalism—like a Tesla—and refusing to give the nonprofit sector any of those permissions—so, by comparison to the Tesla, it's like riding a bicycle. Then the charity can decide which practices suit it and which don't, and which don't violate its sense of mission and ones that further it. But this Puritan attitude—you can't pay people any money, and you can't spend money on fundraising, don't take risks with donor money, all of this stuff—it's killing them."[337]

• Jacob Harold: A Deeper Look

"There are things," says Jacob Harold of GuideStar, "that Charity Navigator could do to make their approach less problematic. For example, they could still cite the overhead ratio, but they could change their algorithm to show that there is such a thing that overhead could be too low. I wouldn't agree with that" because it doesn't address the core issue, "but, Harold says, "it still would be an improvement."

But not much. It just may be that the system—a system that journalists and the public have come to rely on as their one and only way of determining if a charity is worthy of their beneficence—is too broken to be fixed.

If that's the case, though, what kind of system should we have? What would address the core issues of better understanding charities, their work, and their effect on society? If it's too broken, how do we change the system? "The answer," according to Harold, "if it is comprehensive enough, sophisticated enough, and modern enough, it could quite possibly begin to allow us, through the unique role of charities, to see society as a better whole. Because evaluation leads to understanding, which leads to more scrutiny, which leads to effectiveness and efficiency, the answer could permit humankind to actually improve through philanthropic efforts. Yes, really. Age-old, chronic problems—homelessness, racism, environmental degradation, and so many others, as well as their derivatives—could be addressed and even, possibly, solved. Humanity wouldn't live in complete harmony, but its disharmony might be of the kind within which differences would be tolerated, respected even, to give people a better life. No, chronic problems do not have to last forever."

Thinking of it that way is a tall order, but how else to be serious about charities?

∽

On this arduous, hopeful road, we begin by asking if it is possible to create a shared framework for understanding the quality of nonprofit organizations—after all, an essential part of our quest is to get a handle on effectiveness. "And the answer to that is," according to Harold, "a qualified yes. To get there, though, we have to think of the tangible; as a start, we have to think not only at the lofty level of saving the world, but also at the more tangible level of organizing the actual work that must be done." Harold asks, "Given the incredible diversity of the nonprofit sector, is it even conceivable to have a common intellectual framework that coherently compares Harvard University to the ACLU to a homeless shelter? I've come to believe that the answer is no; that is, it's not possible in terms of a star rating." That's the negative portion of the qualified yes. But then there's the other portion.

"There are some things that are common for all charities. For example, every nonprofit, no matter its size or mission, ought to be able to articulate its goals and its strategy, and whatever metrics it thinks are appropriate. It's possible to have a format that is consistent but translating that format into a single rating is where it breaks down," says Harold.

"A metaphor we use at GuideStar is that of a nutrition label. Nutrition labels offer a familiar format for sharing a wide variety of information about packaged food, information that speaks to different questions and different preferences people have. The label doesn't say, for example, that this box of crackers is an 'A' and this box of crackers is a 'C,' but the statistics on the label make it much more efficient to compare the nutritional content of the two boxes of crackers."

Another example Harold suggests as a way of presenting multi-dimensional information can be found in the way Amazon organizes its web site. "Amazon has a star rating, yes, but it has many other ways of helping readers decide which book to buy: personal reviews, professional reviews, a narrative description, sales ranking within a category, or the ability to look inside the book and see a few pages. This way you don't have to judge the book by its cover. There is a multi-dimensional way of thinking and people are perfectly capable of sorting through that. But it has to be presented in a way that's consistent and stable and meaningful enough that people can do it efficiently."

That's one way to look at disparate information, but different charities are more different from one another than is evident with the differences between cracker types. "The analogy weakens when we understand that comparing charities is more than comparing crackers to crackers or books to books, and more like comparing crackers to steak or broccoli, or both. All three are foods, but very different ones, some having more advantages than disadvantages, and to really get the picture, a consumer has to take in all the information. This ends up more of a matrix with components, each with variable values, than a straight line that goes from good to bad."

Harold thinks we need to look at things a little more comprehensively. "First," he says, "get more and better organized external views." By "external" he means the views of those not working at the charity. "There are certain analytical approaches that are appropriate for certain types of nonprofits. For example, a survey to get the perspectives of end beneficiaries is probably the most relevant way to judge a homeless shelter. This is because the beneficiaries are well placed to say whether it was a good experience. But this is not true, for example, for an environmental advocacy group because the end beneficiaries of, for example, the Sierra Club actually have no idea if the Sierra Club is doing a good job of lobbying on Capitol Hill or trying to convince a corporation to change its practices." Still, Harold would like "to get to the point where we have the end-beneficiary perspective on all nonprofits."

Choosing the programmatic terms on which a charity wants to be evaluated, he says, is both an offensive and a defensive move. "It's offensive because it's a way to raise money and increase impact, and it's defensive because if a charity ever comes under criticism, it will be able to say, *Look, this is what we believe is most important about our organization; this is how we believe we should be judged.*"

Also, to secure external views, he suggests compiling perspectives from topic experts. "For advocacy or research organizations, experts are often better positioned to judge the effectiveness of a nonprofit" than the general public is when using only the numbers from an IRS form. Jacob uses the metaphor of a college basketball coaches' poll "where you're surveying experts and taking their qualitative judgments and aggregating them to come to something quantitative." For this, however, there needs to be an agreed-upon set of numbers and quality of experts in each of the numerous areas of mission charities are divided into and a system by which their perspectives can be compiled and analyzed.

A second way to build a better evaluation process, according to Harold, is for the public to judge the clarity of a *nonprofit's self-description.* This idea echoes Thomas Brown's plea for more specificity of ambition. Harold says, "It's possible to judge if a nonprofit has a clear goal and a coherent strategy, to determine whether the metrics it uses seem appropriate." GuideStar has collected the articulation of goals and strategies from about 20,000 charities. "I would love to see people say *a third of these are really good, a third are kind of fine and a third of them are incoherent*—something along those lines." In fact, when Harold is asked to say—in one word—what donors should care about most, he says *clarity.* "Nonprofits have an opportunity to show that they are effective by clearly articulating a goal, a strategy, and a measurement system plan." Again, this doesn't completely solve the problem but it is another component of the solution and would be a way to push nonprofits to be clearer.

This is a tricky area, though, because it's only about the clarity of the *articulation* of the goal. "Giving high marks for that," he says, "is different from saying that the goal itself is a good one or a bad one, which is a personal choice. I can imagine a nonprofit that I totally disagree with having a very clear goal and strategy, and I suppose, as a user I'd have to give them a good rating." Undoubtedly many people would not live up to this ideal, but forcing a charity to articulate its goals certainly should be a step in the process.

Getting a better handle on operational and governance practices would help, as well. In the third step of his way of looking at charity evaluation, he says, "Separate from articulating goals, I think the idea of having nonprofits articulate their practices around governance and transparency is a meaningful approach." To a degree, that is already being done. In addition to requesting financial data from a charity's 990, the Better Business Bureau's Wise Giving Alliance asks charities to provide narratives on governance and oversight, measuring effectiveness, and fundraising disclosures.

Finally, Harold thinks benchmarking programmatic metrics is important. To illustrate, he cites land conservation organizations. "There are thousands of these groups in the United States and you could, for example, compare the number of acres protected." That's easy enough to benchmark and measure. "But the challenge is that some acres are more ecologically meaningful than others, and so this has a potential problem of being misinterpreted." Not all acres saved are equally worthy of preserving. "Just because one organization saves 1,000 acres and another only 500, that doesn't mean the first organization is better." He has no answer to that but says, "I feel we still need to share that data. We need to show it so that it is comparable, but also be clear that we're not making a better-or-worse judgment here. Instead, we're trying to give the user a sense of scale. A nonprofit needs to own its best metrics, in a way that is not judgmental but is still helpful."

While no single suggestion Harold offers is a complete solution, each does, on its own, elevate the discussion past using only the numbers—and subjectively manipulated at that—found on a charity's IRS form, and, combined, add up to a useful whole.

Inherent in such potential revision is the need for perspective, and from more than one source. To address the inevitable subjectivity and consequent feelings of unfairness, Harold says "a charity could, on its website, reference the evaluations of others—how information was compiled and its conclusions—and then provide its own responding narrative."[338]

- **Martin Whittaker: Ranking For-Profits**

In 2016 a young nonprofit called JUST Capital announced the JUST 100, its first rankings of the largest publicly traded companies in the United States. The rankings were based on the issues that Americans care about most, like worker pay and treatment, customer respect, product quality, environmental impact, and more. The JUST 100 was based on values— not revenues or market value—and featured the top three or four leaders in each of several industries. The following year, JUST Capital released its second, more comprehensive, ranking of America's Most JUST Companies, which included the JUST 100 list of the top performing companies across all industries in absolute rank order, as well as the Industry Leader list, which included the 33 top performing companies by sector.

The idea is basic: poll Americans to identify the issues that they care about most when it comes to corporate behavior, evaluate large corporations on those issues, and then rank the corporations. Martin Whittaker, JUST Capital's chief executive officer, says, "We want to capture the public's true definition of a just company."

JUST Capital was started with the help of the investor and philanthropist Paul Tudor Jones, and, in addition to Jones, has the likes of Deepak Chopra and Arianna Huffington on the board. "These folks," says Whittaker of the entire board, "want to have a major impact on the way business and capitalism function."

Jones says that we look at capitalism all wrong. "We as a society have come to view our companies and corporations in a very narrow, almost monomaniacal, fashion with regard to how we value them. We have put so much emphasis on profits, our short-term quarterly earnings, and share prices, at the exclusion of all else. It's like we've ripped the humanity out of our companies."

That concern drove Jones to partner with others to create JUST Capital, and to hire Whittaker to lead the effort. "The mission," Jones says, "is to help companies and corporations learn how to operate in a more just fashion by using the public's input to define exactly what the criteria are for just corporate behavior."[339]

"The special sauce of JUST Capital," Whittaker points out, "is that we don't evaluate or rank the performance of companies on the basis of what we think is important. We measure companies on the basis of issues the public tells us *they* prioritize. JUST Capital gives ordinary people a voice. It's where we get our legitimacy."

He admits that not everyone thinks that's a good idea. "Some people asked me why we're letting the American people decide this," Whittaker says. "*That doesn't make any sense,* they said. *Ordinary people don't know anything about these issues.* These are not ill-meaning skeptics; they tend to be those who have spent their lives as activists, and thought that you couldn't just go to people with a survey and get anything back that made sense." Whittaker acknowledges that's a fair point, but, he says, "It really doesn't do justice to the public's intuitive grasp of what's really important."

JUST Capital partnered with advisors and polling groups, such as the National Opinion Research Center (NORC) at the University of Chicago, to help develop the measuring methodology. Whittaker's team then asked questions of focus groups around the country. "The moderator had a blank piece of paper and said to the people, essentially, what we want to discuss is what you think a just company looks like. Then, without any bias and without leading anyone, we had a discussion, and, organically, it went from there."

The focus-group discussions led JUST Capital to identify several priorities, including worker and customer satisfaction, quality products and services, and the environment. "Each issue, Whittaker says, "captures corporate justness. Each one comprises multiple specific criteria that determine what we actually measure in the model."

~

The 2017 report, entitled "Roadmap for a Corporate America," notes the need for a recalibration of priorities at large companies. "People said putting workers first," the reports says, "is more than twice as important as job creation alone and nearly four times more important than putting shareholders and management first. Americans across the board believed that investors reign supreme, while employees receive the short end of the stick.

"The other key issues Americans want corporations to address: Be responsive and respectful to customers. Create good products. Minimize environmental impact. Support communities in which you're operating (locally and overseas). Commit to ethical leadership. Together, the weighting of each of these issues from the American public form a comprehensive, data-driven roadmap for becoming a more equitable and just company."[340]

With that roadmap, JUST Capital then scores the companies. "We collect and evaluate data from a myriad of different sources on how each company actually performs across the 39 components," Whittaker says. "We do this in as fair, unbiased, and rigorous a way as possible, taking care to gather the best and most reliable information we can." Those myriad sources include "public filings, like 10Ks and company filings, third-party vendors, the government, the press, and third-party experts. JUST Capital collects 120,000 data points across 85 metrics to compile the rankings.

The questions and methodology are revisited annually to catch any changes in mood among the public.

Each company sees its analysis before it is published. "We tell the companies the work we've done and how we've done it," Whittaker says, "we tell them all our sources, and we show them our data on how they stack up."

There is also a process for a company to dispute the findings so it has the chance to comment and provide additional data if necessary. "In the end, though," Whittaker says, "we are the judge on how we score the companies. But it's all fully transparent to the companies. Everybody knows how and why we came to our conclusions."

Transparency to the public is also a large priority. "We want to make sure what we are doing and how we are doing it are accessible and understandable to anyone," Whittaker says. "The idea is that anybody can go on our site and see exactly what we've done, how we've done it, and then find out how any company is doing on the things that he or she cares about."

∿

JUST Capital is a charity, but Whittaker doesn't use the metrics at Charity Navigator as a guide for itself. "We've been trying to establish JUST Capital as a . . . just organization. We pay people very well, for example.

Just because you work in the nonprofit world we don't feel as though you should be underpaid. We are a generous employer and provide great benefits. For example, we have a 12-week family-leave policy—maternity and paternity—fully paid," which, he thinks, beats most Fortune 500 companies. "We do many things that show we walk the talk, and I believe that commitment has made us better at analyzing companies. When you walk a mile in someone's shoes, you realize these things are not that easy; they're not that obvious."

As apparent as it is that JUST Capital sees the potential for the for-profit world to make society better in areas of worker satisfaction, the environment and other public priorities, it doesn't take much imagination to also understand that some of the core thinking at JUST Capital could be adapted to create a better way for the public to understand how donated dollars are being used. Such an understanding might then lead to changes in the way charities operate.

"There's no reason," Whittaker says, "that our system has to apply only to publicly traded companies."[341]

CHAPTER 7

ONWARD

IT'S ONE THING TO CLAIM that our current approach to understanding charities is deeply flawed, but it is quite another to posit a credible alternative. The information sent to the IRS on Form 990 was never intended to be used evaluatively or judgmentally—it was, remember, a way for the IRS to check in on a charity to be sure it publicly discloses its finances, and has not acted as a for-profit entity, with nary an indicator about impact or organizational quality—yet because of its easy accessibility it has come to serve as the primary, and often the only, source of information the public has about charities.

Because of the mostly superficial nature of evaluations these days, we need something else, a way to encourage people to make choices informed by both their hearts and their heads. We need more than we have to shine a light on what really goes on at a charity. Not even the BBB WGA's questions that go deeper than what can be found on a 990 provide what is needed for donors to make a fully informed decision about what is best for them.

The call for an exacting glare might seem counterintuitive, as our hearts instinctively warm at the very mention of the word *charity*. While there is no reason to deny that instinct, it's important that our heads employ a check—although not cynicism—on what we otherwise might think is an unabated effort to change the world for the better. Competent, effective, and trustworthy charity leaders know this, and they proactively address the questions that have emerged over the years.

The good ones ask of themselves, *How would society be worse off if we went out of business?*

≈

Although many people think a calculation is inherently objective, it is not. Just because, for example, we can determine that the sum of three and four equals seven does not in any way address whether those are the numbers we should be adding in the first place. *That* decision is subjective.

Generally, people are cause-driven when they donate, and so, in addition to numbers and data, a proper evaluation needs to include context and narrative, and the process and results have to be fair. Yet the idea of fair is itself subjective and often personal. There is no universally agreed-upon answer, and there probably never will be, to the question of what the right context is and the right amount of information an evaluation should contain. Also, a proper evaluation system must recognize that there are many categories of charities and they simply cannot be compared on a linear scale. In a world where top-ten lists reign supreme, what can be done?

Is there a way we can combine the ideas of Thomas Brown, Richard Feiner, Dan Pallotta, Jacob Harold, and Martin Whittaker—as well as those of others—to build a better system? Can we insist on more specificity and bold ambition? Can we more deeply explore the ways business, government, and the nonprofit sector can work together to solve society's more difficult problems? Can we rid ourselves of the mindset of poverty so a charity can invest in itself, which would be an investment in its mission? Can we insist that charities better articulate their goals and provide their own assessments? If we truly honor the role of charities in society, can we employ the public's wisdom to provide a consensus of what's important?

Can these considerations be included in the way charities are evaluated? Yes.

~

To begin with, charities themselves need to clearly define and disseminate their tangible goals. The food bank, for example, might want to increase the number of meals it serves, or improve the nutritional quality of those meals. A university might want to measure its progress toward an abuse-free campus or to evaluate its classes better. A hospital might want to measure safety improvements, or progress on how it focuses on patient care. As there are over a million charities in the United States the goals they might have are endless, but each charity should publicly articulate them.

A nonprofit called Impact Matters, begun in 2017, acknowledges that nonprofits don't share a single mission. "Each adopts its own," its website says. The organization asks these questions: "Has the nonprofit set forth an actionable mission? Has the nonprofit identified outcomes that tightly reflect its mission? Does the nonprofit use data correctly when analyzing performance? Does the nonprofit use data to improve delivery of its philanthropic services?"[342] This is a good way to begin the evaluation process, for it calls on the charity to do some work.

The key is that the charities need to be honest, clear, and specific. They must realize that filing a form with the IRS does not equal transparency or proper, ethical disclosure.

Yes, a charity also needs to post its financial ratios: the percent of budget to programming, overhead, and fundraising—the efficiency of a fundraising effort, and perhaps other categories—but, to avoid wrongly focusing on anomalies in any one year, as well as to provide long-term context, the data section should include historic trends covering several years of revenues and expenditures. Yes, "relevant" is subjective, and so narrative context is needed, even here amidst the arithmetic calculations. While they should not weigh heavily in a person's overall understanding of a charity, the numbers are not unimportant.

Even that caveat, though, comes with its own caveat. When we think of efficiency—a goal in search of a number, if there ever was one—we think of something done more quickly than not. But quicker is not always better. A suicide hotline, for example, can service more people with shorter calls, but it is well established that the relationship between the caller and the person answering is of paramount importance, and its quality often leads to the difference between life and death. Measuring efficiency, especially when the factors are the same for all charities, can be a fool's errand if not conducted thoughtfully and competently.

While numbers are important, they must be thoughtfully included with other information.

∽

Once they have defined their goals, charities need to publicly assess the progress toward those goals.

Every charity needs to be assessed but the watchdogs, especially as they are currently constituted, with far too little money to do an adequate job, have, at most, examined only a few thousand charities. There are more than one million charities in the United States asking for money from the public. More attention is going to be paid to the big charities where, cumulatively, most of the money goes, but all donors must be honored with an assessment of any charity they want to support.

As with the financial information, goals and assessments should have historical results so that people can see trends and progress, or the lack of progress, over the years.

Part of the financial picture, in addition to how money is spent, is how money, for the larger charities, is invested. Does a charity's endowment portfolio, for example, fit with a donor's social philosophy?

Another metric is the board members' engagement and understanding of their roles. How often members attend meetings could be a metric. Also, how many receive board training would help us understand how serious they are in improving themselves. After all, lawyers, accountants and other professionals must take continuing education courses—and these people have already mastered the basics of their profession, which is not true with board members who are often clueless about their responsibilities. That they are not paid—the norm at nonprofits in the United States—is no excuse for inattentiveness or incompetence.

～

There must be more than just the nonprofit informing the evaluation process. The people a nonprofit serves also need a voice. Students, faculty, museum visitors, hospital patients, animal owners, and veterans—among many other client categories—not only have a stake in a charity's worthiness, the prism through which they view a charity's activities is uniquely situated to assist in assessing that worthiness.

Donors must also be part of the mix. It is their money, after all, that permits a charity to survive and thrive, and donors should be able to voice their concerns, as well as their pleasure, about how their money is used.

The larger public should also weigh in on matters even more fundamental. "You could poll the American public to ask what a just charity or a well run foundation looks like," says JUST Capital's Martin Whittaker. Much of what Whittaker is doing in the for-profit world can be done in the nonprofit world. "What are the things that you would want to know?" he asks. "What values does the public want in its charities?" Also, as JUST Capital tells companies what is happening, charities can be told as well. "As businesses exist to create value, so are charities," Whittaker says. "It's just accomplished in different ways. Businesses are monetized in the form of revenue and profits, and charities are monetized in the form of grants." Also, he points out, the feedback at charities is not as strong or direct. Unhappy customers at for-profits simply discontinue their patronage. "When you buy something, you care deeply that you're getting your money's worth," he says, "but at charities the process of deciding dissatisfaction is a little more complex, and so the feedback is not as strong. "Do people really follow the dollar?" he wonders. "Who's more effective at addressing malaria? Does anyone know? The real magic is in giving donors value for their donations and on creating value."[343] A good evaluative system would provide charities with feedback, available to everyone, on how they are doing compared to the values the public offers up.

~

A responsible overseeing organization of the effort is needed, an organization that would regularly poll the public on matters important to society and monitor outside evaluations from clients and donors, as well as the assessments—both numerical and narrative—the charities conduct. It would not rate charities—for the point, as it always should have been, is to usefully evaluate them—but would include statistical analyses of the assessments resulting in a broad spectrum, likely shown in a bell curve, so the public would see where in a continuum a charity fits, and it would show comparisons of both overall and individual assessments.

This way, Harvard doesn't universally beat out Yale, or anyplace else actually. The Red Cross doesn't beat out the local homeless shelter. A university and a social services agency aren't even in the same category for assessments. It is time we see the charitable sector as composed of organizations that offer different types of services—in our evaluations, as well as in the services they provide—instead of as one big conglomerate.

Visitors to the site of such an overseeing organization should also be able to use it interactively. Some people don't like endowments, for example, because they feel that means too much money is sitting around, but many charities have grown large endowments to prudently ensure a future source of income. This is both a practical and a philosophical question, one that although the charity has answered for itself, ought to be part of an individual's evaluation.

The question for charities, however, isn't only how we can better slice and dice information about them. It's also about learning whether they comport with our personal perspectives and values. Donors and others should be able to interact with the data and narratives on their own terms to determine a charity that is worthy to them. Yes, Carleton really is a far better place than Harvard for many, many intelligent students. The Metropolitan Museum of Art doesn't have what the di Rosa, a small museum in Napa, California has. Comparing them is irrational.

Because any one voice, or cabal of voices, can be unfairly or maliciously driven, the overseeing organization needs to be able to eliminate the extremes from any assessment, and users needs to know the particulars of the process in the event they want to include the extremes.

The overseeing organization would also scrub the Internet to find and include links to news stories about the charity.

With all of this, users could create their own top-ten lists. It would be relevant because it would be theirs.

~

The organization would also act as a thought leader—often in collaboration with other groups, such as the Urban Institute, Independent Sector, the Philanthropy Roundtable and the National Council on Nonprofits—on issues relating to the nonprofit world and philanthropy. Or perhaps it would simply replace some or all of them. Dan Pallotta suggests some of them should merge.[344]

Part of this leadership would mean the organization would investigate charities that are reported to have problems, whether financial, operational, or ethical. The stories in the *Tampa Bay Times* about the worst charities in America were good, but more needs to be done, such as encouraging people to formally complain to the states and to the IRS. At the same time, we need to accept the reality that, regardless of their legal status, state and federal overseers are not doing a good job as watchdogs. And—let's face it—they most likely never will. An overseeing organization, well funded and with a robust and always expanding vision, could do much to fill the gap. *CBS News* could still do a hit job on a charity, but there would be a platform to fight back. Think of how differently the Wounded Warrior Project story might have developed if the public knew it could go to a neutral, competent site that would act as a check on the allegations. If allegations prove to be true, the platform would show that, as well.

The organization, while not endowed with any regulatory authority, would ideally have the resources to investigate, on a global basis, nonprofit activity. For example, it took the *Wall Street Journal*—not the IRS and not any state attorney general—to discover that hundreds of private foundations sidestep laws prohibiting self-dealing and inappropriate business transactions between private foundations and their officers, directors, and substantial donors.[345] While some foundations perform studies, no organization devotes adequate resources to evaluating and researching issues in the nonprofit sector; nor can any claim the authority to do the job. An overseeing organization with the right financial resources, and whose workforce could balance proper professional acumen and ethical understanding, could dig into these issues, along with the media, and then report to regulators and the public any questionable activity.

In short, the following would go a long way toward fixing the evaluation system so people know what's going on at charities:

- The public defines its values for charities.
- The charity publicly defines it goals.
- The charity publicly evaluates its goals.
- The public evaluates the charity's goals.

- Individuals manage their preferences regarding charities' goals and values.

- An overseer manages the process and generates reports.

- In collaboration with other organizations, or not, an overseer is the nonprofit intellectual and policy leader.

- An overseeing organization investigates questionable activity at a charity and conducts broad audits related to policy questions affecting nonprofits and philanthropists.

A gold standard top-level domain might also play a role. The top-level domain is the word after the dot in a web or email address. For most charities that word is "org"; many educational institutions use "edu." Currently there is no requirement that an organization actually be a nonprofit to use either of these domains, and certainly the domain indicates nothing of the organization's worthiness. ICANN, the Internet Corporation for Assigned Names and Numbers, itself a nonprofit, is responsible for authorizing new domains. What if one of them, for example, were "charity"? And what if an organization, in addition to proving that it is legally a charity, could obtain that domain only if it satisfied certain criteria? Two challenges, although not insurmountable, would be to establish fair and useful standards, and to ensure compliance. If that could be done, the overseeing organization, as described here, would be in the best position to define those standards and to ensure that organizations maintained them.

Also, as a thought leader, the organization might study donor behavior, such as what can be found in the premise, regarding donors, put forth by Anand Giridharadas the author of *Winners Take All: The Elite Charade of Changing the World,* in which he argues that donors today are at least as predatory as they are socially concerned, that their charity impulses "monopolize progress and then give symbolic scraps to the forsaken—many of whom wouldn't need the scraps if the society were working right."[346] Exploring and conducting ongoing research on this and other intriguing theses would fit nicely into the purposes of such an organization.

∾

The board of the organization should be both prestigious and engaged. It should consist of appropriately chosen leaders in the nonprofit world, with representation among charities of different sizes, as well as from government and business. It would not be partisan and would include a leader from both liberal and conservative think tanks. The board members would be paid—as for-profit board members are and as nonprofit board members typically are not. Board members would have limited terms.

The mission would include the protection and advancement of the social pursuit of goodness. It would, exploring Richard Feiner's approach, quarterback a process to explore how all three sectors might work better together to improve society.

This can't be done on the cheap, but it should not raise money. To free it from ongoing fundraising or donor pressures, the organization needs to be a fully funded foundation. Taking into account staffing, technology, and research, the project needs the resources to support a healthy budget. Ideally the corpus, and thus the income, would grow so that spending could increase with inflation. In 2017, GuideStar's budget was $13 million, the BBB Wise Giving Alliance's was $2.2 million, Charity Navigator's was $3.4 million and CharityWatch's was a little under $540,000. GiveWell's budget that year, excluding grants it made to charities, was $5 million. Guidestar's budget is the largest in this group, but it is still inadequate for the purposes of this enterprise.

Dan Pallotta notes that the combined budgets of the major players of the top 10 charity associations totaled less than $75 million annually in 2016. "Let's set aside for the moment," he suggested, "how tragic that figure is for a $1 trillion sector to which Americans give $400 billion in charitable contributions alone. If putting together a $75 million merger of 10 organizations is more than we can handle, we should all go home. In just five quarters ending in 2014, Apple spent over $11 billion on 29 acquisitions, not including its acquisition of Beats Headphones for $3 billion. The Kansas City Royals' 2015 team payroll was over $110 million. The budget for any run-of-the-mill Hollywood action movie is three times the scale of what would be required. Can all of the intelligence of the sector's leaders not put together a deal of that scale? We can, of course, continue along the way we are. But if we do, anyone with half a brain can tell you we will never achieve our full potential."[347]

Ideally, the organization would have a singular designation in the tax code that would make it different from a public charity or foundation—or any other nonprofit described in the tax code.

We need this different, expansive point of view to move forward. It doesn't call for the elimination of charities or for the IRS or state attorneys general to abdicate their authority. Much of their activity would stay the same. It simply offers more for people to help society. It's not perfect—no thought process is, and the execution of an idea is always a challenge—and, as more data and experience inform the process, it would improve over time.

It would better respect the public's need to know and society's need for improvement. Evaluating charities intelligently is a crucial step in the process of determining if charities are earning their keep. Furthermore, the process would go a long way to ensure, as Jacob Harold says, that charities are trustworthy.

In the end, though, it's not about making better assessments. It's about making a better world. The evaluation of charities—or even their existence—is not the ultimate objective.

∾

It may seem surprising, irreverent even, that Abraham Lincoln, as Garry Wills argues in *Lincoln at Gettysburg,* saw the United States Constitution, the bedrock of our republic, as only a means to an end, that end being the vision embodied in the Declaration of Independence. "Lincoln," Wills writes, "distinguished between the Declaration as the statement of a permanent ideal and the Constitution as an early and provisional embodiment of that ideal, to be tested against it, kept in motion toward it."[348] Theodore Parker, the Transcendentalist and a contemporary of Lincoln's, saw it much the same way. "The Constitution is only a provisional compromise between the ideal political principle of the Declaration and the actual selfishness of the people North and South."[349]

That's a startling notion, but think of the defect inflicted at the Constitution's birth: slavery. Everyone understood, even at the time the

Constitution was written and ratified, that enshrining the inferiority of other human beings would be divisive; so backhanded was the process, in fact, the word slavery never found its way into the text. "The thing is hid away in the constitution," Lincoln said, "just as an afflicted man hides away a wen or a cancer, which he dares not cut out at once, lest he bleed to death; with the promise, nevertheless, that the cutting may begin at the end of a given time. Less than this our fathers could not do; and more they would not do."[350]

The given time for the cutting, it turns out, was a little less than a century. By 1861 it was clear that the wen was so evil that it needed to be removed. If not, the arc of progress would overwhelm it and the mighty Constitution would be no more than a temporary and failed embodiment of the ideals that made America singular. It and the republic it nurtured would be doomed.

Thus, to give shape to the intangible ideal that "all men are created equal," for which so much blood had been spilled at Gettysburg, in his great speech Lincoln, looking back four score and seven years from 1863, fully ignored 1787, when the Constitutional Convention took place, and led us instead to 1776, when the Declaration of Independence was approved. Lincoln wasn't referring to the country's *legal* birth, but to the country's *ethical* birth, the one where the idea of life, liberty and the pursuit of happiness are inalienable rights was conceived.

As enshrined as it is, the Constitution constitutes little more than a delivery vehicle on a journey to realize our ideals, our permanent aspirations. Ultimately, if it's not up to the job of transporting us to a more perfect union, well then, we might just need a whole new structure.

Does this thinking not mirror the general struggle for improving society? The current nonprofit system is a whole lot less enshrined than the Constitution is. If those who care about the work of nonprofits want to make the world a better place, then is it not true that the American nonprofit structure, so widely admired around the world, is a mere vehicle, useful only until it is not?

The highest ideal in the world of philanthropy is the love of humankind, so let us consider the promotion of that love to be a permanent objective.

As well, let us understand that everything charity leaders do needs to be in the service of that objective. Anything less, if society is to be serious, could render the provisional status of our current nonprofit system, fragile as it is, to an historical one.

This is not a solitary alarm. Josh Freedman, a contributor to *Forbes,* argued in 2013 that, in addition to being so motley, the big problem with nonprofits, especially universities—and with a particular jab at Harvard— is that so many make so much profit. The solution, he says, "is to eliminate the very idea of the nonprofit sector."[351] The conversation on the matter of the role of charities in society and, indeed, whether some charities are really charities, is swelling.

～

For now, though, so as not to get too far ahead of ourselves, let's stick to trying to better understand the efficacy of charitable organizations. Doing that will inform the larger questions of how, or whether, the nonprofit world as we know it should survive.

CHAPTER 8

THE BOARD FAILS WOUNDED WARRIOR PROJECT

Précis

Wounded Warrior Project, begun in 2005, grew quickly after one of its founders, John Melia, resigned in 2008 after making what many on the board felt were some poor decisions. It was also clear that Melia's vision would not be aligned with the growing needs of veterans that WWP was positioning itself to address.

Steve Nardizzi was appointed the new CEO, and Al Giordano the new COO. They brought with them large programmatic ideas for the organization's growth and impact, and established an aggressive fundraising effort to support those ideas.

Over the next decade, the organization grew from offering a handful of initiatives to conducting almost 20 full-scale programs, and from raising under $20 million per year to raising almost $400 million per year.

In support of their vision, the two executives supplemented a traditional fundraising program with an extensive schedule of raw and effective television commercials. They portrayed catastrophically wounded veterans and many of the problems they were experiencing. Even though they were responsible for raising substantial money, the ads attracted criticism, much of it from individuals in or close to the military, because, it was alleged, they discouraged sign-ups.

An analysis of military recruitment during the years in question showed no evidence to support that claim.

While it grew, WWP considerably increased the support it provided to other veterans' organizations.

Some organizations began a drumbeat against WWP because it was growing quickly and becoming more influential. Most organizations that serve the veteran community are relatively small. Also, many have poor administrative reputations.

Jealousy was a factor in the growing dislike of WWP. The aggressive tone of the WWP fundraising program didn't sit well with some people in the nonprofit community.

Some smaller organizations, which were not raising much money, fraudulently linked themselves to WWP. When forced to defend itself in court from the bad behavior of one, WWP was subjected to gratuitously disparaging publicity.

In February 2014, WWP hosted an All-Hands Huddle, an organization-wide conference, at the Broadmoor Hotel in Colorado. Erick Millette, a WWP employee, was happy and enthusiastic about the conference. Everyone else at the organization felt the same.

Millette later heavily and publicly criticized the conference. The criticism included Steve Nardizzi rappelling down the side of the Broadmoor.

While Nardizzi led WWP to much success, at the Broadmoor meeting he overlooked a crucial, if cosmetic, aspect of any modern-day organization: how things look has a bearing on how things are.

His success during the prior decade, as well as his confidence in his leadership abilities, diverted him from the optics of the way he ran the organization.

Nardizzi acknowledges that some of his flamboyant actions while chief executive were problematic, and that they opened the door to criticism.

Among those who didn't like WWP was Admiral Michael Mullen, former chairman of the Joint Chiefs of Staff.

In 2013 Nardizzi had a contentious meeting with Mullen during which Mullen claimed that WWP had no metrics, it was not transparent, the ads victimized warriors, and the organization generally wasn't doing good work.

According to Nardizzi, Mullen admitted that he had never looked at the WWP website prior to complaining about the lack of transparency and program metrics.

Because he disliked the raw content and aggressive schedule of the television ads, Mullen aligned himself with other charities that didn't like WWP.

The meeting was a courtesy by Nardizzi to a former formerly high-ranking member of the military. Mullen had no authority over Wounded Warrior Project, an independent nonprofit organization.

~

In February 2013 CBS aired a WWP public service announcement during the Super Bowl.

That spring, Richard Jones, a senior executive at the CBS Corporation and someone who had a good reputation in the veterans' community, contacted WWP to ask if he could join the board. The thinking was that Jones was at least partly responsible for the Super Bowl placement and thus, in addition to his credibility in the veteran space, should be nominated for a board seat.

Jones was on the boards of two other charities, Dixon Center and the Institute for Veterans and Military Families, whose leaders were antagonistic to WWP.

During his interviews to join the WWP board, Jones did not disclose his relationships with the two charities unfriendly to WWP.

Although Jones was likely instrumental in getting the Super Bowl PSA on the air, it seems his motive was not born of his devotion to WWP; instead, he may have wanted to get on the inside of WWP to better diminish its standing.

~

In 2015 Erick Millette quit his job at Wounded Warrior Project. He joined a closed Facebook page, which was created by disgruntled former employees who posted complaints about WWP. The anonymity encouraged members to create their own singular narrative in what was essentially an echo chamber.

The group's criticisms morphed into a vindictive collusion to take down WWP's staff leadership.

The reason why Millette was unhappy has never been made known publicly. His criticism of WWP amounted to an abrupt, unprovoked about-face in stark and unexplained contrast to his earlier enthusiasm. He refused to respond to questions about this matter.

In June 2015 some of the people in the Facebook group reached out to air their complaints to the *New York Times*. Dave Philipps, a reporter for the paper, then began research for a story.

When Philipps said he was contacted by "a small group of employees and former employees who felt like the leadership at WWP was going in the wrong direction," he had to at least suspect that he was being used in a well-thought out and deliberately planned attack on Wounded Warrior Project. A review of his communications with them makes it clear that he knew he was dealing with an organized group.

Most likely—although this has not been established—Jones alerted the news division at CBS when he heard from WWP staff that the *New York Times* was going to run a story. Even though a "firewall" explanation asserts that an executive at CBS could have nothing to do with news decisions, it strains credulity to think that Jones was not involved.

According to Philipps, *60 Minutes* considered running the story, but there wasn't enough time to conduct proper research.

On January 26 and 27, 2016 *CBS News* ran a three-part story on Wounded Warrior Project. On January 27, the *New York Times*, above the fold on the front page, ran a similar story. The reports would have a devastating impact on WWP.

Many of the allegations made in the reports were either wrong or misleading.

Although Philipps reached out for comments beyond those whose voices constituted the Facebook page, he chose not to include them, even though they far outnumbered the complaints. One person Philipps interviewed, Andrew Coughlin, a WWP staff member as well as a veteran, criticized Philipps in a twitter exchange for Philipps's failure to include his comments in the *New York Times* piece. The interview included Coughlin's statement that Wounded Warrior Project saved his life and his marriage.

Both news organizations could have better vetted Erick Millette, their primary source of allegations, for bias and accuracy, and included the views of the many others that would have countered the prevailing sentiment the news stories conveyed.

Both news organizations relied on Charity Navigator for at least one serious allegation, relating to the reporting of joint cost allocation, to show alleged inefficiencies at Wounded Warrior Project, even though, according to an accounting process required by GAAP (Generally Accepted Accounting Principles) and the IRS, there were no such inefficiencies.

Two categories of sources for the stories—documents and people—were wanting in their veracity.

∾

In addition to questions concerning his motivation to become a WWP board member, Richard Jones had a conflict of interest as the crisis developed. He was actively involved in overseeing WWP's response to the *CBS News* investigation and, as a senior-level employee at CBS, should have recused himself from discussions the board conducted concerning the issue.

Not only did Jones not recuse himself, he actively participated in the interviews Simpson Thacher conducted in the aftermath of the media stories.

Richard Jones refused to answer questions relating to his involvement in the crisis.

∾

Unlike the way the board of the Red Cross responded when that organization came under fire, WWP's board members conspicuously failed to support their two top executives.

In fact, they were silent and they muzzled Steve Nardizzi during this time.

On March 10, 2016, the WWP board announced at a news conference that Simpson Thacher found that "certain allegations raised in media reports were inaccurate."

The WWP board also announced at that news conference that Simpson Thacher found that some policies needed strengthening.

The WWP board also announced at that news conference that Nardizzi and Giordano had been fired. No one on the board could bring himself to look either man in the eye as the news was delivered.

The reason given—to restore trust—has never been substantiated.

The board that fired Nardizzi and Giordano instructed them to do exactly as they did—fundraising, programs, organizational development, and more. Only a few months earlier, board members applauded the men's work and approved substantial bonuses on the basis of that work.

The board did not have the courage to counter the incorrect allegations put forth by the *New York Times* and *CBS News*. As a result, tens of thousands of veterans were negatively affected in one way or another.

Simpson Thacher provided WWP's board only an oral accounting—not a written report—of its financial review in response to the media allegations. It wrote a letter only in response to Senator Charles Grassley's inquiries.

A meeting to discuss differences between the board and Nardizzi was scheduled for mid-March 2016, but it never took place because the two were already gone.

~

Fundraising revenues did not drop, as the board contends, after the news reports, but began to drop immediately following the firings.

By the end of WWP's 2016 fiscal year, six months after Nardizzi and Giordano were fired, fundraising dropped by $70 million. Also, by then programs were dropped or reduced and many people were let go.

By the end of WWP's 2017 fiscal year, fundraising dropped by an additional $91 million.

The fastest growing charity in the United States had, in almost no time at all, become the fastest shrinking charity in the United States.

QUESTIONS UNANSWERED

Peter Honerkamp and Chris Carney, the men who started Soldier Ride, sent an email to Anthony Odierno and Richard Jones. "Unfortunately, the board has repeatedly refused to respond to our inquiries about that decision," they wrote. "We believe silence is the refuge of people who have something to hide."

For Tony Odierno and Richard Jones:

- Why did the board fail to forcefully debunk the allegations made by *CBS News* and the *New York Times*?

- Why was the initial WWP rebuttal that appeared on its website withdrawn in the aftermath of the firings?

- How did CBS learn of the firings of Nardizzi and Giordano before any other media outlet knew?

- How did officials at the Department of Defense learn of their impending dismissal days before it occurred?

- Why were the TV commercials depicting the catastrophically wounded removed from the air as soon as Nardizzi and Giordano were fired—given their effectiveness in garnering donations and given the needs of the catastrophically wounded?

- Do you regret voting to fire them in light of the enormous loss of revenue it caused WWP—and, in turn, the reduction in services to those wounded warriors you had pledged to serve?

- If Nardizzi and Giordano deserved to be fired, why did you not resign given that you were entrusted with overseeing their management?

- Did you at any time communicate with, or act at the behest of, David Sutherland, Admiral Mullen, or others in the military in your interaction with WWP?

- Were you part of a plot, however informally conceived, planned or executed, to change the control and direction of WWP so as to make it more answerable to the military?

- Do you know if there were those in the military who resented WWP because it exposed the failures of the Veterans Administration to care for its own?

And questions for Richard Jones:

- When you were interviewed about joining the board why did you fail to disclose that you were on the board of IVMF and the Dixon Center, both of which were hostile to WWP?

- Are you aware that board members who interviewed you are greatly disturbed by your failure to reveal that affiliation?

- A few days after Steve Nardizzi and Al Giordano were dismissed, you called Erick Millette to thank him for coming forward with his accusations about WWP governance. Given the fact that everyone at WWP knew Millette was lying, why did you do so?

- Given your employment at CBS, why did you not recuse yourself from the board deliberations on whether to fire Nardizzi and Giordano?

- Why did you participate in the Simpson Thacher interviews?

- Why did you claim a CBS camera crew was outside your house trying to interview you in the aftermath of the initial media allegations when they could have simply approached you at your office?

- Did you threaten to resign if the other WWP Board members did not agree to unanimously fire Nardizzi and Giordano?

- Did you inform the news division of CBS that the *New York Times* was doing a story on the management and fundraising practices at WWP?

- Do you in any measure regret how much damage you and the board caused WWP and our wounded warriors by your failure to defend the organization? [352]

Earlier, the entire board received a similar list of questions. Only Tom Johnson, the chief executive officer of Abernathy MacGregor, the firm the board hired to oversee the firings of Nardizzi and Giordano, responded. He wrote, "The board has no additional comments beyond what they have said publicly. The board feels that some of the questions should be directed to CBS, and not to them." [353]

The board did respond, in written form, to a few questions in a podcast aired in September 2016 conducted by Robert Samuel, a producer at the O'Reilly Factor. When asked about the overall critical nature of a report issued earlier in the month, the WWP board said, "Based on the findings of its review and a comprehensive evaluation of the circumstances, the Board lost confidence in the ability of former CEO Steve Nardizzi and former COO Al Giordano to lead the organization because of their conduct and poor judgment. The Board determined the best course of action was to terminate them in order to move the organization forward and restore trust among those who need WWP's services most." *The news release of March 10, 2016 did not say anything about "poor judgment" on the part of either Steve Nardizzi or Al Giordano; in Simpson Thacher's letter to Senator Grassley, nothing was offered to substantiate the claim of poor judgment.*

On the accusation that WWP suffered a deep drop in fundraising not just after the media reports, but after Nardizzi and Giordano were dismissed, the board said, "Based on figures publicly reported by WWP, the decline in fundraising began immediately after exaggerated media reports and continued to accelerate as concerns sparked by those reports continued to take hold among our donor base." *This is not true. Fundraising did not begin to drop until after the firings—not immediately following the news reports. During this time Nardizzi provided weekly updates to the board, which showed that donations were not dropping off.*

The board also ignored the assertion that it was pressured by top Pentagon officials, including Admiral Michael Mullen, to fire WWP's two top leaders, and said it "determined the best course of action was to terminate" Nardizzi and Giordano "immediately in order to move the organization forward and restore trust among those who need WWP's services most." *As has been shown, this statement is highly suspect.*

Finally, to the question of whether Richard Jones had a conflict of interest given his role at CBS, plus his board membership on other charities with antagonistic relationships with WWP, the board said, "Richard Jones is an experienced director who puts WWP's well-being and best interests first."[354] *Note how the statement avoided addressing the conflict-of-interest question.*

~

While some key players in this saga may wish to dispute the accuracy of some of the extrapolations, findings and conclusions described here, it must be remembered that each of them was contacted with questions about all of these matters. No one wanted to talk. No one was willing to explain why things happened as they did.

- After being asked to explain his comments to the media, Erick Millette, the main resource for the pejorative reports, said, "I'm not discussing WWP any longer."[355]

- After expressing discontent of the characterization in an early report of Admiral Michael Mullen's meeting with Steve Nardizzi, Mullen was asked if he wanted to provide his own perspective. He responded, "I have nothing else to add."[356]

- When asked to justify the conclusions in the Simpson Thacher review of Wounded Warrior Project, Paul Curnin, the firm's attorney who signed the letter to Senator Charles Grassley, did not respond.

- When asked if anyone at *CBS News* could address questions about its research and reporting methodology, Al Ortiz, an executive producer of special events at *CBS News*, responded with this: "*CBS News* stands by our reports on WWP as accurate, fair, and properly sourced. I can assure you that our reporting was completely independent, and that we made numerous requests to speak with Mr. Nardizzi, his representatives, and all members of The WWP Board of Directors. Thank you for reaching out to *CBS News*."[357]

- When Dave Philipps was asked if he would answer questions about his research and reporting methodology, he responded with this: "Thanks, but I'm not interested. Good luck."[358]

How Did The Board Fail?

Even though they are often silent and in the background, members of a charity's governing board constitute the most important group of people at any charitable organization. The board has fiduciary oversight and fosters the vision. Many people don't know anything about this group because the one who usually generates the public attention for the organization's accomplishments, as well as for its failures, is the senior staff person.

By law, each board member must adhere to three duties: a duty of care, by ensuring the prudent use of all the assets, including the charity's good will; a duty of loyalty, by making decisions not in his or her self interests; and a duty of obedience, by ensuring that the nonprofit acts lawfully and ethically.[359] Every decision made at a board meeting ought to be in service to those three duties.

Arguably, however, they are too broad to provide much guidance. Other than for obvious crimes, it is difficult to bring legal charges against charitable boards. Their purpose, then, is more aspirational than legal; adherence to them more cultural than statutory. A verdict of liability will most likely be found not in a jury's opinion but in public opinion.

Crises test resolve. The WWP board acted, if not in violation of its three duties, far less diligently than was prudent in responding to the crisis.

≈

Although some employees had criticized Nardizzi and Giordano for creating a toxic culture in which minor offenses and disloyalty were punished, that was not a staff-wide opinion. In fact, the culture was healthy. You don't get to the top of the heap—remember, the staff voted WWP as the number one nonprofit to work for—otherwise.[360] Board members actually echoed that message, with their positive reviews of Nardizzi and Giordano, strong evidence that the board thought both men were performing well.

And then, when the fuse of the media stories was lit, the board froze in the maelstrom. It created the impression that no one was in charge and that there may have been merit to the allegations. The board made the situation worse when it fired the two men and, in the process, provided

294 | WOUNDED CHARITY

contradictory statements: *Nothing really wrong here; we're doing well, actually—but our leaders have to go.*

"Poor judgment" was the essence of the only denunciation of Nardizzi and Giordano in the Simpson Thacher review, but there was nothing to substantiate even that, and much to refute it. The critique was hollow, as Bill O'Reilly discovered when Tony Odierno admitted as much in their Fox interview in March 2016.

It's as if the board wanted to justify a decision already made. It's as if the board was inventing a problem to justify its own poor judgment.

The board knew, at the time, that the media got it wrong, and it didn't take a financial audit to show that. The out-of-context criticism from a small group of anonymous disgruntled former employees and inadequate evaluations from ratings agencies that lacked credibility were only excuses.

How well did WWP's board members really think Nardizzi and Giordano were doing when they wrote their evaluations? Or, how honest were they? Or, how susceptible were they to the news reports? Or, how susceptible to those reports did they *want* to appear, perhaps with the goal of hiding another agenda? Or, were they simply inept?

Or, were the majority railroaded by one person? The matter of Richard Jones's actions must be taken into account. What he did professionally informed what he did as a volunteer, which can be a good thing—until a conflict arises. The media allegations, driven—or at least accommodated—by this pivotal board member in whom other members placed their confidence, averted the public's attention with a false narrative. By not recusing himself, Jones was essentially inserting himself in, as well as influencing, the investigation of what he oversaw at WWP. That has a name: conflict of interest. "You can't serve two masters," Al Giordano says, "He had a duty of loyalty to Wounded Warrior Project, but he also had a duty of loyalty to CBS. He's conflicted. Shouldn't be in the room. Yet he had more to do with the investigation than any other board member."[361]

Intense external scrutiny is valid, but the scrutiny has to also be scrutinized and validated. Knowing and evaluating the source of criticism are as important as knowing and evaluating the criticism itself. Boards should know that. Boards should not automatically cave in to pressure.

There's an old adage that advises organizational leaders to act based on how they would feel if their actions were the subject of a story on the front page of the *New York Times*. That's advice worth taking into account, but it's hardly comprehensive; it's not the same as validly explaining and defending what the *Times* got wrong.

If the board had issues with Nardizzi and Giordano driving faster than their headlights, they should have demanded a discussion with the two men to ensure everyone was on the same page. And, if the board intended to have such a discussion, it should not have fired them beforehand.

Clearly, within certain restraints, the board has the right to do whatever it wants, but, because the aftermath of the allegations was so chaotic, the growth and reputation of the organization suffered dramatically.

Matt Modine, the actor and supporter of veterans' causes, responded with this to the question of whether the allegations that came to light in early 2016, or the firings, affected his feelings about WWP: "It affected my judgment about the leadership in the project," he said. By leadership, he clearly meant the board. "It has not affected my support for the veterans. I'm only sad that the millions of dollars of support they were receiving under Al and Steve's leadership is lost. Al and Steve worked for the veterans."[362]

Richard Levick, a columnist for *Forbes,* addressed this issue in "The Gutting Of Wounded Warrior: How To Kill A Charity." Writing in September 2016, within six months of the firings, he said, "One thing seems irrefutable: not media allegations, but WWP's misguided response seems to have provided the coup de grâce. There's a crisis communications bromide that, to placate the wolves at your door, make a sacrifice. That usually means human sacrifice; i.e., firing people. But herein lies the danger of all bromides: they don't fit all situations." Nonprofits, Levick says, face different expectations from those faced by for-profit companies. "Once trust is broken or a confession made, the trust cannot be regained. Donors will simply make donations elsewhere."[363]

It appears that the firings were the result of timidity. The board consisted of people who were successful in business or the military. It is not inconceivable that this otherwise accomplished group was a degree or two too separated from the rank and file of the veteran community for them to

appreciate that Nardizzi and Giordano instinctively knew what the organization needed to best serve those who returned wounded. Wounded
Warrior Project is a complex bureaucracy, but it is also a warm place where
real and damaged men and women find solace and support.

One long-time donor, a combat-wounded, double-amputee Vietnam
veteran, said when he canceled his monthly donation, "Some of them
[your board members] might have been heroes on the battlefield, but they
are all cowards in the boardroom."

~

Quality governance leadership was absent at a most vital time. Art Taylor,
of the BBB's give.org, says, "The board of directors could have operated a bit
better. By that, I mean it seems they decided at first to stick with Nardizzi.
Then, because of public pressure, they decided to fire both the CEO and
the COO. But they didn't go into any detail as to what, in fact, Nardizzi
and Giordano had done so wrong that they had to be removed. While we
were already monitoring the circumstances, it was at that point that we felt
we needed to list Wounded Warrior Project as an evaluation-in-progress
while we got the facts."[364]

It seems likely that the self-inflicted damage was more than the board
could handle. There can be no doubt that WWP's directors failed in their
leadership. In a real, if not legally indictable, way, they failed in their duties
of care, loyalty and obedience. As they rid themselves of their executive
leadership, they imperiled Wounded Warrior Project. They failed their
organization. And they failed the veterans and the families they depend on.

The good news, if it can be so considered, is that they are not alone.

A 2017 study from Stanford University showed that charities have serious concerns about their leadership. "More than 80 percent of nonprofit
organizations," the study found, "struggle with at least one of the seven
fundamental elements of nonprofit leadership and management, thus ham-
pering their overall performance and their ability to achieve their goals."
The seven fundamental elements are: 1) board governance, 2) funding,
3) impact evaluations, 4) strategy, 5) organization and talent, 6) mission,
and 7) insight and courage. The most problematic area for respondents

was board governance. Over half said their nonprofits had weak board governance." This supported the findings of an earlier report, which said, "Over a quarter of nonprofit directors do not have a deep understanding of their organization's mission and strategy. Nearly a third are dissatisfied with the board's ability to evaluate organizational performance. A majority do not believe their fellow board members are very experienced or engaged in their work."[365]

Wounded Warrior Project was an excellent organization: it employed over 600 people and pretty much every one of them was moving in the same direction; for a few years running, it was the number one nonprofit organization to work for; its programs were extensive, well-funded and had measurably positive impact; in both its fundraising and administration, it had instituted every conceivable best practice. The only thing that wasn't tightened up: the board, which Nardizzi and Giordano could not control.

The board also had no excuse when it came to the damaging publicity. For some years prior to the crisis, Nardizzi had been urging the board to undertake training in crisis management, but they refused. When the allegations were reported in early 2016, Nardizzi cautioned Tony Odierno by telling him that the board needed to be careful in its handling of the crisis. He even wrote a report on what had happened to Livestrong, Boys and Girls Clubs, and Susan G. Komen, and graphed out the scale of the losses as a result of not handling their media crises well.

⁓

Al Giordano thought the whole board, not just Jones, should have been "conflicted out." In March 2016, after CBS ran its piece on the board's expenditures and before he was fired, he met with WWP's general counsel and assistant general counsel, as well as with outside counsel, attorneys from Arnold & Porter. He asked them if the board members were in such an intractably conflicted position that "they should simply be removed and a caretaker board appointed until things could be worked out."[366]

And what about that CBS report? If Jones was the strategist behind the network's damaging coverage of Nardizzi and Giordano, why would he have wanted the news crew to show WWP's *board* in a bad light? After all, he was a member of the board. Wouldn't such a report reflect badly on *him*? Maybe. But it's possible that Jones wanted to put pressure on the board to fire Nardizzi and Giordano; that is, in response to a report where its bad behavior was highlighted, the board could show that it was doing something in response to the entire saga.

And what about Jones's frantic call to Steve Nardizzi, telling him he was "trapped," when the *CBS News* crew was supposedly descending on his home? It's possible that the whole thing was a ruse to get everyone to believe he was the victim—not the author—of the debacle. It's also possible that Jones did not want to show his *employer* in a bad light; CBS, the storied Tiffany news organization that had just been caught ignoring journalistic standards—and at the instigation of Jones, at that.

It was around this time that Jones, even though he was not the board chair, demanded that board members vote unanimously to fire Nardizzi and Giordano—or else he would resign.[367] In this way, he could defend the bad journalism to protect his own interests at CBS, as well as realize his goal of ridding WWP's leadership, which had been a thorn in the side of his favorite veterans' charities—success in his view, perhaps, but, given the severe financial and programming losses that followed at WWP, a pyrrhic victory; and, plainly, honor was nowhere to be seen.

The board's members might have salvaged a sliver of honor, as Giordano suggests, by engaging in a transition strategy to replace themselves. The human sacrifice so common in the wake of a crisis—remember, *bromide*, the word Richard Levick rightly used, means trite and unoriginal—would have had more meaning, and better results, had the board admitted that *it* screwed up, and arranged to replace itself.

John Melia, as well as others, criticized the board for not providing proper oversight. But many others criticized the board for not support-ing its top executives in the face of allegations that were known to be unfounded at the time of the firings. One former board member who spoke on the condition of anonymity said, "The board cut and run—even though they must have signed off on the larger strategic initiatives that Steve and Al put forth. They were partners in all of this. They can't criticize those two without criticizing themselves. They were fired for optics? Yes, they were, weren't they? They put them out to twist in the wind. That was not honorable."

Wounded Warrior Project was the target of a long-marinating hit job. The board, wittingly or not, acted as executioner.

One former WWP employee had an unusual criticism. "I blame Al and Steve," he said. "They should not have listened to the board. They should have told their story to the press. You say they were muzzled? Well, screw that. They should have screamed bloody murder. They should not have listened to the board. All they"—board members—"care about is their reputation. Well, this was more important than their reputation. The lives and livelihoods of veterans were at stake."[368] This is a profound sentiment, which, if considered seriously, creates a profound conflict: the duty of top staff members to be loyal to their board while at the same time their duty to be loyal to their mission. Does staff ever have the right, or the obligation, to mutiny?

∾

Al Giordano was fired in a most ignominious manner, but takes the high road to say, "It's not about me. I still have all four of my limbs. So they fired me? Big deal. Did I take a big hit? Yeah. Did I have to change industries because I'm blackballed now? Yeah. Whatever. But that's not the big thing. How many warriors could have been helped? The scale of the losses is mind-boggling." He mentions the spike in the suicide rate, from a report in the fall of 2018. "We had $100 million in the budget for mental health in our last year. Not to mention the Long-Term Support Trust that was set up to take care of the catastrophically injured for 20 years—and longer— down the road. No more money in that now. Great, we're taking care of a hundred families, but what about the other 800 or 900?" All of this was unnecessary, he says. "And why? Because a couple of guys with stars on their shoulder boards didn't like the ads? What's going to happen to the kid who is now condemned to a government-sponsored nursing home at an inappropriate age? The kid who's too young for a nursing home but there's nowhere else he can go."

Giordano says this with much passion, his focus on the individual human damage WWP's loss of revenues represents. It is a passion born of the authority his family's and his own military service grant him. "My skin in the game is first and foremost taking care of the wounded men and women. First and last. That's why I started this."

Then, thinking about the moment he was fired, "And not one of them could look me in the face."[369]

After it was all over, John Loosen, the former long-time board member, wrote to Giordano:

> Al,
>
> We had a good run. Thanks to people like you, we helped and saved thousands of people from extended catastrophic miseries.
>
> Looking back, I'm surprised we weren't taken down sooner by the establishment. Our forward-looking, unorthodox philosophy changed the prototype on how to run a VSO and deliver services. The establishment (the government and other VSOs) was threatened and wasn't ready for the change, and therefore chose to attack and destroy. Unfortunately they succeeded. Sometimes some people, because of their fear, jealousy and ignorance, would rather destroy no matter what the consequences be.
>
> It's a disgrace and you should be proud of your accomplishments. You regrettably were cut off at the knees by others not worthy to be in the same room with you.
>
> Proud of you and honored to always call you a friend.
>
> John[370]

In January 2019, Charlie Battaglia, another former board member, wrote this to Giordano:

> I would like to think that those of us not on the board at the time of the cases would have acted differently. Throwing Steve and you

under the bus was an admission of guilt that nearly destroyed WWP as well as Steve and your reputations.

Charlie[371]

~

In late September 2018, Tony Odierno and Roger Campbell stepped down from the board and new members were announced. Richard Jones remained.

AFTERWORD

LASTING IMPRESSIONS

Others share John Loosen's and Charlie Battaglia's sentiments. In the wake of what happened, in the summer and autumn of 2016 many people took time to reflect on what it meant to work at Wounded Warrior Project. The following were among the many notes that found their way, unsolicited, to Facebook, as well as personally to Steve Nardizzi. The names have been removed because naming the people could subject them to an unwanted public backlash. When he became CEO Nardizzi signed up for the scrutiny, but they did not.[372]

∽

"I'm sorry it has taken me so long to reach out. Honestly, I was trying to find the right words. But after last week, I realized if I wait to find the right words, I'd never reach out to a lot of amazing people.

"I just want you to know how proud I am to have worked for you and the amazing organization you built. I remember the first meeting we had. You barely knew me, but you had so much confidence in me to do something new with the board presentation. That moment made me so thankful to be on the bus with you and it only built from there.

"I can't even form sentences around my feelings regarding how terribly you and Al were treated. But truly I believe that everything happens for a reason. So I know there is something great out there for you. And I know there are many lucky people out there who will be touched by your leadership.

"Thank you for everything you did for me. I've grown so much through working with you and with WWP, and I hope I can continue to grow and help the organization. We definitely miss you around the office. I hope you are well and finding new work you can be passionate about."

∽

"Our office just had a video conference with the High Commission of UNHCR [United Nations High Commissioner for Refugees] and it was really refreshing. Authentic leaders are inspiring and rare. I was fortunate enough to work for great senior leaders in my previous job—Steven Nardizzi, Jeremy Chwat, Adam Silva and Jennifer Mischla Silva—and blessed once again."

～

"I just wanted to thank you for all that you did for WWP, the warriors and the staff while you were here. Seeing the culture you, Al and the others created was something I've never witnessed in a workplace . . . It was inspiring! To know that the CEO of a company would take the time to come and shoot the shit with all of us new worker bees over dinner blew my mind, and made me feel an importance I had never felt."

"Its with a heavy heart that I'm writing this to you today because I'm reminiscing about the 'good old days' when our culture meant something and we were able to come together as an entire team and bond as family. I miss those times and I am so very sad to see amazing teammates who gave so much be let go so easily and/or move on for personal reasons. It's like watching the end of an era when all you want to do is cling so tightly to it and never let go."

"I know change is inevitable and things can't always remain the same, but I'm struggling today in my role as an Outreach Coordinator because I feel that our culture/family is gone and I'm not sure if there is any way back."

"I know that I have only been with the organization for a brief moment and only got to experience its greatness for a fleeting moment before everything changed, so I can't imagine what pains you went through. But I am forever grateful for your vision and dedication while you were here."

"I'm not sure you'll ever read this but it was important for me to say THANK YOU for creating something beautiful! For creating hope for those without any, for creating friendships and bonds that I will carry with me for a lifetime."

"You impacted a generation, sir, and you created a legacy that cannot be taken away from you. I know that today I am reflective and somber but as a spiritual man I know that this verse will carry me through: 'Being confident of this, that he who began a good work in you will carry it on to completion.'"

～

"I remained quiet when everything started happening at WWP in January. Not out of uncertainty, as I never doubted the integrity of our leadership, but out of the need to process. Even as I left WWP in April I wasn't sure I had fully processed the changes that were in motion. This week brought a wave of sadness as I read post after post of departures and others trying to lift the spirits of those still on the bus.

"I am thankful to have served under the leadership of Steven Nardizzi, Al Giordano, Adam Silva, Jeremy Chwat and Ron Burgess. I'm grateful for the professional growth I achieved under the guidance of Ayla Tezel and Deirdre Galley. During this time of transition and change for my WWP teammates, I am amazed to see the selfless love and encouragement from these same individuals towards those leaving WWP as well as those who remain to serve the mission to honor and empower wounded warriors. THAT is leadership and it is exactly how you develop strong employees who work together to build up an even stronger team.

"To the disgruntled former employees who started this mess along with media outlets that didn't take the time to accurately fact check . . . shame on you."

NOTES

1. Dan Pallotta, "The Way We Think About Charity is Dead Wrong," (Filmed 02.2013) ted.com https://www.ted.com/talks/dan_pallotta_the_way_we_think_about_charity_is_dead_wrong/transcript#t-501692 (Accessed on 07.17.2017).

2. Brian Mittendorf, "Do Nonprofits Really Limit Advertising Because of Pressure to Cut Overhead?" The *NonProfit Quarterly* (04.23.2013) https://nonprofitquarterly.org/2013/04/23/do-nonprofits-really-limit-advertising-because-of-pressure-to-cut-overhead/ (Accessed on 07.18.2017).

3. Phil Buchanan, blog post on the Huffington Post, "Getting the Facts Straight About the Nonprofit Sector" (09.23.2013; updated 11.23.2013) http://www.huffingtonpost.com/phil-buchanan/getting-the-facts-straight_b_3976022.html (Accessed on 07.18.2017).

4. Dan Pallotta, in an email to the author (09.13.2018).

5. Al Giordano, interview with the author (10.13.2018).

6. "U.S. Veterans Organizations by the Numbers," GuideStar (11.2015) https://www.guidestar.org/downloadable-files/us-veterans-organizations.pdf (Accessed on 07.18.2018) Precisely determining the number of organizations that serve veterans can be confusing because, in part, many are groups within other groups. Even officially designated veterans service organizations (VSOs) are divided into those that are Congressionally chartered and recognized by the VA for purposes of processing claims, those that are Congressionally chartered but not recognized by the VA to process claims, those not Congressionally chartered but recognized by the VA to process claims, and, in a fourth category, neither Congressionally chartered nor recognized by the VA to process claims, but which are still are recognized as representing the interests of American veterans.

7. Erick Millette, interviewed by WBZ, Boston (09.10.2013) http://boston.cbslocal.com/2013/09/10/nh-veteran-says-wounded-warrior-project-saved-his-life/ (Accessed on 04.09.2017).

8. Dave Philipps, interviewed by Kelly McEvers, National Public Radio (03.11.2016) http://www.npr.org/2016/03/11/470119942/wounded-warrior-project-fires-top-executives-over-lavish-spending (accessed on 12.22.2016).

9. Unless otherwise noted, the quoted material in the immediately prior pages

are sourced variously from among four reports—three aired by *CBS News* on January 26 and 27, 2016, and one published by the *New York Times* on January 27, 2016:

Chip Reid and Jennifer Janisch, "Wounded Warrior Project Accused of Wasting Donation Money," *CBS News* (01.26.2016). https://www.cbsnews.com/news/wounded-warrior-project-accused-of-wasting-donation-money/ (accessed on 12.12.2016).

Chip Reid and Jennifer Janisch, "Ex-employee: Wounded Warrior Project Conduct "Makes Me Sick." *CBS News* (01.27.2016). https://www.cbsnews.com/news/wounded-warrior-project-investigation-veterans-charity-accused-of-no-follow-up/ (accessed on 12.12.2016).

Chip Reid and Jennifer Janisch, *CBS News* "Charity Watchdogs Question Wounded Warrior's Spending on Vets," *CBS News* (01.27.2016). https://www.cbsnews.com/news/charity-watchdogs-question-wounded-warriors-spending-on-vets/ (accessed on 12.12.2016).

Dave Philipps, "Wounded Warrior Project Spends Lavishly on Itself, Insiders Say" *New York Times* (01.27.2016). https://www.nytimes.com/2016/03/12/us/after-complaints-on-wounded-warrior-project-pressure-from-donors.html (accessed on 12.12.2016).

10. Anonymous, interview with author (09.15.2016).

11. Anonymous, interview with author (10.28.2016).

12. Charity Defense Network, "Material Errors And Omissions Uncovered In Media Reporting On Wounded Warrior Project" (03.17.2016). https://cdn2.hubspot.net/hubfs/2141034/Wounded_Warrior_Project_-_Preliminary_Media_Advisory.pdf (Accessed on 02.22.2017).

13. Justin Constantine, Facebook entry (02.13.2014).

14. Erick Millette, Facebook Screen Shot (02.11.2014).

15. Dave Philipps, in an interview with Kelly McEvers, "Wounded Warrior Project Fires Top Executives Over Lavish Spending," *NPR* (WBUR) (03.11.2016) http://www.wbur.org/npr/470119942/wounded-warrior-project-fires-top-executives-over-lavish-spending (Accessed on 01.28.2017).

16. Al Giordano, interview with the author (12.19.2016).

17. The review was conducted by conducted by Simpson Thacher & Bartlett, a New York City-based law firm, and FTI, a forensic accounting consultant firm, also located in New York City.

18. Steve Nardizzi, interview with author (05.31.2016).

19. "What CBS Didn't Show You" Wounded Warrior Project (01.28.2016).

https://www.facebook.com/wwp/videos (Accessed on 06.27.2018).

20. From transcripts of interview Dave Philipps had with Meghan Wagner and Jon Sullivan (01.22.2016).

21. Al Giordano, interview with author (06.15.2016).

22. Anonymous, in emails sent to top CBS staff (02.26.2016, and 02.28.2016); the author is in possession of the emails.

23. Lauren Hoenemeyer, in an email to Joanne Fried (02.01.2016).

24. Rebecca Koenig, "Amid Capitol Hill Criticism, Red Cross Board '100 Percent' Confident in CEO" Chronicle of Philanthropy (06.23.2016) https://www.philanthropy.com/article/Critical-Haiti-Report/236901 (Accessed on 08.27.2016).

25. Al Giordano, interview with the author (10.13.2018).

26. Steve Nardizzi, interview with the author (11.16.2016).

27. Ed Edmundson, interview with the author (11.17.2016).

28. Walter Reed Army Medical Center in Washington closed its doors August 27, 2011 as part of its merger with the Bethesda National Naval Medical Center.

29. *U.S. News & World Report* http://health.usnews.com/best-hospitals/area/il/rehabilitation-institute-of-chicago-6431012 (Accessed on 01.28.2017).

30. https://www.youtube.com/watch?v=fS1cH5nE-CA.

31. Meredith Asbury, "Honoring America's Veterans" (10.13.2013) www.columbiamo.va.gov/docs/essaycontest2013.pdf (accessed on 11.19.2016).

32. "America's Wars: U.S. Casualties and Veterans," Department of Defense and Veterans Administration (08.2017) http://www.infoplease.com/ipa/A0004615.html (Accessed on 06.27.2018).

33. Kyle Longley, "The Grunt's War," *New York Times* (02.17.2017); https://www.nytimes.com/2017/02/17/opinion/the-grunts-war.html?smprod=nytcore-ipad&smid=nytcore-ipad-share (Accessed on 02.18.2017).

34. "Veterans: Oh, You're Back?" *Time Magazine* (01.12.1968), p.15 http://content.time.com/time/magazine/article/0,9171,837648,00.html?iid=sr-link1 (Accessed on 02.01.2017).

35. "Coming Home: Vietnam Veterans in American Society" Vietnam War Reference Library, The Gale Group (2001); http://www.encyclopedia.com/history/encyclopedias-almanacs-transcripts-and-maps/coming-home-vietnam-veterans-american-society (Accessed on 02.20.2017).

36. Harvard Sitikoff, "The Postwar Impact of Vietnam," *The Oxford Companion*

to American Military History, Oxford University Press (1999) http://www.english.illinois.edu/maps/vietnam/postwar.htm (Accessed on 11.09.2016).

37. Bob Greene, "If You're a Veteran, Were You Spat Upon?" *Chicago Tribune* (07.20.1987) http://articles.chicagotribune.com/1987-07-20/features/8702230346_1_vietnam-veterans-marriages-abducted (Accessed on 02.15.2017).

38. David E. Rosenbaum, "March Against Death Begun By Thousands in Washington," *New York Times* (11.14.1969) p.1 http://query.nytimes.com/mem/archive-free/pdf?res=9B06E3D9153DEF34BC4C52D-FB7678382679EDE (Accessed on 02.13.2017).

39. Jerry Lembcke, *The Spitting Image,* New York University Press; 1998; pg. 4-5.

40. Diane H. Mazur, *More Perfect Military: How the Constitution Can Make Our Military Stronger;* Oxford University Press, (2010) pp. 98-100.

41. Bob Greene; *Homecoming: When the Soldier Returned from Vietnam,* G. P. Putnam's Sons (1989).

42. Stanley Karnow, *Vietnam: A History;* Penguin Books; 2nd edition (1997) p.122.

43. Reggie Cornelia, interview with the author (04.11.2017).

44. Jan Scruggs, interview with the author (01.27.2017).

45. Harvard Sitikoff, "The Postwar Impact of Vietnam," from *The Oxford Companion to American Military History.* Ed. John Whiteclay Chambers II. New York: Oxford UP, 1999. Copyright 1999 by Oxford UP. http://www.english.illinois.edu/maps/vietnam/postwar.htm (Accessed on 11.09.2016)).

46. Chris Carney, interview with the author (01.12.2017).

47. Kevin Boylan, "Why Vietnam Was Unwinnable," *New York Times* (08.22.2017) https://www.nytimes.com/2017/08/22/opinion/vietnam-was-unwinnable.html?action=click&pgtype=Homepage&clickSource=story-heading&module=opinion-c-col-left-region&region=opinion-c-col-left-region&WT.nav=opinion-c-col-left-region (Accessed on 08.22.2017).

48. Bernie Sanders, "If You Think It's Too Expensive to Take Care of Veterans, Don't Send Them to War," Speech before the United States Senate, CSPAN (05.22. 2014) https://www.c-span.org/video/?c4541633/think-expensive-take-care-veterans-dont-send-war (Accessed on 11.16.2016).

49. John Melia, CNN, Interview with Fredricka Whitfield (03.20.2004) http://transcripts.cnn.com/TRANSCRIPTS/0403/20/cnnitm.00.html (Accessed on 04.01.2017).

50. John Melia, 06.01.2008, Wounded Warrior Project History http://www. nonprofitpro.com/article/wounded-warrior-project-history-107420/all/ (accessed on 01.25.2017).

51. Matthew Modine, Digital Hollywood Content Summit (10.22.2014). https:// www.youtube.com/watch?v=2DQnhBzXv7w (Accessed on 07.13.2017).

52. United Spinal Association, "National Veterans Organization Awards $2.7 Million Grant to Aid Wounded Soldiers," News Release (09.26.2005).

53. Helping A Hero; http://www.helpingahero.org/our-heroes/ssg-ryan-kelly (Accessed on 03.03.2017).

54. National Veterans Organization Awards $2.7 Million Grant to Aid Wounded Soldiers" (09.26.2005) United Spinal Association Archives; http://archive. is/Yn2C5 (Accessed on 02.20.2017).

55. James B. Peake, MD, Secretary of Veterans Affairs, in letter to Ronald Drach, board chair of Wounded Warrior Project (09.10.2008).

56. 2013/2014 Directory: Veterans and Military Service Organizations; p. i and pp. 1-38; https://www.va.gov/vso/VSO-Directory_2013-2014.pdf Accessed 02.19.2017).

57. George Vecsey, "A Veteran Unbowed by His War Injuries," *New York Times* (04.23.2008). http://www.nytimes.com/2008/04/23/sports/other-sports/23vecsey.html (Accessed on 11.30.2017).

58. Peter Honerkamp, interview with the author (12.19.2016).

59. Steve Nardizzi, interview with the author (10.27.2017).

60. John Melia, interviewed in "Soldier Ride," a documentary by Matthew Hindra and Nicholas Kraus (2014).

61. Steve Nardizzi, interview with the author (10.27.2017).

62. Reggie Cornelia, interview with the author (04.11.2017).

63. Chris Carney, interview with the author (06.25.2017).

64. Heath Calhoun: Profile Of US Skiing Paralympian For Sochi 2014 (02.18.2014) *Bleacher Report;* http://bleacherreport.com/articles/1959745-heath-calhoun-profile-of-us-skiing-paralympian-for-sochi-2014 (Accessed on 03.03.3017).

65. "A Spoonful of Sugar Helps the Benefits Go Round," Hamptons.com (07.27.2005), http://www.hamptons.com/article.php?articleID=501#. WLr7XRjMzsk (Accessed on 03.04.2017).

66. Beth and Ed Edmundson, interview with the author (11.17.2016).

67. Meghan Wagner, from transcripts of interview with Dave Philipps (01.22.2016).

68. Dave Philipps, "Wounded Warrior Project Fires Top Executives Over Lavish Spending," interviewed on National Public Radio (03.11.2016) http://www.npr.org/2016/03/11/470119942/wounded-warrior-project-fires-top-executives-over-lavish-spending (Accessed on 03.21.2017).

69. Peter Honerkamp, interview with the author (04.26.2017).

70. Matthew Modine, Digital Hollywood Content Summit (10.22.2014) https://www.youtube.com/watch?v=2DQnhBzXv7w (Accessed on 07.13.2017).

71. Wounded Warrior Project Forms 990 from 2005 to 2015

72. John Melia, "Founder Says Wounded Warrior Project Grew Too Fast," News4Jax (03.17.2016) https://www.news4jax.com/news/investigations/wounded-warrior-project-founder-talks (Accessed on 06.11.2018).

73. Steve Nardizzi, interview with the author (06.10.2018).

74. John Melia, *CBS News* (03.30.2016) http://www.cbsnews.com/news/wounded-warrior-project-faces-power-struggle-at-top-of-organization/ (Accessed on 04.10.2017).

75. John Melia, "Founder Says Wounded Warrior Project Grew Too Fast," News4JAX, 03.17.2016 http://www.news4jax.com/news/investigations/wounded-warrior-project-founder-talks (Accessed on 03.28.2017).

76. Ron Drach, interview with the author (03.31.2017).

77. Anonymous, interview with the author (08.10.2017).

78. The 2017 budget for the Department of Veterans Affairs was $180 billion; it employed approximately 350,000 people.

79. Ron Drach, interview with the author (03.31.2017).

80. Eric Howard, interview with the author (05.02.2018).

81. Anonymous, interview with the author (12.07.2018).

82. Anonymous, interview with the author (12.08.2018).

83. Charity Navigator Website; https://www.charitynavigator.org/index.cfm?-bay=content.view&cpid=48 (Accessed on 10.09.2017).

84. Better Business Bureau Wise Giving Alliance, "Standards for Charity Accountability" https://www.bbb.org/us/storage/0/Shared%20Documents/Standards%20for%20Charity%20Accountability.pdf (Accessed on 10.09.2017).

85. CharityWatch; https://www.charitywatch.org/charitywatch-criteria-methodology (Accessed on 10.09.2017).

86. Art Taylor, Jacob Harold, Ken Berger, "The Overhead Myth" (06.17.2013);

http://5770-presscdn-21-69.pagely.netdna-cdn.com/wp-content/uploads/2013/06/GS_OverheadMyth_Ltr_ONLINE.pdf (Accessed on 09.10.2017).

87. Stephanie Lowell, Brian Trelstad, Bill Meehan, "The Ratings Game," Stanford Social Innovation Review (Summer 2005) https://ssir.org/articles/entry/the_ratings_game (Accessed on 08.10.2016).

88. Stacy Palmer, "Is Charity Navigator the 'National Enquirer' of Watchdog Groups?" *Chronicle of Philanthropy* (11.23.2007) https://www.philanthropy.com/article/Is-Charity-Navigator-the/192097 (Accessed on 08.10.2016).

89. Al Giordano, interview with the author, 04.10.2017.

90. Art Taylor, interview with author (03.16.2018).

91. Elvia Castro, Ezra Vázquez-D'Amico, and Rubens Pessanha, "Donor Trust Report," (2018) Better Business Bureau Wise Giving Alliance, pp. 10, 13.

92. Catherine Hollander, interview with the author (10.12.2018).

93. GiveWell Metrics Report—2017 Annual Review (2017) https://files.give-well.org/files/metrics/GiveWell_Metrics_Report_2017.pdf (Accessed on 10.12.2018).

94. Jacob Harold, interview with the author (01.10.2018).

95. Stave Nardizzi, interview with the author (04.18.2018).

96. Steven Nardizzi, "Your Mission or Your Overhead Ratio" Speech at the Bridge Conference (07.11.2014).

97. Art Taylor, interview with the author (03.19.2018).

98. IRS Regulation §20.2031-1.

99. Jordan Ellenberg, *How Not to Be Wrong: The Power of Mathematical Thinking,* Penguin Books, New York (2014) Print; pp. 57-58.

100. Jacob Harold, interview with the author (01.10.2018).

101. Robert D. McFadden, "William Aramony, United Way Leader Who Was Jailed for Fraud, Dies at 84," New York Times (11.13.2011) http://www.nytimes.com/2011/11/14/business/william-aramony-disgraced-leader-of-united-way-dies-at-84.html (Accessed on10.18.2017).

102. Laura Nahmias, Dan Goldberg, Nidhi Prakash, "The Wrecking of A Blue-Chip New York Nonprofit," Politico (03.13.2015) http://www.politico.com/states/new-york/albany/story/2015/03/the-wrecking-of-a-blue-chip-new-york-nonprofit-087679 (Accessed on 10.18.2017).

103. Rachel L. Swarns, "Nonprofit's Chief During Its Fall Seeks $1.2 Million Payday, and Outrage Ensues," New York Times (05.03.2015) https://www.

nytimes.com/2015/05/04/nyregion/as-former-fegs-chief-executive-waits-for-payday-so-do-her-ex-employees.html?_r=0 (Accessed on10.17.2017).

104. Pam Belluck, "Cancer Group Halts Financing to Planned Parenthood," *New York Times* (01.31.2012) http://www.nytimes.com/2012/02/01/us/cancer-group-halts-financing-to-planned-parenthood.html (Accessed on 10.18.2017).

105. Ruth McCambridge, "Komen's Brand Equity Plummets According to Harris Poll: What Other Changes Are Afoot?" *NonProfit Quarterly* (03.27.2012) https://nonprofitquarterly.org/2012/03/27/komens-brand-equity-plummets-according-to-harris-poll-what-other-changes-are-afoot/ (Accessed on 10.18.2017).

106. Ruth McCambridge, "Komen's Folly: A Decline in Fundraiser Ranking Tells the Story in Numbers," *NonProfit Quarterly* (10.30.2015) https://nonprofitquarterly.org/2015/10/30/komens-folly-a-decline-in-fundraiser-ranking-tells-the-story-in-numbers/ (Accessed on 10.18.2017).

107. Ruth McCambridge, "Another Komen Chapter Goes Under amidst Massive Revenue Losses," *NonProfit Quarterly* (07.03.2018) https://nonprofitquarterly.org/2018/07/03/another-komen-chapter-goes-under-amidst-massive-revenue-losses/ (Accessed on07.12.2018).

108. Mission Statement, Help Heal Veterans https://www.guidestar.org/profile/95-2706737 (Accessed on 10.19.2017).

109. David Fitzpatrick and Drew Griffin, "California charity Help Hospitalized Veterans pays $2.5 million fine," CNN (09.06.2013) http://www.cnn.com/2013/09/06/us/california-charity-fine/index.html (Accessed on 10.20.2017).

110. "Abuse of Authority, Misuse of Position and Resources, Acceptance of Gratuities, & Interference with an OIG Investigation National Programs & Special Events," Department of Veterans Affairs—Office of Inspector General (02.05.2010) https://www.va.gov/oig/pubs/VAOIG-09-01492-83.pdf (Accessed on 10.20.2017).

111. Anderson Cooper, "360 Degrees," CNN (09.17.2014) http://transcripts.cnn.com/TRANSCRIPTS/1409/17/acd.01.html (Accessed on 10.20.2017).

112. According to its IRS filing, in 2017 Help Heal Veterans spent 27 percent of its budget on programs, and not all of that was spent to help veterans.

113. Drew Griffin, "VA Moves to Fire Executive Who Used Office for Veterans Charity for Lavish Spending," CNN (11.10.2016) http://www.cnn.com/2016/11/10/politics/national-vietnam-veterans-foundation-donations/index.html (Accessed on 12.23.2017).

114. Spencer Hsu, "Head of Vietnam Veteran Charity Who Embezzled $150,000 Sentenced to Five Months," *Washington Post* (10.05.2017) https://www. washingtonpost.com/local/public-safety/head-of-vietnam-veteran-charity-who-embezzled-150000-sentenced-to-five-months/2017/10/05/ a9593220-aa03-11e7-92d1-58c702d2d975_story.html?utm_term=.01f775896b5e (Accessed on 12.23.2017).

115. Pennies for Charity—Where Your Money Goes (11.2017) https://www.charitiesnys.com/pdfs/pennies-for-charity-2017.pdf (Accessed on 08.15.2018).

116. Kris Hundley and Kendall Taggart, "America's Worst Charities: America's 50 Worst Charities Rake in Nearly $1 Billion for Corporate Fundraisers," *Tampa Bay Times* and the Center for Investigative Reporting (06.06.2013) http://www.tampabay.com/topics/specials/worst-charities1.page (Accessed on 10.23.2017).

117. Aaron Couch, "AMC Drops 'Worst Charity' From 'Breaking Bad' Fundraising Website," *Hollywood Reporter* (08.22.2013) https://www. hollywoodreporter.com/news/breaking-bad-amc-drops-worst-612717 (Accessed on 03.22.2018).

118. Many professionals who examine charity beyond the information found on a 990 are skeptical when costs associated with overhead and fundraising are unrealistically low.

119. The calculations conducted by CharityWatch, as are those at Charity Navigator, are problematic for reasons explained both earlier and later in the text. While the author doesn't agree with Mr. Borochoff's number here (54 percent of WWP's budget devoted to programming), his explanation regarding Disabled American Veterans and the Disabled American Veterans Charitable Service Trust is both accurate and illuminating.

120. Unattributed, "Follow the Money: Beware of Groups that Pass Your Donations to Inefficient Charities," CharityWatch (06.03.2016) https:// www.charitywatch.org/charitywatch-feature/169 (Accessed on 09.02.2016).

121. Al Giordano, interview with the author, 04.10.2017

122. Unattributed, "Charity Watchdog Groups and Nonprofit Fundraising Costs Ratings," Carr Riggs & Ingram, (06.15.2014) http://www.cricpa.com/nonprofit-fundraising-costs-ratings/ (Accessed on 08.10.2016).

123. Brian Mittendorf, "Natural Disasters, Aid Groups, and Donor Questions," interviewed by Amy Costello on a podcast for the *NonProfit Quarterly* by Tiny Spark, (10.26.2017) https://nonprofitquarterly. org/2017/10/26/natural-disasters-aid-groups-donor-questions/?utm_ source=Daily+Newswire&utm_campaign=ef231f4d16-EMAIL_ CAMPAIGN_2017_10_26&utm_medium=email&utm_term=0_94063a1 d17-ef231f4d16-12333785 (Accessed on 10.26.2017).

124. Marcus Baram, "Veterans Charity Fraud: Despite Widespread Outrage, Groups Continue To Abuse Public Trust," *Huffington Post* (08.29.2011) https://www.huffingtonpost.com/2011/06/29/veterans-charity-fraud_n_886259.html (Accessed on 01.05.2018).

125. Dan Corry, "In the Charity Sector, Impact Is Everything, (02.25.2014) *The Guardian* https://www.theguardian.com/voluntary-sector-network/2014/feb/24/charity-impact-measurement-results-outcomes (Accessed on 08.18.2016).

126. The author interviewed almost 40 individuals who had been or were employed at Wounded Warrior Project at the time research was being conducted for this manuscript.

127. Ed Edmundson, interview with the author (11.17.2016).

128. Steve Nardizzi, interview with the author (10.27.2017).

129. Nidhi Sahni, Laura Lanzerotti, Amira Bliss, and Daniel Pike, "Is Your Nonprofit Built for Sustained Innovation?" *Stanford Social Innovation Review* (08.01.2017) https://ssir.org/articles/entry/is_your_nonprofit_built_for_sustained_innovation?utm_content=229097daaf-71568cd076330b09b3d970&utm_campaign=Six%20Elements%20for%20Building%20Innovation%20Capacity&utm_source=Robly.com&utm_medium=email (Accessed on11.28.2017).

130. Dave Philipps, "After Complaints on Wounded Warrior Project, Pressure From Donors," *New York Times* (03.11.2016) https://www.nytimes.com/2016/03/12/us/after-complaints-on-wounded-warrior-project-pressure-from-donors.html (Accessed on 01.04.2018).

131. Jacob Harold, "Myths, Misconceptions, and Mistakes: The Wounded Warrior Project" *GuideStar* (02.10.2016) https://trust.guidestar.org/myths-misconceptions-and-mistakes-the-wounded-warrior-project (Accessed on 12.28.2017).

132. Roger Woodworth, interview with the author (10.03.2016).

133. Charles Battaglia, "Opinion: Wounded warrior project deserves support," (8.4.2016) http://www.military.com/daily-news/2016/08/03/opinion-wounded-warrior-project-needs-and-deserves-support.html (Accessed on 08.19.2016).

134. Charles Battaglia, interview with the author (08.04.2016).

135. Charles Battaglia, "Wounded Warrior Project Deserves Support," Military.com (08.03.2016) https://www.military.com/daily-news/2016/08/03/opinion-wounded-warrior-project-needs-and-deserves-support.html (Accessed on 04.04.2018).

136. Gary Morton, "Best Nonprofits to Work for in 2013," *Nonprofit Times* (04.01.2013) http://www.thenonprofittimes.com/wp-content/uploads/2013/04/BestPlacesToWork_20132.pdf (Accessed on 05.22.2018).

137. Trevor Dombeck, interview with the author (05.08.2017).

138. Scott Alpaugh, interview with the author (07.28.2017).

139. Doug White, "Wounded Truth: A Report Addressing the Allegations Made Against The Wounded Warrior Project In January 2016" (09.06.2016) https://drive.google.com/file/d/0B_8d70VSOvbgdGtXZHlVVXRUb3c/view (Accessed on10.19.2018).

140. Matthew Modine, interview with the author (07.15-17.2017).

141. Wounded Warrior Project website, https://www.woundedwarriorproject.org/mission/board-of-directors/anthony-odierno (Accessed on 04.15.2018).

142. Harvey Naranjo, interview with the author (11.14.2016).

143. Ed Darack, "Extortion 17, Seal Team Six And What Really Happened On The Deadliest Day In The History Of Naval Special Warfare And The U.S. War In Afghanistan" (08.31.2017) http://www.newsweek.com/extortion-17-seal-team-six-navy-seals-afghanistan-conspiracy-theories-names-657841 (Accessed on 03.11.2018).

144. Although it is still colloquially known by this name, in 1987 SEAL Team 6 was dissolved. A new unit named the "Naval Special Warfare Development Group" was formed as SEAL Team Six's successor.

145. Arlington National Military Website; http://arlingtoncemetery.net/cgcampbell.htm (Accessed on 03.11.2018).

146. Cindy Campbell, interview with the author (11.13.2016).

147. Cindy Campbell, letter to the editor "Thank You for Putting the Spotlight on Such a Great Organization—Wounded Warrior Project," jdnew.com (03.20.2015) http://www.jdnews.com/20150320/worthwhile-cause-to-fulfill-mission/303209888 (Accessed on 03.12.2018).

148. Cindy Campbell, in an email to Dave Philipps (02.02.2016).

149. Dave Philipps, in an email to Cindy Campbell (02.02.2016).

150. Cindy Campbell, in an email to Dave Philipps (02.03.2016).

151. Beth Edmundson and Eric Edmundson, interview with the author (11.18.2018).

152. Chip Reid, "Wounded Warrior Project on Charity Navigator's Watch List" *CBS News* (01.30.2016) https://www.cbsnews.com/news/

wounded-warrior-project-on-charity-navigator-watchlist-cbs-news-investigation/ (Accessed on 05.15.2017).

153. Reporting on misleading reports is a way to give credibility to misinformation, and is a main ingredient in the way "fake news" is disseminated. See "Operation Infektion" *New York Times*, https://www.nytimes.com/2018/11/12/opinion/russia-meddling-disinformation-fake-news-elections.html?emc=edit_ty_20181115&nl=opinion-today&nlid=188979720181115&te=1#one (Accessed on 11.15.2018).

154. Ken Berger, interview with the author (06.03.2016).

155. Charity Navigator website; https://www.charitynavigator.org/index.cfm?-bay=content.view&cpid=4247 (Accessed on 05.22.2018).

156. Al Giordano, interview with the author, 04.10.2017

157. Sandra Hurtes, Letter to the Editor, *New York Times* (01.30.2017), https://www.nytimes.com/2016/01/30/opinion/lavish-spending-by-the-wounded-warrior-project.html?_r=0 (Accessed on 05.15.2017).

158. Steve Nardizzi, interview with author (10.27.2017).

159. Alexis Buchanan and Ruth McCambridge, "Wounded Warrior Project: The Fundraising Factory Issue," Nonprofit Quarterly (02.01.2016) https://nonprofitquarterly.org/2016/02/01/wounded-warrior-project-the-fundraising-factory-issue/ (Accessed on 05.17.2017).

160. Chip Reid, "Top Wounded Warrior donor calls for CEO's resignation" *CBS News* (03.03.2016). https://www.cbsnews.com/news/top-wounded-warrior-project-donor-calls-for-ceos-resignation/ (Accessed on 08.23.2017).; in the video, WWP board chair Anthony Odierno is shown avoiding CBS reporters.

161. Steve Nardizzi, interview with the author (06.15.2016).

162. Al Giordano, interview with the author (03.27.2018).

163. Fortune Editors, "The World's 19 Most Disappointing Leaders," *Fortune* (03.30.2016) http://fortune.com/2016/03/30/most-disappointing-leaders/ (Accessed on 03.02.2018).

164. Steven Nardizzi and Al Giordano, "Why We Shouldn't Have Made Fortune's 'World's Most Disappointing Leaders List,'" Fortune (04.08.2016) http://fortune.com/2016/04/08/worlds-most-disappointing-leaders-wounded-warrior-project/ (Accessed on 03.02.2018).

165. Sean Norris, "Wounded Warrior Project Investigation: What *CBS News* Got Wrong" NonProfitPRO (01.28.2016) http://www.nonprofitpro.com/article/investigation-blasts-wounded-warrior-project-for-wasting-millions/ (Accessed on 05.20.2017).

166. Jacob Harold, "Myths, Misconceptions, and Mistakes: The Wounded Warrior Project" GuideStar (02.10.2016). https://trust.guidestar.org/myths-misconceptions-and-mistakes-the-wounded-warrior-project (Accessed on 12.28.2017).

167. Anonymous, in an email to Ayla Tezel (02.01.2018); the author is in possession of the email.

168. Chip Reid and Jennifer Janisch, "Wounded Warrior Project Execs Fired," *CBS Evening News* (03.10.2016). http://www.cbsnews.com/news/wounded-warrior-project-ceo-and-coo-fired/ (Accessed on 05.31.2017).

169. Erick Millette, "Ex-Wounded Warrior Employee on Execs' Firing: 'It Feels Good'" *CBS Evening News* (03.11.2016). http://www.cbsnews.com/news/ex-wounded-warrior-project-employee-on-execs-firing-it-feels-good/ (Accessed on 06.01.2017).

170. Dave Philipps, "Wounded Warrior Project's Board Fires Top Two Executives," *New York Times* (03.10.2016). http://www.nytimes.com/2016/03/11/us/wounded-warrior-board-ousts-top-two-executives.html (accessed on 12.11.2016).

171. News Release, Wounded Warrior Project Board of Directors (03.10.2016).

172. Steve Nardizzi, interview with the author (11.16.2016).

173. Dave Philipps, "After Complaints on Wounded Warrior Project, Pressure From Donors," *New York Times* (03.11.2016) http://www.nytimes.com/2016/03/12/us/after-complaints-on-wounded-warrior-project-pressure-from-donors.html (accessed on 12.11.2016).

174. Bill O'Reilly Staff, "Podcast: Ousted Wounded Warrior Project Executives Speak Out," Bill O'Reilly No Spin News (09.30.2016) https://www.billoreilly.com/b/Podcast:-Ousted-Wounded-Warrior-Project-Executives-Speak-Out/574230005396901283.html (Accessed on07.30.2017).

175. Dave Philipps, interviewed by Kelly McEvers, National Public Radio (03.11.2016). http://www.npr.org/2016/03/11/470119942/wounded-warrior-project-fires-top-executives-over-lavish-spending (accessed on 12.22.2016).

176. As recounted in *The Daily Howler* (07.11.2000). http://www.dailyhowler.com/h071100_1.shtml (accessed on 01.04.2017).

177. On November 20, 2017, eight women who were employees of, or aspired to work for Rose accused him of "contriving to be naked in their presence, groping them, and making lewd phone calls." The accusations, which were made in a report in The Washington Post, dealt with conduct from the late 1990s to 2011. CBS, PBS, and Bloomberg terminated their contracts with Rose the following day.

178. Anthony Odierno, "Wounded Warrior Project chair on recovery from spending scandal," *CBS Morning News* (03.14.2016) http://www.cbsnews.com/news/wounded-warrior-project-chairman-anthony-odierno-search-new-executive-after-lavish-spending-scandal/ (Accessed on 06.01.2017).

179. Because of the publicity surrounding several legal settlements involving sexual harassment allegations, which led to more than 50 advertisers leaving his show, in April 2017, a little more than a year after his interview with Tony Odierno, Bill O'Reilly was fired from his position as a prime-time host on Fox News.

180. Anthony Odierno and Bill O'Reilly, interview; The O'Reilly Factor, *Fox News* (03.14.2016).

181. Senator Charles Grassley in a letter to Anthony Odierno, chairman of the board of Wounded Warrior Project (03.18.2016).

182. Paul Curnin, in a letter to Senator Charles Grassley (04.05.2016).

183. Steven Nardizzi and Al Giordano, "A Further Response to Senator Grassley's Questions about Wounded Warrior Project," The Wounded Truth (05.29.2016). https://www.thewoundedtruth.com/single-post/2016/05/29/A-Further-Response-to-Senator-Grassley's-Questions-about-Wounded-Warrior-Project (Accessed on 06.29.2017).

184. Senator Charles Grassley, in a letter to Anthony Odierno (05.16.2016).

185. Wounded Warrior Project webpage https://www.woundedwarriorproject.org/mission/executive-staff/michael-linnington (accessed 08.26.2016).

186. Anonymous, interview with the author (07.22.2016).

187. Scott Paltrow, "U.S. Army Fudged Its Accounts by Trillions of Dollars, Auditor Finds" (08.19.2016). http://mobile.reuters.com/article/idUSKCN10U1IG (Accessed on 08.27.2016).

188. Leo Shane III, "In the Wake of Scandal, Wounded Warrior Project Outlines Significant Overhaul," *Military Times* (08.31.2016); https://www.militarytimes.com/2016/08/31/in-the-wake-of-scandal-wounded-warrior-project-outlines-significant-overhaul/ (Accessed on 09.12.2017).

189. Michael Linnington, in an interview with Dianna Cahn, "Wounded Warrior Project Donations Drop $70 million, But CEO Says Charity Is on the Rebound," *Stars & Stripes* (05.08.2017); https://www.stripes.com/wounded-warrior-project-donations-drop-70-million-but-ceo-says-charity-is-on-the-rebound-1.467376#.Wacakq3Mzsm (Accessed on 08.30.2017).

190. Eric Miller, "Wounded Warrior Project Sees a Drop in Donations," *First Coast News* (05.04.2017). http://www.firstcoastnews.com/news/local/data/

military/wounded-warrior-project-sees-a-drop-in-donations/436906107 (accessed on 08.25.2017).

191. Emily Wax-Thibodeaux, "Wounded Warrior Project cleared of 'spending lavishly,' report finds," *Washington Post* (02.08.2017). https://www.washingtonpost.com/news/checkpoint/wp/2017/02/08/wounded-warrior-project-cleared-of-spending-lavishly-report-finds/?utm_term=.7b1b4b72733c (Accessed on08.30.2017).

192. Better Business Bureau Wise Giving Alliance; http://www.give.org/charity-reviews/national/veterans-and-military/wounded-warrior-project-in-jacksonville-fl-3806 (Accessed on 01.30.2017).

193. Art Taylor, interview with the author (03.19.2018).

194. Michael Linnington, in an interview with Joy Purdy, WJAX (08.04.2016). http://www.news4jax.com/news/investigations/new-wounded-warrior-project-ceo-to-be-completely-accountable

195. Charity Navigator, https://www.charitynavigator.org/index.cfm?bay=search.comments&orgid=12842 (accessed on 02.17.2017).

196. Wounded Warrior Project IRS Form 990 from fiscal years 2015 and 2016.

197. Notes to Consolidated Financial Statements (p. 26); Wounded Warrior Project (09.30.2016).

198. Wounded Warrior Project Board Book (09.27.2016) pp. 27-31.

199. Michael Linnington, "Former Wounded Warrior CEO Accuses Board of Dishonesty About State of Charity's Finances," *Chronicle of Philanthropy* (08.26.2016). file:///Users/doug1/Documents/1%20Book%20-%20WWP/Media%20Reports/2016%2008.26%20Chronicle%20(Nardizzi%20Accuses%20Board%20of%20Dishonesty).webarchive (Accessed on 05.15.2017).

200. Al Giordano, interview with the author (12.19.2016).

201. "Total Revenue" WWP Board Book (09.27.2016).

202. Al Giordano, interview with the author (10.13.2018).

203. Charles Grassley, in a letter to members of the Senate Judiciary and Finance Committees (05.24.2017).

204. Dianna Cahn, "Senator's Findings: Wounded Warrior Project On the Tight Track After Addressing Problems," *Stars & Stripes* (05.25.2017) https://www.stripes.com/senator-s-findings-wounded-warrior-project-on-the-right-track-after-addressing-problems-1.470251 (Accessed on 04.07.2018).

205. Leo Shane III, "In the wake of scandal, Wounded Warrior Project outlines significant overhaul," *Military Times* (08.31.2016) https://www.military-times.com/2016/08/31/in-the-wake-of-scandal-wounded-warrior-project-outlines-significant-overhaul/ (Accessed on 07.25.2018).

206. Chip Reid, "Charity Watchdogs Question Wounded Warrior's Spending on Vet." *CBS News* (01.27.2016) https://www.cbsnews.com/news/charity-watchdogs-question-wounded-warriors-spending-on-vets/ (Accessed on 09.17.2017).

207. Wounded Warrior Project Long-Term Support Trust, IRS From 990 (2017).

208. Mark Hrywna, "Revenue, Program Spending Decline Again At Wounded Warrior Project," *Nonprofit Times* (04.23.2018) http://www.thenonprofittimes.com/news-articles/revenue-program-spending-decline-wounded-warrior-project/ (Accessed on 05.02.2018).

209. Anonymous, in a 2016 memo in the author's possession

210. Peter Honerkamp, interview with the author (04.24.2018).

211. Peter Honerkamp, email to Michael Linnington (02.06.2017).

212. Christian Conte, "Wounded Warrior makes Best Nonprofit to Work For list," *Jacksonville Business Journal* (04.08.2011). https://www.bizjournals.com/jacksonville/news/2011/04/08/wounded-warrior-makes-best-to-work-for.html (Accessed on 12.12.2017); also Kutak Rock, LLP, "Wounded Warrior Project Values Employees," (04.10.2014). http://www.kutakrock.com/wounded-warrior-project-values-employees-04-10-2014/ (Accessed on 12.12.2017).

213. Steve Nardizzi, interview with the author (11.16.2016).

214. Dave Philipps, in an email to the author (08.15.2016).

215. Steve Nardizzi, interview with the author (11.16.2016).

216. Dave Philipps, in an email to the author (08.15.2016).

217. Steve Nardizzi, interview with the author (11.16.2016).

218. The author is in possession of the screenshot for these posts.

219. Anonymous, interview with the author (01.15.2018).

220. Biography of Dave Philipps http://www.biographies.net/bio/m/0ch4z_2 (Accessed on 10.24.2017).

221. Biography of Chip Reid https://www.cbsnews.com/team/chip-reid/ (accessed on 10.24.2017).

222. Jack Murtha, "In Separate Investigations, CBS and The *New York Times* Reveal the Inner Workings of Wounded Warrior Project," *Columbia*

Journalism Review (01.28.2016) https://www.cjr.org/hit_or_miss/nyt_wounded_warrior_project_cbs.php (Accessed on 10.02.2017).

223. Andrew Marantz, "Main Streamers," *The New Yorker* (12.11.2017), p.85.

224. James Brady died on August 4, 2014 at the age of 73. No cause was specified, although District of Columbia police told CNN that his death was ruled a homicide, the result of the shooting 33 years earlier.

225. Tony Schwartz, "TV Networks Quickly Supply Vivid Documentation of Assassination Attempt" *New York Times* (03.31.1981). http://www.nytimes.com/1981/03/31/us/tv-networks-quickly-supply-vivid-documentation-of-assassination-attempt.html?emc=eta1 (accessed on 09.13.2016).

226. "1 PM"; Walter Cronkite documentary about the JFK Assassination https://www.youtube.com/watch?v=tkiBRcdH_Pc (accessed on 03.20.2016).

227. Leslie Moonves; quoted by Robert Reich, "These Three Trump Enablers Made This Election Season Unbearable," *Salon* (11.07.2016). http://www.salon.com/2016/11/07/robert-reich-these-three-trump-enablers-made-this-election-season-unbearable_partner/ (Accessed: 12.11.2016). On September 9, 2018, Moonves, the chairman and CEO of CBS, resigned shortly after *The New Yorker* published accounts from six women with allegations of sexual assault or misconduct, following allegations by six other women in July.

228. "*Trustees of Dartmouth College v. Woodward*" https://www.law.cornell.edu/supremecourt/text/17/518#writing-USSC_CR_0017_0518_ZO (Accessed on 01.28.2017).

229. Richard Current, "It Is … A Small College … Yet, There Are Those Who Love It," *American Heritage* (August 1963; Volume 4, Issue 5) http://www.americanheritage.com/content/%E2%80%9Cit-%E2%80%A6-small-college-%E2%80%A6-yet-there-are-those-who-love-it%E2%80%9D (Accessed on 10.08.2018).

230. Marcus Baram, "Veterans Charity Fraud: Despite Widespread Outrage, Groups Continue To Abuse Public Trust," *Huffington Post* (08.29.2011) https://www.huffingtonpost.com/2011/06/29/veterans-charity-fraud_n_886259.html (Accessed on 01.05.2018).

231. Dave Boyer, "VA Still Plagued by Problems Two Years After Scandal," *Washington Times* (04.03.2016) https://www.washingtontimes.com/news/2016/apr/3/va-still-plagued-by-problems-two-years-after-scand/ (accessed on 01.03.2018).

232. Department of Veterans Affairs Access Audit - System-Wide Review of Access - Results of Access Audit Conducted May 12, 2014, through June 3,

2014; https://www.va.gov/health/docs/VAAccessAuditFindingsReport.pdf (Accessed on 01.03.2018).

233. Lisa D. Ordóñez, Maurice E. Schweitzer, Adam D. Galinsky and Max H. Bazerman, "Goals Gone Wild: The Systematic Side Effects of Over-Prescribing Goal Setting," (working paper) (2009) http://www.hbs.edu/faculty/Publication%20Files/09-083.pdf (Accessed on 01.03.2018).

234. Ron Carucci, "Four Ways Your Leadership May Be Encouraging Unethical Behavior," *Forbes* (06.14.2016). https://www.forbes.com/sites/roncarucci/2016/06/14/four-ways-your-leadership-may-be-encouraging-unethical-behavior/#1b8df3c55c03 (Accessed on 01.03.2018).

235. Michael Mann, "Mission Betrayed: How the VA Really Fails America's Vets," *Encore Press* (2017), p. 5.

236. Anonymous, interview with the author (05.30.2017).

237. Michael Pearson, "The VA's Troubled History" (05.30.2014) http://www.cnn.com/2014/05/23/politics/va-scandals-timeline/index.html (Accessed on 01.03.2018).

238. Quentin G. Aucoin, "Report of Administrative Investigation - Conflict of Interest and Violation of Ethics Pledge, Office of the Secretary, Washington, DC– Report No. 14-02190-293 (2014-02190-IQ-0088) (07.21.2016) https://www.va.gov/oig/pubs/admin-reports/advisory-14-02190-293.pdf (Accessed on 01.03.2018).

239. Donovan Slack, "Illegal VA policy allows hiring since 2002 of medical workers with revoked licenses," *USA Today* (12.21.2017) https://www.usatoday.com/story/news/politics/2017/12/21/va-policy-years-allows-hiring-medical-workers-revoked-licenses-violatiohiring-policy-breaks-breaks-l/971058001/ (Accessed on 01.09.2018).

240. Sally Pipes, "The VA's standards just hit a new low," *Washington Examiner* (01.09.2018). http://www.washingtonexaminer.com/the-vas-standards-just-hit-a-new-low/article/2645380 (Accessed on 01.09.2018).

241. Lisa Rein, "Veterans Affairs Chief Shulkin, Staff Misled Ethics Officials About European Trip, Report Finds," *Washington Post* (02.14.2018) https://www.washingtonpost.com/politics/veterans-affairs-chief-shulkin-staff-misled-ethics-officials-about-european-trip-report-finds/2018/02/14/f7fbc020-0c3a-11e8-8b0d-891602206fb7_story.html?utm_term=.b7529a2f9352 (Accessed on 02.14.2018).

242. Nicholas Fandos, "Veterans Affairs Secretary Is Latest to Go as Trump Shakes Up Cabinet," *New York Times* (03.28.2018) https://www.nytimes.com/2018/03/28/us/politics/david-shulkin-veterans-affairs-trump.

html?hp&action=click&pgtype=Homepage&clickSource=story-heading&module=first-column-region&region=top-news&WT.nav=top-news (Accessed on 03.28.2018).

243. Donovan Slack and Andrea Estes, "Secret VA Nursing Home Ratings Hide Poor Quality Care From the Public," *USA Today* (06.17.2018) https://www.usatoday.com/story/news/politics/2018/06/17/secret-va-nursing-home-ratings-hide-poor-quality-care/674829002/ (Accessed on 06.18.218)

244. Rosye Cloud, interview with the author (10.31.2016).

245. Eric Hartley, "Lawsuit by Norfolk's First Veteran Liaison Says City Fired Him for Raising Ethical Concerns," *Virginian-Pilot* (11.28.2016) https://pilotonline.com/news/government/local/lawsuit-by-norfolk-s-first-veteran-liaison-says-city-fired/article_65c40cec-8361-505e-acef-b9cec6b15052.html (Accessed on 03.02.2018).

246. Rosye Cloud, interview with the author (03.22.2018).

247. Justin Shur, attorney for Rosye Cloud, in a letter to William Tully, Investigator, Office of Inspector General, Department of Veterans Affairs (08.19.2016).

248. Julia Perkins and Conor Dirks, in a memo to Shaw Bransford & Roth, P.C. (03.17.2016).

249. Rosye Cloud, interview with the author (03.22.2018).

250. Leo Shane III, "Top VA Benefits Official Pummill Retires," *Military Times* (06.16.2016) https://www.militarytimes.com/veterans/2016/06/16/top-va-benefits-official-pummill-retires/ (Accessed on 03.02.2018).

251. Letter from Rosye Cloud to Curt Coy, Deputy Under Secretary, Office of Economic Opportunity (04.11.2014).

252. Rosye Cloud, in an email to the author (12.01.2018).

253. Justin Shur, attorney for Rosye Cloud, in a letter to William Tully, Investigator, Office of Inspector General, Department of Veterans Affairs (08.19.2016).

254. The Lenzner Firm, "Rosye Cloud Exonerated by Veterans Affairs OIG" (12.15.2016) https://www.prnewswire.com/news-releases/rosye-cloud-exonerated-by-veterans-affairs-oig-300379410.html (Accessed on 03.02.2018).

255. Rosye Cloud, in an email to the author (10.18.2018).

256. Phillip Longman, *Best Care Anywhere: Why VA Health Care Would Work Better For Everyone,* 3rd Edition, Berrett-Koehler Publishers (2012) pp.4, 6.

257. Guy McMichael, interview with the author (08.07.2017).

258. Tim Mak, "Wounded Warrior Project Under Fire," *Daily Beast* (09.26.2014) http://www.thedailybeast.com/articles/2014/09/26/wounded-war-riors-project-under-fire.html (Accessed on 12.13.2017).

259. Art Taylor, interview with the author (03.16.2018).

260. Adam Ashton, "Wounded Warrior Project sues a veteran critic in Gig Harbor," *The News Tribune* (02.09.2015); http://www.thenewstribune.com/news/local/military/article26253748.html (Accessed on 03.31.2017).

261. Ronald B. Leighton, "Wounded Warrior Project, Inc., Plaintiff, v. Gordon Alex Graham, Defendant," Consent Judgment, Permanent Injunction And Order (06.01.2015) https://www.woundedwarriorproject.org/media/1898/graham_order_consent_judgment_060115.pdf (Accessed on 07.12.2018).

262. Tim Mak, "'Wounded Warrior' Charity Unleashes Hell—On Other Veteran Groups," *Daily Beast* (05.04.2015) http://www.thedailybeast.com/articles/2015/05/04/wounded-warrior-charity-unleashes-hell-on-other-veteran-groups.html (Accessed on 01.04.2018).

263. Ruth McCambridge, "Is Wounded Warrior Project a 'Neighborhood Bully' Among Veterans' Groups?" (05.05.2015) https://nonprofitquarterly.org/2015/05/05/is-wounded-warrior-project-a-neighborhood-bully-among-veterans-groups/ (Accessed on 09.30.2016).

264. Steven Nardizzi, "Your Mission or Your Overhead Ratio" Speech at the Bridge Conference (07.11.2014).

265. The jury determined the $500,000 awarded in punitive damages by estimating that half of Nardizzi's time for two years was wasted on fighting WWFS's shenanigans; thus, a little more than a year of Nardizzi's salary.

266. Wounded Warriors Family Support website, https://www.wwfs.org (Accessed on 04.01.2017).

267. Between July 2016 and August 2017, the author spoke to 13 individuals on this topic who would not speak on the record for attribution.

268. John Copeland and David Sutherland, "The Sea of Goodwill" (01.15.2010). http://fifnc.org/programs/Sea_of_Goodwill.pdf (Accessed on 10.02.2016).

269. Chris Carney, interview with the author (11.17.2017).

270. Anonymous, interview with the author (11.20.2017).

271. Rosye Cloud, interview with the author (01.31.2016).

272. David Coleman, "US Military Personnel 1954-2014," Data sourced from the Defense Manpower Data Center, Office of the Secretary of Defense,

U.S. Department of Defense http://historyinpieces.com/research/us-military-personnel-1954-2014 (Accessed on 09.11.2017).

273. Thomas Spoehr and Bridget Handy, "The Looming National Security Crisis: Young Americans Unable to Serve in the Military," The Heritage Foundation (02.13.2018) https://www.heritage.org/defense/report/the-looming-national-security-crisis-young-americans-unable-serve-the-military (Accessed on 03.07.2018).

274. Al Giordano, interview with the author (08.23.2016).

275. Steve Nardizzi, interview with the author (10.27.2017).

276. Dan Pallotta, "Uncharitable," (2008) Tufts University Press, p. 102

277. Trace Adkins, Wounded Warrior Project (published on *YouTube* 11.25.2016) https://www.youtube.com/watch?v=8zpGSlOFAgY&t=25s (Accessed on 12.01.2017).

278. Wounded Warrior Project TV Commercial 'Eric' (published on *YouTube* on 04.08.2014) https://www.youtube.com/watch?v=Q_eRlp2Aj00&t=3s (Accessed on 12.01.2017).

279. Wounded Warrior Ad (published on *YouTube* on 12.27.2013) https://www.youtube.com/watch?v=AREgX7aX3ak (Accessed on 12.01.2017).

280. Beth Edmundson, interview with the author (11.18.2018).

281. Steve Nardizzi, interview with the author (05.31.2016).

282. John Molino, in an email to the author (09.21.2016).

283. Michael Mullen, in an email to the author (05.08.2017).

284. Barak Obama, "President Obama Welcomes the Wounded Warrior Project's Soldier Ride" (04.18.2013) https://www.youtube.com/watch?v=k-9jQNkNkK3k (accessed on 08.20.2017).

285. Erick Millette, "NH Veteran Says Wounded Warrior Project Saved His Life" WBZ (09.10.2013) http://boston.cbslocal.com/2013/09/10/nh-veteran-says-wounded-warrior-project-saved-his-life/ (accessed on 07.20.2017).

286. Erick Millette's Facebook page (04.26.2014).

287. Martha Franklin, et al.; The Wounded Warrior Project Survey (2014) https://www.woundedwarriorproject.org/media/2433/2014-wwp-alumni-survey.pdf (Accessed on 12.05.2017). The quoted comments can be found on pages 117 and 118 of the report. The statistics that formed the basis of the interviewer's question and Millette's response can be found on page 18 of the report.

288. Erick Millette, in an interview with Ken Mitchell, Mission Radio

(09.25.2014) https://missionsradio.podbean.com/e/interview-with-the-wounded-warrior-project/ (Accessed on 12.05.2017).

289. Justin Constantine's Facebook page (02.13.2014).

290. Dave Philipps "Wounded Warrior Project Spends Lavishly on Itself, Insiders Say," *New York Times* (01.28.2016) http://www.nytimes.com/2016/01/28/us/wounded-warrior-project-spends-lavishly-on-itself-ex-employees-say.html (Accessed on 09.04.2017).

291. Erick Millette declined to be interviewed for this book.

292. Mike Landrum, interview with the author (10.27.2018).

293. Erick Millette, in an email to the WWP personnel manager (08.13.2014).

294. Chip Reid, "Top Wounded Warrior donor calls for CEO's resignation," *CBS News* (03.03.2017); http://www.cbsnews.com/news/top-wounded-warrior-project-donor-calls-for-ceos-resignation/ (Accessed on 05.10.2017).

295. Anonymous, in an email to Gayle King; the author is in possession of the email.

296. Ayla Tezel, Executive Vice President, Communications at WWP, in a letter to Al Ortiz, Executive Director at CBS (01.27.2016).

297. Anonymous, in an email to Tony Odierno (02.01.201); the author is in possession of the email

298. The comments in this section are composed of an amalgam of interviews the author had with several people familiar with the relationship between Steve Nardizzi and board members.

299. John Loosen, interview with the author (06.26.2017).

300. Steve Nardizzi, in an email to the author (12.01.2017).

301. Steve Nardizzi, interview with the author (10.27.2017).

302. Steve Nardizzi, in an email to the author (12.01.2017).

303. "Wounded Warrior Project 2015 CEO Leadership Assessment Summary Report" (09.14.2015).

304. Al Giordano, interview with the author (06.10.2018).

305. "Wounded Warrior Project 2015 COO Leadership Assessment Summary Report" (09.14.2015).

306. In 2013, the William J. Clinton foundation was renamed the Bill, Hillary & Chelsea Clinton Foundation; in 2015 it was again renamed, this time to the Clinton Foundation

307. Victoria Bjorklund and Jennifer Reynoso, "Governance Review of the

William J. Clinton Foundation" (12.03.2011) https://www.scribd.com/document/327595685/Clinton-Foundation-Internal-Governance-Review?irgwc=1&content=27795&campaign=VigLink&ad_group=1726779&keyword=ft500noi&source=impactradius&medium=affiliate (Accessed on 10.31.2017).

308. Charles Ortel, as quoted from the Daily Caller News Foundation in "BOMBSHELL: Clinton Foundation Donors Expected 'Benefits In Return For Gifts," *The Daily Caller* (10.14.2016) http://dailycaller.com/2016/10/14/bombshell-clinton-foundation-donors-expected-benefits-in-return-for-gifts/ (Accessed on 10.31.2017).

309. John Kass, "At the Clinton Foundation, You Can Smell the Meat a-Cookin," *Chicago Tribune* (08.31.2016) http://www.chicagotribune.com/news/columnists/kass/ct-hillary-clinton-foundation-0901-20160831-column.html (Accessed on 10.30.2017).

310. Richard Painter, "The Real Clinton Foundation Revelation," *New York Times* (08.31.2016) https://www.nytimes.com/2016/08/31/opinion/the-real-clinton-foundation-revelation.html (Accessed on 10.31.2017).

311. "A Confidential Summary of the March 2016 Verbal Report to the Wounded Warrior Project, Inc. Board of Directors," p. 7; attached to a letter written by Paul Curnin of Simpson Thacher & Bartlett to Josh Flynn-Brown, Investigative Counsel to the Senate Judiciary Committee (09.12.2016).

312. This information is accessed on each organization's 2015 or 2016 IRS Form 990.

313. Chip Reid, "Wounded Warrior Project on Charity Navigator's Watch List," *CBS News* (01.30.2017) https://www.cbsnews.com/news/wounded-warrior-project-on-charity-navigator-watchlist-cbs-news-investigation/ (Accessed on 10.31.2017).

314. IRS Form 990, Vassar College (2105) http://www.guidestar.org/FinDocuments/2016/141/338/2016-141338587-0e1c9ff1-9.pdf (accessed on 02.01.2018).

315. Steve Nardizzi, interview with the author (10.27.2017).

316. Al Giordano, interview with the author (10.12.2018); the precise amount the forensic accounting examination covered over the six-year period was $1,245,408,087.

317. Al Giordano, interview with the author (10.13.2018).

318. "Economic Impact," National Council of Nonprofits, https://www.councilofnonprofits.org/economic-impact (Accessed on 02.27.2018).

319. Unattributed, "Political Nonprofits (Dark Money)" Center for Responsive Politics, https://www.opensecrets.org/outsidespending/nonprof_summ. php (Accessed on 02.27.2018).

320. Marc Gunther, "Rich charities keep getting richer. That means your money isn't doing as much good as it could." *Vox* (04.24.2017) https://www.vox. com/the-big-idea/2017/4/24/15377056/big-charities-best-charities-evaluation-nonprofit (Accessed on 02.27.2018).

321. "A National Imperative: Joining Forces to Strengthen Human Services in America," Oliver Wyman, SeaChange, Alliance for Strong Families and Communities, American Public Human Services Association (2017) p. 4 http://www.alliance1.org/web/resources/pubs/national-imperative-joining-forces-strengthen-human-services-america.aspx (Accessed on 02.27.2018).

322. Adam Meyerson, "America's Givers Are Disappearing," *Washington Examiner* (04.18.2018) https://www.washingtonexaminer.com/opinion/ op-eds/americas-givers-are-disappearing?dm_i=4WBE,30AA,23BUB-J,BP84,1 (Accessed on 08.29.2018).

323. Nicholas Kristoff, "Is the Business World All About Greed?" *New York Times* (01.24.2018) https://www.nytimes.com/2018/01/24/opinion/davos-corporate-social-impact.html (Accessed on 01.25.2018).

324. Thomas Brown, interview with the author (01.17.2018).

325. David Gelles, "Inside the Revolution at Etsy," *New York Times* (11.25.2017) https://www.nytimes.com/2017/11/25/business/etsy-josh-silverman.html (Accessed on02.10.2018).

326. Nicholas Kristoff, "Is the Business World All About Greed?" *New York Times* (01.24.2018) https://www.nytimes.com/2018/01/24/opinion/davos-corporate-social-impact.html (Accessed on 01.25.2018).

327. Frank Bruni, "Corporations Will Inherit the Earth," *New York Times* (02.10.2018) https://www.nytimes.com/2018/02/10/opinion/sunday/ corporations-will-inherit-the-earth.html?emc=edit_tnt_20180210&nlid=1889797&tntemail0=y (Accessed on 02.18.2018).

328. Nicholas Kristoff, "Is the Business World All About Greed?" *New York Times* (01.24.2018) https://www.nytimes.com/2018/01/24/opinion/davos-corporate-social-impact.html (Accessed on 01.25.2018).

329. Manpower Demonstration Research Corporation. In 1974 the Ford Foundation, along with six government agencies created MDRC to implement and document the results of programs intended to help the poor.

330. This information was compiled from the MDRC website. "Key Partners

in NYC's Social Impact Bond," (undated) https://www.mdrc.org/key-partners-nycs-social-impact-bond (Accessed on 01.24.2018).

331. "Impact Evaluation of the Adolescent Behavioral Learning Experience (ABLE) Program at Rikers Island," Vera Institute of Justice (07.2015) https://storage.googleapis.com/vera-web-assets/downloads/Publications/impact-evaluation-of-the-adolescent-behavioral-learning-experience-able-program-at-rikers-island/legacy_downloads/ABLE-summary.pdf (Accessed on 01.24.2018).

332. Donald Cohen and Jennifer Zelnick, "What We Learned from the Failure of the Rikers Island Social Impact Bond," *Nonprofit Quarterly* (08.07.2015) https://nonprofitquarterly.org/2015/08/07/what-we-learned-from-the-failure-of-the-rikers-island-social-impact-bond/ (Accessed on 01.23.2018).

333. James Anderson and Andrea Phillips, "What We Learned From the Nation's First Social Impact Bond," *Huffington Post* (07.02.2016). https://www.huffingtonpost.com/james-anderson/what-we-learned-from-the-_1_b_7710272.html (Accessed on 07.03.2017).

334. Richard Feiner, interview with the author (12.29.2016).

335. Dan Pallotta, interview with the author (10.17.2017).

336. CNN, Situation Room Transcript (03.12.2010) http://transcripts.cnn.com/TRANSCRIPTS/1003/12/sitroom.03.html (Accessed on 02.05.2018).

337. Dan Pallotta, interview with the author (10.17.2017).

338. Jacob Harold, interview with the author (01.10.2018).

339. Paul Tudor Jones, "Why We Need to Rethink Capitalism," TED Talk (03.2015) https://www.ted.com/talks/paul_tudor_jones_ii_why_we_need_to_rethink_capitalism (Accessed on 01.30.2018).

340. Roadmap for America: JUST Capital's 2017 Survey Results" JUST Capital (2017) pp. 1, 8 https://com-justcapital-web-v2.s3.amazonaws.com/wp-content/uploads/2017/11/JUST_Capital_RoadmapCorpAmerica_Final_111017.pdf (Accessed on 02.01.2018).

341. Martin Whittaker, interview with the author (01.31.2017).

342. ImpactMatters website; https://www.impactm.org/about/vision (Accessed on 05.18.2018).

343. Martin Whittaker, interview with the author (01.31.2017).

344. Dan Pallotta, "Opinion: Dan Pallotta Says Major Nonprofit Groups Should Merge," *Chronicle of Philanthropy* (05.16.2016) https://www.philanthropy.com/article/Opinion-Dan-Pallotta-Says/236486 (Accessed on 07.19.2018).

345. Andrea Fuller, "Private Charitable Foundations Give Lavish Rewards to Insiders," *Wall Street Journal* (05.31.2018) https://www.wsj.com/articles/private-charitable-foundations-give-lavish-rewards-to-insiders-1527613467 (Accessed on 05.31.2018).

346. Anand Giridharadas, "Winners Take All: The Elite Charade of Changing the World," (2018), p. 4

347. Dan Pallotta, "What the Nonprofit Sector Needs To Reach Its Full Potential," *Harvard Business Review* (05.13.2016); https://hbr.org/2016/05/what-the-nonprofit-sector-needs-to-reach-its-full-potential (Accessed on 05.05.2018).

348. Gary Wills, *Lincoln at Gettysburg*, Simon & Schuster (1992) p.101

349. Theodore Parker, *The Collected Works of Theodore Parker Slavery volume 5*, p.216

350. Gary Wills, quoting Abraham Lincoln, *Lincoln at Gettysburg*, Simon & Schuster (1992) p.101.

351. Josh Freedman, "Are Universities Charities? Why The 'Nonprofit Sector' Needs To Go," *Forbes* (10.10.2013). https://www.forbes.com/sites/joshfreedman/2013/12/10/the-nonprofit-sector-should-not-exist/#7b51b7077501 (Accessed on 07.25.2017).

352. Peter Honerkamp and Chris Carney, in an email to Anthony Odierno and Richard Jones (09.19.2017).

353. Tom Johnson, interview with the author (08.30.2016).

354. Written responses to "Podcast: Ousted Wounded Warrior Project Executives Speak Out," Bill O'Reilly's No Spin News Excerpt (09.30.2016). https://www.billoreilly.com/b/Podcast:-Ousted-Wounded-Warrior-Project-Executives-Speak-Out/574230005396901283.html (Accessed on 12.18.2017).

355. Erick Millette, in a Facebook exchange with the author (07.19.2016).

356. Michael Mullen, in an email to the author (05.08.2017).

357. Al Ortiz, in an email to Peter Honerkamp (03.03.2017).

358. Dave Philipps, in an email to the author (03.10.2017).

359. "Board Roles and Responsibilities," National Council of Nonprofits https://www.councilofnonprofits.org/tools-resources/board-roles-and-responsibilities (Accessed on 05.25.2017).

360. Gary Morton, "Best Nonprofits to Work For 2013," *Nonprofit Times* (04.01.2013) https://www.thenonprofittimes.com/wp-content/uploads/2013/04/BestPlacesToWork_20132.pdf (Accessed on 05.25.2017).

361. Al Giordano, interview with the author (10.13.2018).

362. Matt Modine, in an email to the author (07.19.2017).

363. Richard Levick, "The Gutting Of Wounded Warrior: How To Kill A Charity," *Forbes* (09.12.2016) https://www.forbes.com/sites/richard-levick/2016/09/12/the-gutting-of-wounded-warrior-how-to-kill-a-charity/#138eb7df405b (Accessed on 02.13.2018).

364. Art Taylor, interview with the author (03.19.2018).

365. Stanford Survey on Leadership and Management in the Nonprofit Sector (11.2017) p.2, http://www.engineofimpact.org/wp-content/uploads/2017/11/Stanford-Survey-on-Nonprofit-Leadership-November-2017.pdf (Accessed on 11.25.2017).

366. Al Giordano, interview with the author (03.27.2018).

367. Anonymous, interview with the author (04.20.2017).

368. Anonymous, interview with the author (08.14.2018).

369. Al Giordano, interview with the author (10.13.2018).

370. John Loosen, in an email to Al Giordano (09.29.2018).

371. Charlie Battaglia, in an email to Al Giordano (01.11.2019).

372. The author is in possession of each name.

INDEX